In the Shadow of Death

Previously published in this series by Yad Vashem:

Enzo Tayar, *Days of Rain*

Alan Elsner, *Guarded by Angels: How My Father and Uncle Survived Hitler and Cheated Stalin*

Isabelle Choko, Frances Irwin, Lotti Kahana-Aufleger, Margit Raab Kalina, Jane Lipski, *Stolen Youth: Five Women's Survival in the Holocaust*

Hadassah Rosensaft, *Yesterday, My Story*

Gabriel Mermall, Norbert J. Yasharoff, *By the Grace of Strangers: Two Boys' Rescue During the Holocaust*

E.H. (Dan) Kampelmacher, *Fighting for Survival*

Hersch Altman, *On the Fields of Loneliness*

Flora M. Singer, *Flora, I was but a Child*

Israel Cymlich, Oskar Strawczynski, *Escaping Hell in Treblinka*

Moty Stromer, *Memoirs of an Unfortunate Person: the Diary of Moty Stromer*

Menachem Katz, *Path of Hope*

Leib Reizer, *In the Struggle: Memoirs from Grodno and the Forests*

Mordechai Lensky, *A Physician Inside the Warsaw Ghetto*

Marcel Tuchman, *Remember, My Stories of Survival and Beyond*

Published by the United States Holocaust Memorial Museum:

Adam Boren, *Journey Through the Inferno*

Margaret Bergmann Lambert, *By Leaps and Bounds*

Joseph E. Tenenbaum, *Legacy and Redemption: A Life Renewed*

In the Shadow of Death

JOSEPH FOXMAN

YAD VASHEM AND
THE HOLOCAUST SURVIVORS' MEMOIRS PROJECT
New York • Jerusalem

This book is published by Yad Vashem, the Holocaust Martyrs' and Heroes' Remembrance Authority, c/o American Society for Yad Vashem, 500 Fifth Avenue, 42nd floor, New York, New York 10110-4299, and P.O.B. 3477, Jerusalem 91034, Israel

www.yadvashem.org

and

The Holocaust Survivors' Memoirs Project
in association with the World Federation of Bergen-Belsen Associations, Inc.

The Holocaust Survivors' Memoirs Project, an initiative of Nobel Peace Prize laureate Elie Wiesel, was launched through a generous grant from Random House, Inc., New York, New York. Publication of this book has been made possible by an additional generous grant from Nancy and Matthew Mintzis.

Cover photos and all other photographs courtesy of Abraham Foxman

Library of Congress Cataloging-in-Publication Data

Foxman, Joseph, b. 1905.
In the shadow of death / by Joseph Foxman.
p. cm.
ISBN 978-0-9814686-5-5
1. Foxman, Joseph, b. 1905 2. Foxman, Joseph, b. 1905--Family. 3. Foxman, Abraham H.--Childhood and youth. 4. Holocaust, Jewish (1939-1945)--Lithuania--Vilnius--Personal narratives. 5. Jewish children in the Holocaust--Lithuania--Vilnius. 6. Jews--Lithuania--Vilnius--Biography. 7. Jewish ghettos--Lithuania--Vilnius--History--20th century. 8. Vilnius (Lithuania)--Biography. 9. World War, 1939-1945--Lithuania--Vilnius. 10. Holocaust survivors--Biography. I. Title.
DS135.L53F68 2010
940.53'18092--dc22
[B]
2010054299

Typesetting: Judith Sternberg
Produced by Offset Nathan Shlomo Press

Printed in Jerusalem, Israel.

TABLE OF CONTENTS

FOREWORD

By Abraham Foxman

Of the many fateful decisions my parents made as they tried to keep one step ahead of the Nazis, none was more fraught with anxiety and fear than their decision to give away their one-year-old son.

It was perhaps the most unnatural decision a parent could make. They entrusted my life to my Polish Catholic nursemaid, a woman they had known for only a short time. They did so on a leap of faith, a belief that I would have a better chance of surviving outside of the burgeoning Jewish ghetto of Vilna under the protection and care of the devout Catholic woman who loved me as her own.

It was an incredible risk, and a dangerous calculation. Yet it worked. Turning the narrative of most hidden children and survivors of the Holocaust on its head, I was reunited with both my parents after the war. Unlike the fate of so many families and parents of so many other children, my family unit – because we separated – survived and was reunited intact.

The story of my father's survival is told in the following pages, his memoirs, which have never been published until now.

My father, Joseph, and my mother, Helen, protected me in my youth from hearing about the tough decisions and hard sacrifices they had made during the war years. And after we had left Europe for good and settled into our new life in the United States, they spoke a great deal of their experiences, but not to me.

I did not know that my father, a historian by avocation, had written down, in exacting Yiddish, recollections of his experiences in Lithuania and elsewhere in Eastern Europe. His memoirs describe in careful detail how he repeatedly cheated death in the work camps, in the factories, in the ghetto. Imagine my surprise when, years later, I came across these papers as I was going through his personal effects. I had had no idea that these memoirs existed. My mother and father had never spoken of them.

Many survivors were reluctant witnesses and did not speak about their experiences for a long time after the war. I think that this was partially because they wanted to protect their children from the pain and suffering and anguish they had gone through and had personally witnessed. And it was partially to protect themselves from having to relive what had happened. But their reluctance did not stop their children from asking questions, picking up clues, and making observations from the facts around them.

As I grew older, I began to try to understand why it was that I had survived, why I had been spared the fate of 1.5 million other Jewish children who perished in the Nazi inferno. During the war I had been kept safe, protected, fed, clothed, and happy by my nanny. She had me baptized and took pains to love and care for me. She took me to church every Sunday and kept my Jewish identity hidden.

I had many questions for my father. And there were many answers, both spoken and unspoken. The realization, for example, of how alone we were when I celebrated my Bar Mitzvah. My friends and classmates were surrounded by many dozens, if not hundreds, of family members — the aunts, uncles, cousins, grandparents, and siblings who crowded the *shuls* of Brooklyn to celebrate the most important rite of passage into Jewish adulthood. For my Bar Mitzvah we could barely fill the living room of our one-and-a-half-bedroom apartment — and the guests were friends, not family.

My parents answered some of my questions about Europe and the war with simple yesses and nos. But they were never able to explain what I saw as the biggest question of my life: How could they have given me away? I asked this sometimes in disbelief, and sometimes in anger. My parents were never able to explain this most unnatural decision, which not only saved my life, but theirs as well.

Another question that I struggled with while growing up — and that I ultimately was mature enough to ask my father — was the question of his unflagging and seemingly unquestioning faith in God. How, after everything that had happened to him in Europe, after the killings and the scenes of death he had witnessed, after the near total annihilation of his family and of European Jewry, how could my father believe in and revere God? And how could he make the decision so easily to bring me back to my Jewish roots, my *Yiddishkeit*, after I had been returned to my parents for good.

I was born in 1940, in Baranowicz, Poland. Under the protection of my nanny, I had been baptized in Lithuania as a Catholic boy named Henryk Stanisław Kurpi, the names of my nanny and my patron saint. I had gone to church every Sunday, and, when passing through the city of Vilna, I would cross myself when I passed a church. When I met a priest, I kissed his hand; when we saw a Jew, I had been taught to spit at him.

After the war my father slowly reintroduced me to my Jewish roots without apparent compunction, remorse, or anger at God. His decision was a great mystery to me until, years later, I asked him about his faith. The answer surprised me. He told me that the evil that had created the *Shoah* was not God's – it was man's. Essentially, it was man's inhumanity toward man. This idea is reflected in his memoirs, in which he recounts the moments in his survival odyssey when he truly believes that God intervened to spare his life and the lives of his wife and child. My father saw faith in those interventions, and he was unafraid to express his sincere belief in miracles.

The first time my father took me to *shul* was in Vilnius on Simchat Torah. I guess it was because he figured I'd like it, since it is a joyous festival full of singing and dancing. A Soviet officer in uniform, who was Jewish, came up to my father and asked if he could include me in the dancing. He put me on his shoulders and began to dance, saying, "This is the Jewish flag." The Jewish children picked me up and danced with me, and I came home and told my mother, "Hey, I like the Jewish church!" It was the beginning of my return to Judaism.

Incidentally, sixty-five years later, I would meet this officer again. Unbeknownst to my family and me, the soldier had moved to the United States, where he became an Orthodox rabbi and an educator. We were reunited in his home in Detroit, Michigan, in April 2010. His name is Rabbi Leo Goldman, and he was ninety-one at the time of our meeting.

Something else I didn't understand for a long time was my parents' insistence that I retain my fond memories and love for Bronisława Kurpi, my nanny, the woman who saved my life. This was even after everything that had transpired to taint the relationship, and though we were unable to stay in touch with her after the war. Why, I wondered, would they permit me to keep her memory alive, and even to hold on to photos of the woman who once claimed me as her son, and who after the war had done everything to keep me from being rightfully returned to my parents? She had had me kidnapped twice, and had told terrible lies to the Soviet authorities about my father in an effort to have him imprisoned. There had been a painful custody battle, of which to this day I have no memory, so searing, so emotionally traumatic was this ordeal on the psyche of a five-year-old boy. We had left Eastern Europe to get away from all of this and more, yet my parents obstinately insisted on keeping her memory alive.

When I finally gathered up the courage to ask my father about my nanny, the answer again surprised me, and served as a powerful and early life lesson. "Son," he told me in Yiddish, "Everything in excess is no good – too smart, too stupid, too nice, too poor…"

Here was a good woman who had suffered from too much love. And too much love sometimes transforms itself into hate. Yet my parents wanted me to remember for the rest of my life the woman who had risked her life so that I could live.

Years later I recalled this important lesson when I represented the Anti-Defamation League at an audience with Pope John Paul II. I told him the story of my survival and asked him to bless my nanny and her loving acts of generosity. I consider myself fortunate every day thanks to my nanny's human decency; fortunate that a woman who could barely read and write could say "no" at a time when so many others gave up and gave in when Nazi henchmen came for the children.

Another question I had occasion to ask my father resonates deeply within these very pages. It came up as I was working on an undergraduate paper on the history of and the living conditions in the Vilna ghetto.

Why, I asked my father, did people in the ghettos go to such lengths to keep diaries of what was happening to them? I didn't understand how people bartered bread for paper, when a piece of bread meant the difference between life and death; how people could barter soup, when soup was the only meal they had that day.

My father's answer was that they feared that no one would know that they had lived. He explained that, in the Jewish tradition, we had an obligation of *Zahor* and *Yizkor*, to remember and to eulogize and preserve the memory of the dead.

This is the most important message and lesson of the Holocaust and, for me, explains everything about why my father felt it necessary to put pen to paper and to write about his experiences.

There are many universal questions that arise out of the evil of the Holocaust; there are no easy answers and, perhaps, there will never be. But our children and our children's children need to understand how it happened, why it happened so that they can carry on the imperative of *Never Again*.

If the legacy to our children means anything, it means that never again should anyone, anywhere be put in jeopardy. It means that we have an obligation to stand up and say "no" when confronted with antisemitism, bigotry, or prejudice. I only wish that my father had lived to see the day that his memoirs were finally published and to see the day when his grandchildren and great-grandchildren would ask the same questions to which I had sought answers all those many years. For them he lives on in these pages.

New York, New York
October 12, 2010

INTRODUCTION[1]

By Leah Aharonov

Joseph Foxman's memoirs about his experiences during World War II concentrate on his narrow escapes from death, the help he received, and his gratitude each time he managed to survive. He did not linger on many biographical details, except those that had some bearing on the episodes he describes.

Joseph and Helen Foxman (Fuksman) were married in Warsaw, Poland, in 1935. Helen Radoszycka had grown up in Warsaw. She finished her studies in the *gymnasium* and then worked in her mother's business until her marriage. When Germany attacked Poland, on September 1, 1939, Helen was pregnant. Her husband was visiting a sick brother in Baranowicze, which was occupied by the Soviet Union, and her mother insisted that she leave Warsaw and join him. One of her older brothers escorted her on the journey, and it took them four weeks to cross the Soviet border. They were sent back three times at gunpoint by the Germans. Finally, they crossed separately, and Helen stayed

1 The Introduction is based on sources provided by Abraham Foxman: Interview with Helen Foxman, in Brana Gurewitsch, ed., *Mothers, Sisters, Resisters: Oral Histories of Women Who Survived the Holocaust* (Tuscaloosa and London: University of Alabama Press, 1998), pp. 33–46; Abraham H. Foxman, *Never Again? The Threat of the New Anti-Semitism* (New York: HarperCollins, 2003), pp. 78–88; and Joseph Foxman's testimony at the Jewish Historical Institute, which appears in the Appendix below.

with her in-laws in Baranowicze until Abraham Henoch Fuksman was born on May 1, 1940.

After the child was born, they knew they had to leave. The Soviets had already arrested Joseph's father several times, and they, as refugees, were in danger of being arrested and deported to Russia, as had happened to other Jews and refugees. The authorities had actually come to take Helen, but she had a letter from the doctor attesting to the fact that she was hemorrhaging after the birth, so they left her and the child. Joseph, however, had to go into hiding. Finally they were able to leave; they went to Slonim with the few belongings they were able to take with them. In Slonim Joseph began working for the Soviet regime as a bookkeeper. Through a relative they found a room to live in, but the conditions were difficult, especially with an infant. Food was scarce, and the baby was often sick. Joseph worked in a forest far away and came home only on Saturdays, having to return on foot on Saturday night.

Helen's brother came from Vilna and talked them into going there, even though it meant crossing the border illegally again. The Red Army had entered Vilna on September 9, 1939, but handed the city over to the Lithuanians a few weeks later. Later, in July 1940, Lithuania, including Vilna, also became a Soviet republic.

Helen first went with the child, as it took a few months for her husband to obtain permission to leave his work. Finally, they agreed to let him go, and he received papers from the Russian doctor at his workplace confirming that he had to go to Vilna to see a specialist. He reached Vilna only a few days before the Nazis entered the city on June 24, 1941. They were not allowed to live in the city, so they found an apartment about eight miles away. The baby was now a year old, and Helen could not take care of him because she had to go to work. Someone recommended a Polish woman who took care of young children, and Helen left the baby in the care of Bronisława (Bronia) Kurpi (Kurpa) while she was at work. Bronia was a humble servant girl, poorly educated and not very healthy. She was deaf in one ear and had a weak heart. She was a devout Catholic but totally devoted to little Abraham.

In late June 1941, the Germans and the Lithuanian administration that had been established issued a series of anti-Jewish decrees. Jews were ordered to wear the yellow star, obey a curfew, and remain off certain streets. Several thousand Jews were murdered in the nearby Ponary forest during the *Aktionen* carried out in July, August, and the beginning of September. The "ghettoization *Aktion*" took place on September 6, 1941, and through the ensuing night. Two ghettos were established: 30,000 Jews moved into ghetto number 1; and 9,000 into ghetto number 2. Jews with work permits (*Scheinen*) were placed in ghetto number 1; all the others were in ghetto number 2. The latter was soon liquidated, and the Jews were massacred at Ponary.

The Foxmans postponed moving into the ghetto until they had settled what to do with the baby. While they were packing their belongings in order to move into the ghetto, Bronia asked what would happen to the child. Helen said, "Whatever happens to us will happen to the child." Then Bronia said, "Give him to me. I'll take him." The parents looked at each other, and when Joseph said, "OK. Take him," the decision was made. They gave Bronia almost all their possessions – furniture, clothing, bedding, and a considerable amount of money. After she carted away the belongings, she took the baby. He was thirteen months old at the time. Unknown to them then, this arrangement would last for four years.

The Foxmans entered the larger ghetto with 180 rubles between them. As all the Jews had already been incarcerated ten days before, they feared they would be arrested, attacked, or killed on the way. After they finally made it in by pretending that Joseph was ill, it was difficult for them to find a place to live, as all the living quarters were already taken. By chance they met a woman that Joseph knew from Baranowicze, and she took them in. Soon after, Joseph was given work in a factory not far from the ghetto, in the mountains of Szuszkin in the suburbs of Snipiski in Vilna. The work there consisted of sorting exploded ammunition materials into piles of copper, brass, iron, and tin. These were then loaded onto freight cars headed for ammunition factories in Germany. The work was very dangerous, as any unexploded material could still go off at any time. Joseph also worked in a factory that produced makeup and perfumes and later soap, shoe paste, and floor paste.

As soon as Bronia found out where Joseph was, she started coming to his workplace to ask for more money. She also began nagging him for a written statement that the Foxmans were giving her the child as her own. He wrote something down, but the next day she reappeared in anger demanding that Helen also sign. After she received this paper, she took the child to be baptized. She named him Czesław Henryk Kurpa and registered him as her own son. Then she started coming to the ghetto gates to ask for money. Finally, Joseph agreed to give her 5,000 rubles every month, which was a considerable sum. The only way he could get that much money was by smuggling food and goods into the ghetto, as did Helen, which was very dangerous.

Every night there were *Aktionen*. The men who worked were given pink residence permits for their families. Since Joseph had one for his wife (who did not work) and his child (in case they would have to take him back at one point), they used the child's permit during *Aktionen* to protect a young teacher from the Beth Yaakov seminary.

Joseph also belonged to the Revisionist Zionist group in the ghetto underground, led by Jewish policeman and underground figure Joseph Glazman. The Revisionist Zionist group was active in Jewish defense efforts, and Joseph Glazman, a leader of the Betar youth group, took over the leadership of the Revisionists in the Vilna ghetto. On January 21, 1942, at a meeting in his home, the United Partisan Organization (FPO), a coalition of Zionist youth movements and Communist party groups, was formed. Glazman became part of the FPO command staff. The resistance groups in the Vilna ghetto did not have the support of the majority of the ghetto population and never mounted a full-scale uprising against the Nazis. However, the idea of self-defense and struggle was born there and inspired Jews in other ghettos to resist in one form or another.

Before the final liquidation of the ghetto in September 1943, some Jews escaped to the forests and joined partisan groups that fought independently or under Soviet command. Glazman left the Vilna ghetto in July 1943, and formed a Jewish partisan group in the Narocz forest. They fought first under Soviet command and then under the Lithuanian partisans. Glazman was killed fighting the Germans on October 7, 1943. Joseph and Helen were supposed to join a group in the forest but did not; they later heard that the Jews in the group had been killed.

Sometime in 1943, they received news that the ghetto in Warsaw was being liquidated, and that fighting was going on. Most of Helen's family had been interned there and were killed, but she did not know under what circumstances. Her youngest brother was being hidden by a Christian woman in a small town on the outskirts of Vilna but was denounced, taken to the Vilna ghetto, and murdered at Ponary.

Helen used to leave the ghetto almost every week to see the baby. She would remove the yellow star from her clothes and walk out of the ghetto with a group of workers. She then walked to Bronia's house. It was very far, but

Helen had to see how the baby was being cared for. He recognized her but did not know who she was. She was not allowed to go near him or hold or kiss him. For him Bronia was his mother, and he called her "Mama." He thought his biological parents were an aunt and uncle.

In this book Joseph Foxman relates the incident involving a high official in the Lithuanian police, Court Examiner Julian Boyka, who turned out to be Bronia's brother. When he realized that the boy she called her son was really a Jewish child, he confronted Joseph and demanded that the child be brought into the ghetto. Not knowing what to do, the father asked the advice of a lawyer, Abram Dimitrovsky, who told them it would be best if Frau Kurpi and "Henryk" leave Vilna immediately. Word was passed to them, and they escaped to a summer house five miles outside the city, where they went into hiding. The tension and uncertainty surrounding this episode are described in Chapter 2.

In late summer of 1943, the rest of the people living in the Vilna ghetto were liquidated. On August 4 and 24, and September 1 and 4, 1943, more than 7,000 men and women were deported from Vilna to concentration camps in Estonia. Some were sent to Klooga, a subcamp of the Vaivara camp in northern Estonia, near Tallin. Joseph Foxman realized the situation was ominous and told his wife they had to be prepared to separate. He was chosen to go to the train station to clean out railroad cars and decided he would not return to the ghetto. He got word to his wife that he was hiding outside somewhere. Helen bribed someone at the gate and also left the ghetto. She went to the factory where her husband had worked. There she learned that they had helped him get away. Helen, not knowing where to even begin to look for him, just sat down in the adjacent open field. A fellow worker threw her a note saying that after dark he would show her where her husband was. Suddenly, Bronia came by with the baby. She knew everything that was happening in the ghetto and had come to see Joseph. She took Helen home with her, and at night Helen returned to the factory and was taken to her husband's hiding place in a loft. Thereafter, every night she would come and bring him food.

Helen was able to establish a false identity as an Aryan. She spoke Polish well and looked like a Gentile, and so, with Bronia's help, she was able to obtain the necessary papers that enabled her to get work. Bronia got a place to live on the outskirts of Vilna, and Helen went to live with her and Abraham. She got a job in a bookbinding shop. The work entitled her to ration cards and soup for lunch. Once a Jewish shop, it was now run by Germans who employed Polish women.

When it got very cold, the superintendent at the factory took Joseph into his home. Joseph paid the man 5,000 rubles a month from the money he had made while working outside the ghetto and from smuggling goods into the ghetto. The superintendent and his wife gave Joseph no food, and he lived on the bread that Helen brought him every day and an occasional glass of tea from the owner. On the occasions that the people left the house, Joseph snuck food left for their cat and dog.

Even while Helen stayed with Bronia, she suffered from her outbursts. Every few days she threw Helen out of the house, sometimes even with the child. Throughout the time that Helen stayed with her, she paid her what she asked for and gave her whatever she needed. On the whole Bronia treated the child well. She fed him and kept him clean, but if he made any sign of even leaning toward Helen, Bronia would spank him. Nevertheless, he was very close to her and would hug and kiss her.

Abraham was raised as a Catholic. After he was baptized, he was taught all the prayers, went to church regularly, and wore a small cross around his neck. He became quite devout. As part of his religious education, he was also taught to despise Jews, and he took this very seriously. As the boy was circumcised, Bronia tried to keep him at her side as much as possible. He was not allowed to play with other children or to go to nursery school. Even so, the child was suspected by a Lithuanian policeman of being Jewish and was taken to the Gestapo three times. Bronia told them the Russians had taken his parents away, and she had promised herself that she was going to raise him and thus save him. It was even her intention that he become a priest.

In 1944, the Russians liberated Lithuania, and Joseph came out of hiding. Finally, the child was free to play and go to school. He went to kindergarten, where he learned Russian, which was among the first signs of the Sovietization of the country.

When Joseph arrived at Bronia's house, the child was afraid to go to him. While the child knew him, he did not know he was his father. Bronia was surprised at Joseph's return, as Helen had tried to keep his existence a secret from her so that she would not harm him in any way.

There was little available housing, so when Helen and Joseph rented an apartment, Bronia came to live with them. After having saved the child, she was regarded as part of the family. They lived together as a family even as the struggle for custody of the child unfolded.

Abraham's father carefully and slowly tried to wean him away from Catholicism and back to Judaism. In September 1945, some four months after the liberation, his father took him to a synagogue for the first time. It was Simchat Torah, a joyous holiday with music, singing and dancing. When they returned home, Abraham told Bronia, "I like the Jewish church, because they sing and dance there."

During the year that the four of them lived together the boy attended both synagogue and church, but little by little the father began introducing Jewish traditions. The cross was replaced with a fringed prayer garment, and Hebrew prayers were recited instead of the Latin liturgy.

But Frau Kurpi did not yield easily. She decided to fight to keep the child – and to keep him Catholic. First she went to the local Soviet officials to accuse the father of having collaborated with the Nazis, which could have led to his execution. Indeed, he was arrested and interrogated, but, as there was no evidence to back up the charge, he was released after several days. Soon the father was appointed commissar of a local factory – the same factory in which he had worked while in the Vilna ghetto. Now Frau Kurpi claimed he had stolen government property. Again, he was arrested, and again he was freed after several days. The third denouncement was a claim that he had stolen soap and shoe polish from the factory; however, by this time the authorities dismissed the accusation immediately. Realizing that the underlying motivation for all the false claims was an attempt to get rid of the biological parent in order to keep the child, one of the officials suggested that the parents take the nanny to court in order to establish their parental rights legally.

A custody suit ensued – even as the four continued to live together. Since the facts were more or less clear-cut, the nanny first claimed that the parents were imposters. This was easily disproved. Then she claimed the child was her illegitimate son and not related to the Foxmans. Once again they were able to bring witnesses to repudiate the claim. Eventually the nanny admitted that the first two statements had been lies, but then she appealed on the ground that she was saving the child's soul for the Catholic Church. Fortunately, the atheist Soviets were not impressed. Finally the court rendered the verdict that custody be granted to the biological parents. By now the nanny was angry, jealous, and very resentful of the real parents. In a last-ditch attempt she had several of her relatives kidnap the child and hide him. But the parents were able to find him and then got some Jewish acquaintances who lived in the same housing block to kidnap him back.

At this point they realized they had better leave Europe altogether, even though it was hard for the child to leave Bronia. They left Vilna at the end of 1945, for Lodz, Poland. The Foxmans left Bronia everything, all their belongings. They even asked her to come with them, since they felt grateful for all she had done for the child. They also realized that had the child been with them, they, too, would have perished. Moreover, she had hidden Helen with her and the child for a year, so she had really saved their lives as well.

The Revisionist Zionists helped them, and eventually they arrived in Austria, in the American zone. They lived in a DP camp for three and a half years. Joseph was sick most of the time, although he was head of the camp in Bad Gastein. The family wanted to go to Palestine but could not get a certificate from the British authorities. Although there was considerable "illegal" immigration to Palestine, as Abraham was only four and a half, they did not think they could subject him to the harsh conditions this entailed. Finally, they received papers from relatives in the United States. Joseph rejected this option three times, until he finally agreed to accept the papers. Ironically, in 1935, the Foxmans had actually received certificates to enter Palestine, but Helen had not wanted to leave her family in Warsaw. She had presented Joseph with an ultimatum, insisting that if he wanted to go, he would have to go alone, as she would not marry him.

In the United States they first lived on the Lower East Side in New York, then bought a farm in New Jersey, but eventually moved back to New York. Joseph worked at a variety of jobs, suffering from the physical conditions at many of them because of his ill health. After many years he worked at YIVO as a research associate in history and became director of CYKO, a Yiddish book publisher, and finally established a Yiddish book distributing company. He wrote many articles on the Holocaust and contributed to many publications. Helen worked for twenty years for the Barton's candy company.

Abe Foxman is National Director of the Anti-Defamation League of B'nai B'rith. Foxman reflected on the story of his experience as a hidden child as a strange one, "in which compassion, love, faith and heroism are blended with selfishness, deceit, cruelty and pain."[2]

2 Foxman, *Never Again?*, p. 87.

Despite all the trouble Bronia had caused their family, the parents forgave her because what had mattered most was that she had risked her own life in order to save their child. They remained in touch with Frau Kurpi, writing to her from the DP camp and then from the United States. They even sent her money and packages. But she never wrote back, and, in 1958, the postal authorities informed them that she had passed away.

CHAPTER 1

JEWISH SOLIDARITY

Time, they say, brings justice. But among the unmerciful consequences and injustices of the passage of time is that it causes us to forget. This must not be permitted to happen. We must oppose the "law of time" and the verdict of anonymity. It is incumbent upon every individual who survived the Hitler cataclysm to record and to immortalize his/her Holocaust experiences – those that s/he witnessed with his/her own eyes, or even those that s/he heard about with his/her own ears. It is a national obligation.

This then is a record of several such episodes that I experienced in the ghetto of Vilna, that "city in Israel." Ten times I stood in the shadow of death, and each time I was saved it was purely by accident. It was difficult for me to hope and, even more so, to believe that fate would allow me to relate what I went through – but I did, indeed, remain among the living. Therefore, in a desire to fulfill the meaning of the verse, "I did not die, but I lived," I will relate those experiences that I retained in my notes and in my memory since they occurred.

I lived through it all in the city of Vilna, the "Jerusalem of Lithuania," the city of the Vilna Gaon,[3] of the *Ger Tzedek*,[4] of YIVO,[5] the cradle of the Jewish labor movement, of Hirsh Leckert,[6] of Jewish national movements, of 101 prayer houses and study halls, of the Jewish publishers The Widow and the brothers Romm.[7] All the Jewish cultural transmigrations had taken place in this city; it was where the fathers of Hebrew and Yiddish literature lived and worked; it was the birthplace of the Jewish Labor Bund, and the city of the Tziyyone Tzion Conference and its historic declaration against the "Uganda plan."[8] It is the only city in the world that contains a memorial to Moses – al-

3 The reference is to Elijah ben Shlomo Zalman, known as the Vilna Gaon (Genius) or Elijah of Vilna, and also by his Hebrew acronym *Gra* ("Gaon Rabbi Eliyahu") (1720–1797). He was one of the most exceptional rabbinical figures of recent centuries and a leader of the *mitnagdim*, the opponents of Hasidism.

4 A *Ger Tzedek* is a true, sincere convert to Judaism. The author's reference here is to Valentin Potocki, the son of one of the most prominent noblemen in eighteenth-century Poland, Count Potocki. He became interested in Judaism and decided to convert, moving to Amsterdam, where many Jews who had been Marranos had returned to Judaism. He eventually returned to Vilna, which was then part of Poland, where his true identity was discovered. He was executed in 1749, for violating the law prohibiting conversion to Judaism.

5 YIVO, the Yiddishe Wissenshaflicher Institut (Yiddish Scientific Institute), was founded in Vilna in 1925. It boasted a major Jewish Studies library and counted many major Jewish scholars among its associates and staff. YIVO relocated to New York in 1940.

6 Hirsch Leckert (1879–1902) was a Jewish shoemaker who attempted to assassinate the governor of Vilna in 1902, because the governor had ordered the beating of all Jews who had participated in the May 1 demonstrations. The governor was wounded, and Hirsch Leckert was executed by hanging.

7 The Widow and the Brothers Romm was a famous Jewish publishing house in Vilna, founded in the late eighteenth century by Barukh ben Yosef Romm. The publishing house was managed by Romm's grandsons, David, Hayyim, and Menachem, and later also by David's widow Deborah, during much of the nineteenth century. Their most famous and influential publication was the "Vilna Shas" edition of the Talmud, published in 1886, which is still recognized as the authoritative version of the Talmud and commentaries.

8 The Uganda Program was a British proposal, in 1903, to give a portion of British East Africa to the Jewish people as a homeland. Having failed to receive a charter for large-scale Jewish settlement in Palestine, and in light of the growing antisemitism

beit on the top of the cathedral. It was the most Jewish city in the world – with a broad network of Jewish elementary, vocational, and high schools, musical societies, daily newspapers, and periodicals. The largest Jewish library in Europe was to be found there, as was the famous Vilna Troupe. This was a city where even Jewish poverty looked you proudly in the eye, like a rich man's wife, while every street, every alley, every corner was a monument to generations of Jewish suffering and pain. It was also the city of Jewish protest, rebellion, struggle and heroic resistance, the city in which every paving stone is sanctified with Jewish blood, the city of Itzik Wittenberg and Joseph Glazman.[9] Vilna, it can be said, will proudly and justifiably occupy a place in Jewish history equal to Safed, Massada, Betar, and Tel Hai; it will forever remain a symbol of Jewish martyrdom and Jewish resistance, because in Vilna, for the first time, the idea of self-defense and struggle was born, an idea that inspired the Jewish ghettos all over Europe.

Vilna, September 1941. The Jewish population of the city has been reduced to one-quarter of its original number. Thirty-thousand people had been squeezed into two ghettos – ghetto number 1 and ghetto number 2, or the "Big Ghetto" and the "Small Ghetto." As a refugee from Warsaw, five days before the war,

and violence against Jews, especially in Eastern Europe, highlighted by the Kishinev Pogrom in 1903, Theodor Herzl borught this proposal to the Sixth Zionist Congress in Basel that year. The proposal encountered intense opposition among many Zionists and was rejected by the Seventh Zionist Congress in 1905. Tziyyone Tzion was a movement of mostly East European Jews that arose in 1903, in opposition to the Uganda proposal, insisting that the only place for Zionist settlement was in the Jewish people's ancient homeland, the Land of Israel.

9 Yitzhak Wittenberg was the commander of the FPO, the armed Jewish underground in the Vilna ghetto and a leader of the Lithuanian communist underground in the city. Josef Glazman was a Betar leader, a Jewish policeman in the ghetto, and one of the deputy commanders of the armed underground in the ghetto. Wittenberg was sought by the Germans, was arrested by the Judenrat in 1943, freed by the underground, and then turned himself in to protect others from Nazi vengeance. He was murdered by the Germans. Glazman fled the ghetto in July 1943, together with other members of the underground and fell in battle as a partisan in October 1943. For information on Vilna during the Holocaust and on the various personalities and events, see Yitzhak Arad, *Ghetto in Flames: The Struggle and Destruction of the Jews in Vilna in the Holocaust* (Jerusalem: Yad Vashem and the Anti-Defamation League of B'nai Brith, 1980).

I was shunted from Slonim to Vilna with my wife and one-year-old son Abraham. I am one of the "lucky" ones. We live in the "S.S.S.R," the name jokingly given to the larger ghetto as an acronym of its four main streets: Szawelska, Szpitalna, Straszuna, and Rudnicka.

I am "lucky," because the large ghetto is considered more "secure" than the smaller one. I was granted the right to live in this more secure ghetto because of my work pass, which was stamped with the word *Facharbeiter* ("skilled laborer") and the "birdie," as the ghetto people called the emblem of German authority, with its eagle and swastika. I have a "secure job" in the ammunition storehouses, which had been blown up by the retreating Red Army in the Szuszkin Mountains in Sznipeszuk (Snipiski).

My job is under the supervision of an old German, a retired World War I sergeant (*Feldwebel*), a drunk and an antisemite. He was also the boss over two other work locations, and, together, the three places "employed" about 2,000 Jews.

In the office of the *Deutscher Einheit*, which supervised these three important locations, three Jews were made responsible for the Jewish workers there: Kaplan Kaplanski, a well known Folkist leader in pre-war Vilna; Dr. Salwe Gurian, a refugee from Warsaw; and Dr. Gurian in the Szuszkin Mountains location, where about 500 Jews worked. The work consisted of sorting the exploded ammunition materials into piles of copper, brass, iron, and tin. Then it was loaded onto freight cars and transported to ammunition factories in Germany.

The work was very dangerous, because among the materials were still unexploded charges that could go off at any moment. The work was performed in the open, with no protection from the burning sun or the pouring rain. The workday was ten hours straight, without a break, except for the time needed to drink the bitter "coffee" and the watery soup that was distributed to us. The last workers could still be waiting in line for their pitiful portion when the whistle would blow to return to work.

Every visit of the *Feldwebel* to the Szuszkin Mountains brought fear and apprehension to the Jewish workers, as, after each of these visits, dozens of workers would receive a notice of dismissal. One man was not standing up straight enough; another was not working quickly enough, and so on. The ramifications were greater than simply loss of employment. This meant the loss of the work pass, and loss of the work pass meant the person no longer had the right to live in ghetto number 1. Unemployed Jews would be resettled by the Judenrat and the Jewish Police in ghetto number 2, which was raided by the Gestapo, the SS, and the Lithuanian Police almost every night. Hundreds of Jews would be imprisoned overnight in the jails and in the morning would be transported by truck to the Ponary Forest where they were shot.

Every visit by the *Feldwebel* was also a warning that a new "contribution" was to be made by the Jewish workers. Every day a collection would be taken up, and people would sell their last small possession just to be able to "contribute" the required sum. Otherwise one was in danger of losing his job. At every roll call the *Feldwebel* would openly blackmail them with talk about there not being enough work and that the entire place might be shut down. Somehow the decree was always postponed after the collections were taken.

One day I was transferred from a loading gang to a sorting gang that worked close to the ammunition dump. This spot was also close to the kitchen, where a big kettle of coffee was cooking. It was late in the afternoon, and I had not eaten anything all day. With my lips parched, my stomach empty and churning, my head pounding, and a terrible taste in my mouth, the aroma of the coffee was more than I could bear – and there was still an hour or so before the coffee would be distributed.

I doubled over with cramps. I could not stand up. I left my post and lay down on the soft grass about ten yards up the side of a hill. Within five minutes I heard the familiar whistle for a roll call. With great effort I managed to get to my feet and stumble to the usual place. Most of the workers were already lined up, looking pale and frightened. The news was spreading up and down the lines. *Herr Feldwebel* had decided to pay a sudden visit.

The second whistle blew. Everyone had to stand in line, erect, just like soldiers in military formation. In the distance we could already see the *Feldwebel* and Brigade Leader Gurian, accompanied by a squad of soldiers.

His step, deliberate and unhurried, his head high, and his face flaming with malice and alcohol, the *Feldwebel* approached our ranks. His manner and Dr. Gurian's pallor were signs that something was wrong. No doubt some new decree was about to come down violently on our heads. We stood in fear, our hearts trembling, our eyes fixed on the drunken *Feldwebel*, in whose hands now lay the fate of 500 Jews. Would he again threaten us with closing the work location? Why was it taking him so long to start speaking? The redness in his face had flowed down to his neck. His eyes were murderous. If he had started to foam at the mouth, it would not have surprised us.

Finally, his words began to beat upon our heads – lousy workers, dirty Jews, Jewish shit. After a few minutes of convulsive screaming that he would slaughter us all like scabby dogs because we were lazy, and because we sabotaged the work, he pulled a revolver out of his holster and thundered: "The Jew who was sleeping on the hill before, let him come forward!"

Deathly silence. No one moved. He began to scream again, brandishing his revolver. "The man was wearing a dark shirt! Let him step out of the ranks!" Still no one moved.

There was a brief, whispered exchange between the *Feldwebel* and Dr. Gurian, and then the latter appealed to the Jewish workers. He mentioned various matters about the work, about food rations, about discipline, and especially about the incident of the man sleeping on the grass. If that individual did not come forward now, or if the other men did not reveal his identity, then every tenth man would be shot. Glancing in the direction of Yankele Polikanski, an infamous "hero" of the Vilna underworld, as if he was uncertain whether he could trust him, Dr. Gurian said, "*Yehudim b'li pakhad u'bli moreh*" ("Jews, don't be afraid"). With the exception of those five Hebrew words, his entire speech had been in German.

Again, the reply was silence. The men were buffeted by fear of the consequences and by hope that it would all end with a new "contribution." The *Feldwebel* waited five more minutes, then put his revolver back in its holster, and declared: "You are all dismissed from your jobs. You will return to the ghetto immediately."

It struck the workers like a blow. They all knew the consequences of losing their work passes. Nevertheless, not one of the 500 men came forward to reveal the name of the "sleeper." Such an incident could have happened only in Vilna. Jews from other places would not have been able to pass the test. From my sad experiences in the ghettos and camps, I am familiar with cases where Jews, to save their own lives, volunteered their services to the murderers and even helped them in their bloody work of killing other Jews..

Later that evening, in what was once the concert hall of the music society at 6 Rudnicka Street, a meeting took place of all the workers in the Szuszkin Mountains in order to discuss the new situation. However, it really never reached an actual discussion, because Kaplan Kaplanski, the chairman of the Brigades Council in the ghetto, took the floor and made the following incredible report:

> I spoke with the *Feldwebel* and he told me something my ears found hard to believe. He was delighted with the action and the deportment of the Jewish workers, by their stoicism and their beautiful silence. He has never seen anything like it before in his whole life, the *Feldwebel* said. He thinks it showed admirable courage. He forgives the entire brigade, including the man who was caught sleeping. Everyone will be permitted to come to work tomorrow as before.
>
> For myself, I'm glad that such fine behavior took place in my work location. I want to express my own personal thanks to my brother Jews. My special thanks to Dr. Gurian for his alertness and his splendid fulfillment of his responsibility to the group. I'm proud that such a thing happened in Vilna. It is in the tradition of Vilna. If we are destined to survive, we will record this heroic deed in the history of Vilna Jewry.

Survivors have informed me that Kaplan Kaplanski died of cold and starvation in the German labor camp at Stuthoff. With these lines I carry out his last will and testament.

CHAPTER 2

SAVING AVROM FROM THE GESTAPO

The Vilna Ghetto, the summer of 1942

I and three other Jews were working in the chemical factory, DAIVO, which belonged to a Lithuanian named Klimas. Originally, it had been the Jewish "Chemios Is Airbiniai," known in Vilna as "The Refugee Factory," established in 1940 by five Jewish chemical engineers, refugees from Warsaw, in the building of the former Bletskin Printing plant at 23 Stefanska Street. The Jewish workers in the factory were employed at the hardest and dirtiest jobs. They reported for work two hours earlier than the non-Jewish workers, and quit two hours later – and they received no wages or any special ration cards.

Klimas, who was given the factory as a gift for "special services" to the German occupying power, understood that merely by giving us employment and the right to a work pass he was fulfilling his obligation as our employer. Resigned to our fate, we allowed ourselves to be exploited, satisfied with the knowledge that at least we had an *Arbeitsplatz* (a place to work), which "protected" us and gave us the right to receive a bread ration from the ghetto administration.

One evening, returning weary, starved and dispirited to my room in the ghetto after seventy-two hours of backbreaking labor, I found the Jewish ghetto policeman Zhamask waiting for me. He informed me that he had an order from his commander to bring me at once to the Ghetto Police Headquarters. Several minutes later I found myself in the main office of the Ghetto Police. They asked me to sit down at a table across from a high official of the Lithuanian Gestapo, Court Examiner Julian Boyka (a Polish-Lithuanian). Assisting him was the prosecutor of the Jewish ghetto court, Nusenboim (an apostate) and the ghetto policeman Niko Dreisen.

In a calm and leisurely fashion, Boyka took a revolver out of his holster and laid it on the table in front of him. Then he said something to me in Lithuanian. I replied in Polish that I did not understand Lithuanian. "Please," he said to me, "choose whatever language you wish – Russian, Polish, German, even Yiddish. I know them all."

I chose Russian. In the most polite way imaginable, Examiner Boyka began by warning me that I must tell the truth, the whole truth, and nothing but the truth; otherwise, at the first lie in which he caught me, he would shoot me on the spot. Then he proceeded in the precise manner of a trained examiner:

> Your name is Foxman, Joseph. Your wife's name is Hela. You come from Warsaw. You now live in the ghetto on Szpitalna Street, in the Doctor's block, #7, Apartment 17. You work in the DAIVO factory on Stefanska Street, #23. You have and support, outside the ghetto, a boy two-three years of age. The child stays at the home of a Polish woman by the name of Bronisława Kurpi, who lives on Makowa Street #76 in a basement apartment. And don't try to deny it, because I know everything about it.
>
> If you wish, here are a few signs. Today Frau Kurpi visited you at the factory and you gave her a kilo of laundry soap of a bright brown color and four boxes of soap powder. A week ago you gave her four yards of material for a dress, along with some elastic for garters.

As he said this, he put his leg up on the table and showed me the garters on his own socks. They were made of the same material that I had in fact given to the nursemaid of our little boy Avrom a few days before. Indeed, she was keeping him hidden for us outside the ghetto.

The examiner continued:

Frau Kurpi is my sister. I had not seen her for more than ten years. I was certain she was in Warsaw because that's where she was when the war broke out, but recently I met her by accident in the street here and was very happy to see her. She told me that she had gotten married and that she had a healthy, smart little boy; that her husband had been mobilized into the army at the beginning of the war and now she didn't know where he was. I have never visited her home because I'm always too busy, but she visits me frequently. The boy, whose name is Heniusz, is quite advanced for his years. I took a liking to him as if he were my own child.

So imagine my dismay when I accidentally discovered that this child — whom I love so dearly and with whom I have so much fun — is a Jewish child. It hurt me very much. And it hurt me that my sister, a simple Polish Catholic woman, could permit herself to save and raise a Jewish child, bringing such a terrible stain upon our family. If the fact is discovered by anyone else it can result in a lot of trouble for me personally, considering my position in the Security Court. No one will ever believe that I didn't know that my own sister's child, who spends so much time with me, is a Jewish child. I will most certainly be accused of covering up the whole matter. Believe me, Foxman, if it weren't for the fact that I really love that boy, I'd have killed him myself long ago…

And I must say that I've wondered at times how it was possible for my sister, an ordinary servant-girl without any education or cultural background, and with so many physical problems — she's deaf in one ear and has a weak heart — how such a woman could be the mother of such a bright, good-looking child who understands everything and speaks like a grownup. I would often try to get her to talk about her husband who was supposedly a prisoner of war of the Germans, and every time she'd tell me a different story. That's what made me suspicious eventually that my sister didn't even have a husband; that the boy was hers all right, but was an illegitimate child. But when I discovered the boy was Jewish, everything fell into place.

> And now, I want that child back in the ghetto – within twenty-four hours – otherwise he'll be shot as a Jew who was hiding in the city and living as a Christian. I'll do it myself, even though I love the boy. And my sister will also have to be shot for the crime of hiding a Jew. And you and your wife are accomplices, of course, and will suffer the same consequences. So tomorrow evening, at this time, I'll be in the ghetto. I want to see that child right here in the Police Station. Also, I'll want 200 gold rubles and a gold watch. Otherwise –

All the while this Gestapo brute was talking, I felt as if I were sitting on hot coals. I knew that everything he was saying was true, but I sat there like a sphinx, determined to give no sign that I was the boy's father. He had begun the "conversation" calmly and politely, and he finished it in the same manner. As I sat there, staring at this cold-blooded executioner in white gloves, I also appeared to be listening "calmly."

Lighting a cigarette, he asked me what I had to say for myself. My heart was pounding, but I tried to keep my voice steady.

> Everything I heard you say, sir, is correct. I do know Frau Kurpi. The things you mentioned – I gave her. It's also true that the boy she's taking care of is a Jewish child, and that she often visits me at the factory. Only one thing is not accurate: that the child is mine. He's not. The boy belongs to my wife's sister, whose name is Kazimirowska and who is also from Warsaw. Seven days before the war they were rounded up by the Bolsheviks and sent to Siberia. The child and his nursemaid – Frau Kurpi happened to be outside of Vilna that day – they were in a villa in the Kolonia Magistraczka – and the boy was there, miraculously left behind.
>
> My wife and I asked Frau Kurpi to give the child to us, but she refused, insisting she would return the child only to his parents. If she could not do that, then she would keep him for herself as her own child. The next time I talked with her again about the boy, instead of a reply she took an envelope out of her purse and showed me a paper stamped by the Catholic Church; the docu-

> ment says that Bronisława Kurpi had baptized her son and named him Henryk Czesław Kurpi.
>
> After all that has happened, I believe the boy belongs more to Frau Kurpi than to me, although I am the child's uncle. But if you want me to take the boy with me into the ghetto, I'll be glad to do it. And if he is destined to stay alive, we will be forever grateful to you for getting back for us this member of our family who was taken away from us and baptized without the consent of the parents or anyone in his family. So far as the 200 gold rubles are concerned, not only do I not have them now, but I never in my life have even seen such a sum of money. And that is all I can tell you, sir.

As I finished, his calm, almost serene manner suddenly vanished. His face reddened, and, pounding on the table with his fist, he shouted:

> It makes no goddamn difference to me whether the boy is yours or your sister's! It's enough for me that he's Jewish! Tomorrow evening he must be back in the ghetto! And I can't help you do it; if I do, he'll be taken somewhere else! And I must have that money, just as I said!

Then he pointed to the door, and, in a calmer voice again, he said, "*Auf Wiedersehen*, until tomorrow..."

The next morning I did not go to work. I ran around to various people, and they all gave me the same advice: We'll help you bring the child back into the ghetto. Even if only one person in authority knows about this situation, it's not safe for the boy to stay in the city another day. About the money, give him whatever you have, and we'll try to scrape up the rest.

Uncertain about what course to follow, my wife and I went to see the secretary of the Police Commander in the ghetto, Abraham Dimitrowski. A lawyer from Kovno, he was one of the most honest and decent people in the Vilna ghetto. Dimitrowski took a personal interest in our problem and promised to do what he could.

Several hours later, when we returned, he advised us that it would be best if Frau Kurpi and the child left Vilna immediately and stayed away as long as possible. But they must leave today, at once, so that for the Gestapo man it would appear that she had really adopted the child and, fearful of losing him, she had taken him and run away. True, I would be risking my life under this plan, but it was the only way out of the situation. To bring the child back into the ghetto now would mean sentencing him to a certain death, and my wife and I, having admitted to a connection to the child, would also be victims.

That evening, at the appointed hour, when I reported at the police station to see Examiner Boyka, Frau Kurpi and the boy were no longer in Vilna; they were already hidden in a summer home five miles outside the city. My wife had also left the room where we were living. When I was called into the office, I found not only the examiner but also the lawyer Dimitrowski there. This made me feel a bit more secure, because this was a man who not only wanted to help me but also save my son. I will never be able to express in words how grateful I was to him at that moment.

He also conducted the interrogation. Boyko sat at the table, apparently reading over a document. I told Dimitrowski that while the child was not mine, he was still a close member of the family. As I had wanted to carry out the order of the *Herr* Examiner, I had gone to Frau Kurpi's residence with ghetto policeman Perzer that afternoon to bring the child back into the ghetto. (I had in fact gone to the house with the policeman, but only in order to warn her that she and the child were in great danger and must leave Vilna at once.) When I got there, I continued, I found the place locked and learned from a neighbor that Frau Kurpi had gone away early that morning and had taken the child with her.

I could see that my words made no impression at all on Examiner Boyka. Evidently he had already been informed of this development. Apparently he had also been informed by Dimitrowski that I was penniless, because, when I finished my explanations, all he did was hand me the document he had been reviewing and ask me to sign it. I glanced at the statement. It affirmed that my wife and I had no children, and that we did not know the whereabouts of the Kazimorowski child who had been left in the city when the family had been taken away by the Bolsheviks. My hand trembled as I signed the statement, because I had no idea what kind of trick this might be. But after I signed it, the Examiner pointed to the door without another word. I was free to go.

The next morning Dimitrowski shook my hand and wished me *mazal tov*. The matter had been settled in the best possible way. I could rest easy. We would live to see better times and tell the story with a happy ending.

And so it has turned out. My son, my wife, and I, and our dear friend Dimitrowski were lucky enough to survive. I have kept my promise and have told the story with the happy ending.

CHAPTER 3

ABSENT WITHOUT LEAVE FROM BENZINÓWKA

Summer, 1942

I was working at the Deutsches Reichs Lufwaffe *placówka* (work place) near Legjanszna Street, where several hundred Jews were employed. In the ghetto this place was called "The Benzinówka." The chief brigadier of the Jewish workers was the infamous Viktor Oberhartz, a refugee from Warsaw. During the tragic period of the raids in the ghetto, he had been assistant to Police Chief Jacob Gens,[10] actively and assiduously helping the Gestapo and the SS. For his services to the Third Reich in creating the "New Europe," he was awarded a document that designated him a "Useful Jew." He was thus exempted from wearing the yellow patch, was allowed to walk on the sidewalk, to ride a bicycle, to buy provisions for his family directly from the Germans, and was granted other privileges.

10 Jacob Gens (1905–1943) had been the chief of the Jewish Police in the ghetto until his appointment as head of the Judenrat, with the title "Representative of the Ghetto," in July 1942. He had been a Revisionist Zionist and had served as a lieutenant in the Lithuanian army. Gens was married to a Lithuanian Christian woman and could have evaded incarceration in the ghetto, but he chose to enter the ghetto voluntarily. Initially he was popular among the ghetto residents.

In a certain report to the authorities by Brigadier Oberhartz concerning the various projects in the Benzinówka, this loyal lackey noted that four Jewish workers had not reported for work for the last five days. That same day the Ghetto Command received an order from the Gestapo giving them up to twenty-four hours to produce the four Jewish workers mentioned in Oberhartz's report. Their names were listed precisely, as were the numbers on their work passes. They were to be brought to the notorious Lukiszki prison on the charge of having sabotaged the work. It was very well known in the ghetto that hardly anyone ever returned from Lukiszki.

Mine was among the four names on the order. I was then sick in bed under the care of Dr. Kaplan, a well-known Vilna specialist in stomach ailments, who had diagnosed an inflamed gall bladder. He had brought me to the ghetto hospital on Szpitalna Street, but after four days of tests and examinations had sent me home. At that time the hospital was being frequently raided, with patients being removed to Ponary, so, in that respect, it was a bit safer to be at home.

On my first day at home, my friend Haskel Basok came to visit me. The first thing he told me was a shattering secret: His son Chaim, who was an official in the Ghetto Administration, had informed him that the chief of the Jewish Work Police in the ghetto had just received an order from Gens to produce the four "missing" workers of the Benzinówka and that among those names was Foxman, Joseph.

My friend's advice was that I should get dressed immediately and find a place to hide, because at any moment a member of the Work Police could come storming in to arrest me. He added that my wife's turn would come a few days later. What would happen to our little boy then?

Without a moment's hesitation, I replied, "No!" I knew that if the police could not find me, they would arrest an innocent man. Their orders were to produce four men, and the Gestapo didn't really care what their names were. I refused to be the cause of an innocent man's death.

My friend left. The door had hardly closed behind him when I had another bedside visitor. This time it was ghetto policeman Kabatznik. His "sickbed greeting" was: "Foxman, I have an order to bring you in to the Ghetto Police Headquarters right now!"

Having been forewarned, I replied calmly, "I'm seriously ill. This is my sixth day in bed. I'm not even permitted to get out of bed unless my doctor says so."

In the meantime, my wife Hela had run to ask Dr. Kaplan for a note certifying that I was seriously ill and could not leave my bed. But, amazingly, Dr. Kaplan, one of the most beloved doctors in the ghetto, a man of noble character, refused to write the note. When he found out the reason for the urgency, he thought his cooperation would place him and his wife in danger. Try as she would, Hela could not convince him that his fears were groundless, that giving me the "certificate" would bear no reflection on him.

Meanwhile the ghetto policeman remained sitting by my bed, waiting for my wife to return with Dr. Kaplan's note. When she came in with her eyes red from crying and told us the story, he ordered me to get dressed at once and come with him. Hela ran out again, this time to see the police doctor and ask him for help. But again she returned empty-handed. She ran to the Work Police, to the Ghetto Command, whoever she could think of, but to no avail. Everyone listened and shook their heads.

The curfew hour had arrived, and, as Jews were forbidden to appear on the streets, the policeman had no choice but to spend the night at my bedside.

At five in the morning, again Hela began running from one place to another – again with no results. The Gestapo officer had already arrived in the ghetto in order to ascertain how matters stood with the four Benzinówka workers. He waited until noon.

The same day a report was delivered to the Gestapo: Three of the wanted men had been brought to the prison, and the fourth was actually sick and had been unable to work. Attached to the report was a note from Dr. Szedletz, director of the Ghetto Hospital, that I had in fact been a patient in the hospital for four days, under the treatment of Dr. Kaplan, that I was still very ill and unable to work.

Once more I had had a narrow escape.

CHAPTER 4

SAVING FEYGL

In late 1941, as a laborer in the Construction Commando at the Reichs Fur Factory "Kailis," I was issued a yellow pass, which meant that the bearer and his wife and children were temporarily "safe." During the second *Aktion* of the yellow passes (the first one took place on Black Friday, October 24, 1941), all workers and ghetto officials with yellow passes were "resettled" from the larger ghetto, through the gate on Jatkowa Street, to the smaller ghetto ("Number 2"), from where the inhabitants had already been deported.

In an attempt to save a Jewish child with our yellow pass, my wife and I took with us as our "daughter" one of the teachers from the Brokower Beth Yaakov Seminary, Feygl Bogesz, whose father was a rabbi from a small town in Volhynia. When we got to the gate, I showed my documents to the SS officer and explained that I was Foxman and that my wife and daughter were with me. He took one look at my wife and Feygl and sneered, "Which one is your wife, and which one is your daughter?"

My wife was then thirty-four years old and looked much younger; Feygl was twenty-four and looked older. When I pointed out who was who, the SS officer asked me another question: "How old is your wife, and how old is your daughter?"

I replied that my wife was thirty-eight, and my daughter eighteen. This was so patently untrue that he said: "You and your wife can go out, but your 'daughter' stays here," and he motioned her in the direction of the courtyard gate near the Butchers' Synagogue. My wife and Feygl burst into tears and loud wailing. My wife kissed the officer's hand, pleading with him not to take away her only child; she was our whole life, and we would not be separated from her. If she had to stay, so would we.

His lips twisted in a cruel grin. "*Ja, Ja, bitte*," and he pointed to the policeman standing at the courtyard gate. At this point, Herr A? [*sic*] the brigade leader of the Labor Detachment, intervened and said, "I know them from before the war, and I know they had an older daughter." The SS man, however, refused to accept his testimony and insisted we were trying to trick him. As punishment for our attempted deception, all of us would stay there in the ghetto.

Suddenly there was a commotion and an outcry on the other side of the gate. A boy of thirteen or fourteen had jumped from a window on the seventh floor. The SS officer ran to see what was going on. Taking advantage of the opportunity, my wife and "daughter" and I ran out toward the street leading to ghetto number 2 and melted into the crowd.

Feygl stayed with us until September 1943, when the Vilna ghetto was finally liquidated. It is quite possible that she was among the women who were sent to Estonia and from there to her death.

CHAPTER 5

SURVIVING SMUGGLING

Every unexpected official visit to the ghetto usually meant some very unpleasant surprise. In an attempt not to be taken off guard, a secret telephone was set up in the office of the *Torwache* (Gate Watch) linked to the office of the Jewish Police in the ghetto, whose function it was to maintain "order" at the gate. The *Torwache* was headed first by the infamous Oster and later by the equally infamous Meir Levas.[11] Whenever one of the German bigwigs arrived at the ghetto gate, the Jewish Police inside the ghetto would immediately know who the "guests" were. (The most frequent visitors were Maurer, Weiss, Kittel, Meyer, and Langbauer.[12])

11 The reference is apparently to Rafael Oster (Aster in some sources), who was the first commander of the *Torwache*. He was promoted and transferred to a more senior position in February 1942, and was succeeded by Meir Levas. Oster later became the head of the criminal police in the ghetto.

12 Franz Murer (his name appears incorrectly as Maurer in some sources) was a SS officer who served as the "Jewish expert" (*Judenreferent*) in the German civilian government in the Vilna district and oversaw the ghetto. Martin Weiss was a *SS Hauptscharführer* who commanded a murder unit in Ponary from the summer of 1941, and continued to serve in the district SS with responsibilities in the Vilna ghetto. Bruno Kittel, known as "the butcher of Vilna," headed the Jewish section of the Gestapo in Vilna from June 1943, and oversaw the liquidation of the ghetto in September 1943. He succeeded Murer as head of the Jewish section. Langbauer is apparently a reference to *SS Obersturmführer* Rolf Neugebauer, who commanded the Vilna SIPO and SD office from early 1942 to October 1943.

On one of his "walking tours" on the way to the ghetto, Maurer noticed from a block away that several persons carrying packages had been allowed into the ghetto without being stopped and searched. When Maurer entered the ghetto, he went straight to Gens, head of the ghetto administration, and ordered him to have Levas report to him immediately. When Levas appeared, Maurer asked him for the names of the men who had been on duty at the gate five minutes earlier. Levas went out and returned in a few moments with the information: on duty had been Chaim Lusko and Mordecai Bernstein.

After writing their names in his notebook, Maurer ordered that the two policemen be brought to Lukiszki Prison at ten the next morning. Their crime: helping to smuggle food products into the ghetto. The two policemen were jailed, but were later freed after some "intervention."

The control at the gate thereafter was greatly tightened. On the day in question, Maurer himself was present at the checkpoint when the labor brigades returned to the ghetto from their work places outside. Every worker was searched. As they had no prior warning, many of them had no chance to get rid of the things they were smuggling in. They were punished on the spot with twenty-five lashes on their bare backs. Some fell unconscious and were sent to hospitals.

The results of this tightening of "security" at the ghetto gate were felt almost immediately. The hunger in the ghetto worsened, and the public soup kitchens were swamped. Yet those who worked outside the ghetto somehow still managed to find food for their families. When the whippings also failed to stop the smuggling of foodstuffs, Maurer ordered even those found with a few potatoes or a bit of flour to be sent to the ghetto jail, Liszko.[13] On several occasions Weiss suddenly appeared in the ghetto and demanded that all those in the Liszko jail be turned over to him, regardless for what "crime" they had been arrested. Soon the fear of being sent to Liszko was just as great as being sent to Lukiszki.

One day during this period of tightened control at the ghetto gate, I decided I simply had to get out of the ghetto and find some food for my wife and "family" – which at that time consisted of several Beth Yaakov teachers, the wife of the Rakiske [Rokiškis] rabbi, and two young Hasidim who, because they were Sabbath observers, could not work outside the ghetto. On a dark

13 The reference is to the ghetto prison on Lidzki Street.

night after curfew, "Big Yankel" (who worked in the German glove factory) and I went out through the "blind door" in a courtyard on Szpitalna Street. We were able to buy some flour and put it into the "compresses" wrapped around our bodies.

On our way back to the ghetto, a cry of "Halt!" and the blinding beam of a flashlight stopped us in our tracks. Before us stood a giant of a "Klump" (as the Lithuanian cops were called). He fired a number of questions at us: who were we? where were we coming from? what were we carrying? After searching us and confiscating 500 rubles from my pocket, he took us to the Sixth District police station, which had jurisdiction over the ghetto.

After asking us a few questions and writing down the answers, they ordered us to strip. Stark naked, we were locked into a small room with barred windows and a cement floor, and not even a stick of furniture. In the morning they gave us our clothes, but not our boots. Every few hours the door would open, and a policeman would "visit" us. They gave us nothing to eat or drink. In the evening we were again ordered to strip.

The second day was just like the first, with still nothing to eat or drink. On the third morning we were again given our clothing but not our boots. Instead, they gave us each a pair of old worn-down shoes. We wouldn't need our boots where we were going, the policeman jeered.

Some time later we were honored by the arrival of the German Police *Kommisar*, the Lithuanian chief of police, and a Jewish policeman named Szmulewitz from the *Torwache*. They took us to the office of the ghetto gate. The German and the Lithuanian left, and Szmulewitz took us into another room. We learned that the Lithuanian police had sent a report about us to the Gestapo, and the Gestapo had ordered that we be incarcerated in the Lukiszki prison. After a great deal of effort by Szmulewitz, we were released.

After three days of hunger, thirst, cold, and fear, I returned to my family completely spent. On the Sabbath I went to the synagogue and, for the fifth time, "*bentched gomel*," a prayer of thanks for deliverance from impending disaster. This same Szmulewitz, one of those rare Jewish ghetto policemen who acted selflessly to help others survive, had so many friends among the Lithuanians that he was even able to hide from the Nazis during the liquidation of the Vilna ghetto.

CHAPTER 6

DISCOVERING MASS GRAVES

By order of the *Feldwebel*, forty Jewish workers from the destroyed ammunition storehouses in the Szuszkin Mountains were transferred to a "work project" in Burbiszki. Since only seven men volunteered for this transfer, lots were cast for the balance. I was among the thirty-three others.

The project consisted of building a barrier of concrete posts and barbed wire around Burbiszki Square. And since we were actually working several hundred meters away from the square, we were able to establish contact with some young peasant boys who pastured cows in the nearby meadows. These Christian youngsters, eight to twelve years old, gradually befriended us. Every day they would sell us (at a good price) potatoes, bread, and vegetables. When they had learned to trust us, they confided that about 200 meters from our work place there were several mass graves of some 200 Jews who had been shot by the Lithuanian police.

This was seven months after the ghetto had been established in Vilna. Day by day, the number of the people in the ghetto decreased, with the victims finding their eternal rest in mass graves in the Ponary forest. Yet rumors persisted in the ghetto that all those Jews who had been seized and deported were now in labor camps. At a time when the word "Ponary" had already become an abomination in the ghetto, certain "interested parties" were circulating stories about a "second ghetto" in Ponary where Jews lived and worked. It never even occurred to anyone that tens of thousands of human beings could be slaughtered in cold blood.

With the permission of the German authorities, the Ghetto Administration set up a Postal Section under Dr. Zemach Feldstein, a prominent Zionist leader and educator who had been director of the Hebrew *gymnasium* (high school) in Kovno. Through this postal system many refuges from Warsaw communicated with their families and friends in the Warsaw ghetto. The letters were not too horrendous – or perhaps an "unknown hand" let through only the "good letters" and destroyed the others.

I, too, communicated with my wife's family in the Warsaw ghetto, and we exchanged many letters. From these letters we learned that there was a ghetto in Warsaw with half a million Jews. However, the knowledge that such a ghetto had existed in Warsaw and other cities for three years also prevented us from accepting the idea that Jews were being massacred and that Polish Jewry was on the verge of extinction. People preferred to believe the "good" things rather than the unthinkable news that the deported Jews were no longer alive. Nor did we know that many of the letters that arrived at police headquarters had been obtained either by deception, blackmail, or force, and that most of the Jews in the ghetto believed the "facts" contained in those letters.

The first call of the Polish Workers' Party (the Communist party) to the Jewish population in the Vilna ghetto was, in fact, not a call to resistance or rebellion, but simply to disregard what their "providers" and misleaders were telling them. The call was a blunt declaration that all those Jews who had been picked up during the raids, all those who had been arrested after the big "provocation," all those who had been deported on Yom Kippur, all those from the "second ghetto," and all those who had been taken out of the ghetto and had not returned had all been taken to Ponary by the Lithuanian police and the Gestapo. Ponary was not a labor camp, but a death camp, and anyone who was taken to Ponary had gone to his death.

The "other side" was not asleep either. Every day new "documents" and "proofs" and "facts" were fabricated and disseminated. The end of these illusions, however, was brought about by the tragic discovery of two mass graves in Burbiszki. Two days after the discovery, we chose a suitable time, when all the workers had gone to the kitchen for their so-called lunch. A group of five men – Kadish, Epstein, Foxman, Gurian, and Shura – went to the site with small shovels. We did not have to dig very deeply before our shovels uncovered the bodies. The disorder made the shock even worse. The bodies were sitting, lying down, standing, entangled in each other. They had been killed recently enough for us to make out their features and the colors of their clothing. After verifying the manner of their death, we re-covered the sacred graves of these martyrs.

The very same day we spread the news of our discovery among the Jewish workers in Burbiszki. By evening the 20,000 Jews in the ghetto were already talking about it. Finally, they began to realize that all the previous "actions" of the Germans had been carried out not for the purpose of recruiting "workers" but to round up candidates for execution. The "fact" of the mass graves at Burbiszki was more than sufficient proof.

Several days later the head of the Gestapo demanded that the ghetto police find those individuals who had dug up the graves of the executed "Communists." The Germans – especially the Gestapo and the SS – were extremely concerned that no witnesses be left to their murderous activities. For that reason they would mercilessly eliminate any and all possible witnesses, even those who had served them with utmost loyalty.

Learning that the Gestapo had put a price on their heads, Dr. Shura, Epstein, and Kadish fled to Lida with a group of escapees. Dr. Gurian and I stayed behind in the ghetto. Dr. Gurian resigned from his work in the Council office, and I was dismissed from my work in Burbiszki. The office of the Jewish Police reported to the Gestapo that, upon investigation, they had found that the guilty parties had already fled from the ghetto and could not be found.

For many long weeks Dr. Gurian and I lived in daily fear of death. Not until the Gestapo chief was recalled and the Burbiszki "project" was abandoned did I again – for the sixth time – go to the Lubavitcher *shul* at 9 Szpitalna.

CHAPTER 7

SURVIVING ESCAPE ROUTES

By the end of 1941, the 80,000 Jews in Vilna had already been reduced to one-quarter of that number. The German *Aktionen* and raids were still taking place. Every *Aktion*, every raid, had been designated its own name by the population: the Yom Kippur *Aktion*; the *Aktion* of the skilled workers; the *Aktion* of the white passes; and so on. The remaining Jews in Vilna lived in perpetual fear that tomorrow the hand of the German authority or the Lithuanian police would reach them; that no one would escape.

At that time, however, there was an "escape route" to cities and ghettos where the living conditions were economically and politically "better" than in Vilna – probably because they were part of the Third Reich. Whatever the reason, the Jews there were at first treated better than we were in Vilna. For example, in Warsaw, Bialystok, and Grodno, the mass annihilation of the Jewish population took place a few months later than in Lida, Baranowicze, or Slonim.[14]

14 It is interesting to note the perspective that conditions were better elsewhere. Whereas it was true that systematic physical annihilation had begun earlier in Vilna than in Warsaw, the day-to-day conditions in the Warsaw ghetto were far worse than those in Vilna. Whereas Vilna had experienced the murder of the majority of the Jewish community, followed by a relatively stable ghetto period, the Jews of Warsaw experienced horrendous living conditions that caused the death of more than 20 percent of the ghetto population before the deportations to Treblinka began in July 1942 (Ed.).

The major "escape route," therefore, went to Warsaw, Bialystok, and Grodno. Once a week, often twice, large trucks of the Deutsche Reichspost (the German postal service) drove into Vilna, and, when they left, they carried inside them about sixty passengers. This "action" of transporting Jews from Vilna to Bialystok and Warsaw was headed by the son of Rabbi Karol of Warsaw. The trucks were driven by German army chauffeurs and were escorted by Wehrmacht officers. Most of the escapees were refugees from Warsaw who were going "back home." Among those who escaped this way were Dr. Osias Solowiejczyk, former Senator Jacob Trackenheim, former Sejm Deputy Leyb Minzberg from Lodz, and other prominent personalities.

The escape route to Lida, Baranowicze, and Slonim was conducted by several groups who took the passengers out in trucks belonging to the Pen-Centros Company, escorted by Lithuanian officers. They would be dropped off at Lida, and from there they would try to find further transportation. These passengers were provided with all the necessary documents and passes to get them through the checkpoints. All went well with this "action" until the Gestapo got wind of it. During one such smuggling operation, all the passengers were seized, along with their escort, and sent to Ponary.

Although I was in possession of a yellow pass, which "assured" the bearer and his family of staying alive for a given period, I decided to leave the Vilna ghetto. I made the necessary financial arrangements with the "escape route" to take my wife and me to Lida. From there I would be smuggled out in a beer truck to Slonim, where many of my family were still living. (My brother Chaim, his wife Sheyne, and their daughter Sarah; my sister Sarah Stoliar and her husband Menahem and their son Isak; my younger brother Shlomo, a journalist; my sisters Fanya and Rachel, who both worked in a hospital as nurses; our relatives Garfinkel, Miletski, Weinberg, and others.)

It was the evening of October 24, 1941. All the passengers who were supposed to ride to Lida were waiting with their suitcases in a dark courtyard at 76 Rudnicki for the truck, which was due to arrive at eleven o'clock. Two hours after the appointed time – two of the longest hours in my life – we finally heard the horn of the approaching vehicle. The truck stopped at the ghetto gate, its headlights flooding the street with bright light, and frightening us even further. With trembling fingers we helped each other put on our knapsacks and waited impatiently to enter the truck.

At that moment we were given the bad news: Chief of Police Gens had issued an order forbidding any vehicle from entering or leaving the ghetto that night. To all our appeals and offers of "compensation" the guards had one reply: orders are orders.

Shattered and exhausted, we all returned to our homes and to the continued prospect of daily terror. Of all the passengers I was the only one with a yellow pass; the others had white passes or no passes at all. None of us slept that night, but, in the morning, when we met in the street, we shook hands and congratulated each other: we had learned that the truck that was supposed to take us out had been stopped by the police and Gestapo outside the ghetto, and that the two Jews who were leading the operation, along with two Lithuanians in police uniforms and the driver, had all been arrested and faced certain death.

Through an accidental order of Police Chief Gens, forty-two Jews had been saved from death, including my wife and I. That was the last truck that ever took anyone out of the Vilna ghetto. That escape route had been eliminated.

Having grown up among *Hasidim*, I was so accustomed to their mode of prayer that, whenever I felt nostalgic for a bit of *Yiddishkeit*, I would go to the *minyan* of the Kaidanover *Hasidim*, which met in a small room on the second floor of 1 Szawelska. So it was there that I went once again, after this lucky turn of events, to worship and to "*bentch gomel*" for the seventh time....

CHAPTER 8

"SMUGGLING" MILK

The winter of 1942 in Vilna was exceptionally cold and snowy. The supplies of firewood in the ghetto had long ago been exhausted. People were burning furniture, doors, attic beams, stair treads, whatever they could get their hands on. Everything flammable was being used to warm frozen limbs or to cook our skimpy fare. The ghetto was being cleaned out of every spare bit of lumber. The meager supply of firewood that the Ghetto Administration received for a whole month was barely enough for two or three days. People wore their overcoats indoors and slept in their clothing – and still could not get warm.

For hot meals the Jews in the ghetto hit on the idea of taking their pots to the bakeries and having the food cooked there at a slight charge. These bakeries, which sold bread at a price fixed by the Judenrat and the police, received sufficient firewood for their needs. There were not enough bakeries, however, to accommodate so many pots. Women waited in line in front of these places for hours in order to cook a meal for their husbands and children who were out working and would come home late in the evening. But often enough they would have to return to their homes with the food uncooked, as the lines were so long.

One Sunday morning (an official day of "rest"), having eaten no hot food for a week, I ventured outside the ghetto with a friend to see if we could buy some wood somewhere. On the way we met Yisroel Leibowitz, a worker in the glove factory. His two young children were sick, and he was going out to look for a bit of milk for them.

As we were returning home – my friend and I with the bundles of kindling on our shoulders, and Leibowitz with 2 liters of milk under his arm – we were stopped by a German officer who demanded to see our passes permitting us to leave the ghetto on a Sunday. Since we had no such passes, he searched us thoroughly right in the middle of the street. He found nothing, except what we were carrying openly. We had the impression that he was about to let us go, but his attitude changed instantly when he saw the milk.

"Lousy swine!" he bellowed. "We shed our blood on the front lines, and our wounded men suffer in the hospitals without milk because you damned Jews buy up all the milk and butter for yourselves! You ought to drink poison, not milk!"

And he began to beat Leibowitz hysterically on the face and head, until his victim fell bleeding to the ground. Prostrate at the feet of his tormentor, Leibowitz begged for mercy, pleading that he was a productive worker in a German factory and that he needed the milk for his sick children.

My friend also began to plead for mercy, appealing to the German's "better nature." When he tried to kiss the German's hand, he received such a blow from that same hand that he, too, fell to the ground. I stood frozen to the spot, unable to utter a word.

"*Nein*!" the officer screamed. "All three of you will be shot like dogs for this smuggling! To Gestapo headquarters!"

And he proceeded to march us, beaten and helpless, through the streets, each of us certain that this was the end. My mind felt numb, except for the thought that tomorrow I would be lying in a damp grave at Ponary. I held on tightly to a vision of the two most precious things in my life – my wife in the ghetto and my son on the Aryan side with the Christian woman. This I would take with me to Ponary and keep fresh in my mind to the very last breath.

I remember thinking: how cheap human life is today, and how trivial the price of a Jew – three Jewish lives for two bottles of milk and a bundle of kindling. And our Jewish God in heaven, the God of mercy and compassion, whom we serve with prayer, praise, and thanksgiving, is blind and deaf to our sufferings.

"Halt!" The sharp command broke into our tragic thoughts. We were at the building of the Lithuanian Regional Commissariat. The German officer spoke for a few moments with the sentry and then said to us: "Beat it! And don't ever let me catch you out here again!"

Astounded, we bowed low, but did not budge. Not until he repeated his command did we start moving away slowly. In my heart I recited my last confession of faith, as I was certain that at the next moment I would fall dead with a bullet in my back. We had heard so many such stories. But we walked further and further away from the German, until we turned into another street, and we saw no one was following us. At that point we took a deep breath and hurried back to the ghetto, more dead than alive.

To this day the end of that episode is a puzzle to me. I cannot explain it. What caused that officer who had beaten us unmercifully and who was ready to strangle us with his own hands to finally let us go free?

That Sabbath I went to the Butchers' *shul* on Diznienska Street to "*bentch gomel*" for the eighth time.

CHAPTER 9

"SMUGGLING" FLOUR

High above the main gate of the Vilna ghetto on Rudnicki Street, across from the Church of All Saints, illuminated at night by a large electric light, hung a huge sign in German: "Bringing foodstuffs into the ghetto is strictly forbidden. Anyone found guilty of violating this regulation will receive the death penalty. By order of the Commandant of the City of Vilna."

Despite this order, the Jews of the Vilna ghetto did everything within their power to smuggle life-sustaining food products into the ghetto. Legal and illegal methods were used; all sorts of tricks were invented in order to provide one's family with such things as bread and potatoes.

The Jewish workers in the chemical factory (this writer among them) devised a scheme for smuggling potatoes and cornmeal into the ghetto. On Konska Street there was a Polish theater (I think the name was Nowoczi), and one of the actors was a Pole named Jerzy Sawicki. For a short time he had worked in the same chemical factory as a general laborer in order to receive a work card from the German Labor Office.

To this theater we would transport, in a horse and wagon driven by the Polish worker Strelowski, 50 kilograms of flour in five large sacks. We would do this in broad daylight, as if we were bringing some supplies ordered by the theater.

In the evening, when the play was over, and the audience, actors and stage hands had left, Sawicki and another actor would stay behind and move the five sacks of flour or potatoes up to the attic, which led to another building. There we would be waiting to pick up the "corpse" (as we called a bundle that was smuggled into the ghetto). (I should note here that the driver and the actors did not do this for purely humanitarian reasons but received a considerable amount of money.)

One day, when we were smuggling in such a "corpse," we had with us, in addition to the driver, another worker from the factory named Basok. The trip was proceeding smoothly, and we had already unloaded four of the five sacks into the theater. When I went out to pick up the fifth one, I got one of the worst scares of my life. Standing beside the wagon was a high-ranking police official. I was wearing my work clothes with the yellow patch in front and on my back.

With a smug, sarcastic grin, as if he had apprehended some dangerous criminals, he asked me what we Jews were doing in that theater building and what we were unloading. Showing him my work card, I explained to him that my friend and I worked in the chemical factory, ZAWA, and that the director of the factory, Herr Klimas (a well-known name to the police) had ordered us to deliver these bags of lime and gypsum to the theater, which was being renovated. My partner confirmed my story in good Lithuanian, as the driver nodded his head.

This incident took place two days after the Jewish opera singer, Lara Lewicka, and another person had been stopped by a policeman while leaving the tailor shops outside the ghetto. When a pound of beans and a half-pound of butter was found on them, the policeman sent them to police headquarters, from which they were transferred to Ponary. If two Jews had paid with their lives for a pound of beans and a half-pound of butter, what punishment would my friend and I receive for smuggling in 50 pounds of flour?

Basok and I spoke to the policeman "calmly and slowly." One did not have to be a psychologist, however, to recognize that we were all atremble and that our hearts were pounding. In another moment he would find the fifth sack, which was still in the wagon, check its contents, and our fate would be sealed.

But for some reason he did not do that. He believed our story. Perhaps he believed us because I spoke with him in Russian, not Polish. The Lithuanians hated the Polish language so much that even those who knew Polish would pretend not to understand it. That's how deep-seated the antagonism was between Lithuanians and Poles in Vilna. Or perhaps it was because my friend spoke to him in a good Lithuanian. Sometimes that meant a lot. Or perhaps he believed the driver, who sat there nodding his head artlessly in agreement with everything we said. Or perhaps it was the magic word "Klimas," a name familiar to every police officer in Vilna.

Whatever the reason, the policeman believed us and took his leave of us in Lithuanian. However, that was the last time we could use the theater as a smuggling point. It had served us well. In four weeks we had brought in 200 kilograms of flour.

On the Sabbath following this incident I worshipped at the Yagitche *shul*, pledged a sum of money to the "Winter Relief" fund when I was called up to the Torah, and, for the ninth time, "*bentched gomel.*"

CHAPTER 10

"SMUGGLING" PEOPLE

When the shortage of firewood reached catastrophic proportions, the Ghetto Administration came to an agreement with the German commandant by which certain areas of a nearby forest could be used as a source of supply – subject, however, to the following conditions:

(1) the work in the forest must be done only by Jews;
(2) the supervision over this Jewish work brigade would be by the Jewish Police;
(3) a minimum quota would be set for each worker;
(4) the worker would not be allowed to return to the ghetto until he completed his norm;
(5) 50 percent of the finished firewood produced would go to the city proper; the other 50 percent would go to the ghetto.

Chief of Police Gens accepted all these conditions, and the Judenrat established a special department for "Exploitation of the Forest." It was headed by L. Greenstein, a refugee from Warsaw and a former dealer in second-hand furniture and scrap metal. The supervision over the Jewish work brigades was entrusted to the infamous commander of the Ghetto Police, Kalisz, also a refugee from Warsaw, and his deputies, Lucien Salzwasser and A. Auerbach. Their attitude toward the Jewish workers was not any more lenient than that of the SS or the Gestapo.

In order not to increase the number of ghetto policemen, whose contingent was already full, the chief of police mobilized a number of able-bodied Jewish officials to serve in the forest. Among them was my brother-in-law Ari. He was given a cap with a blue-and-white band and a Star of David armband and was sent off to a place 40 kilometers from Vilna. A month and a half later we still had had no word from him. My wife and I became more and more uneasy about her brother, and we began knocking on doors of various officials. But everywhere we received the same reply: all those who had gone off to the forest to work were in good health; as soon as they fulfilled their work norms they would return to the ghetto.

One evening, as I returned home from work outside the ghetto, my wife came out to greet me with the good news that she had received a letter from her brother. It had been brought into the ghetto by a Christian woman who was now waiting in our apartment. The letter, in her brother's handwriting, was very encouraging, especially since, in these abnormal times, not to hear from someone for almost two months was a cause for great concern.

Our optimism, however, was tempered by another worry: the young woman, Miss Pileczka, from a village near the forest, had received the letter from my brother-in-law with specific instructions to give it to any one of the Jewish workers who were returning to the ghetto. Miss Pileczka, however, was extremely interested in seeing what the ghetto looked like from the inside. She wanted to meet us and bring back personal regards to my brother-in-law. As she had heard about the starvation in the ghetto, she also had decided to bring us a gift of provisions. And this no one would agree to take from her to deliver to us.

She therefore tried – successfully – to attach herself to a group of Jewish workers who had returned to the ghetto late that evening. But it was impossible for her to leave the ghetto in the evening; she would have to wait until morning. So there was nothing else for her to do but stay with us overnight.

This was not such a simple thing in those days. It so happened that the night before there had been a Gestapo raid on Szpitalna Street, and among those arrested was a certain Adolf Segal and a Polish woman who had brought him food from the outside. They were both shot at Ponary – she for smuggling and he for "racial defilement." We therefore had good reason to be apprehensive about our situation.

It should also be noted that, in the event of a Gestapo raid, every occupant of every room had to be accounted for, and the names of the occupants were posted outside the door.

At two o'clock in the morning, two Jewish policemen, accompanied by a Lithuanian officer, knocked at our door and demanded to see our "documents." Miss Pileczka, not having any documents, was ordered to get dressed and go with the police. As the person responsible for the apartment, I, too, was ordered to go with them for violating the order prohibiting non-authorized persons from staying in any of the rooms. My attempts to "negotiate" with them proved to no avail. We were both taken to jail. I was put in the men's section; the Polish woman in the women's section.

The only other person in the men's section was a young man who, despite the late hour, was sitting up on his cot, lost in thought. My entrance startled him, but he stood up and offered me his hand. After hearing my story, he told me his. He was a native of Bialystok. At the outbreak of the war, he had been studying at the yeshivah there. He had come to Vilna in the last truck of the Deutsche Reichspost, hoping to bring his two "refugee" sisters back to Bialystok. With the escape route cut off, they all remained stuck in Vilna. He didn't have a *groszy* in his pocket.

The night before, during a "control check," he had been found with no documents except the one that identified him as a resident of Bialystok. To make matters infinitely worse, he had a revolver in his possession. He had already been interrogated twice by a Jewish policeman named Levin and had been beaten mercilessly.

When he felt a little better, he got up, went to a corner of the cell for a bottle of water, and washed his hands. He held out the bottle to me to do the same. Then he said: "The rabbi with whom I studied in Bialystok told me once: 'If, God forbid, you are ever in a mortally dangerous situation, you must recite the following prayer.'" He then recited the prayer that calls upon God for help and protection from evil.

"I have followed the rabbi's advice," concluded the young man, "and it has always helped me. Last night a truck drove up to the jail from the Aryan side. Five minutes later the jail was empty of prisoners – except for me. Later I learned that the Gestapo hangman Weiss was on that truck. Wash your hands and recite the prayer with me."

I did as he asked and recited the "*V'shomraini*" ("watch over me") prayer after him three times, word for word.

Several hours later a young Jewish policewoman entered and ordered us to follow her. She led us into the office of the prison warden, who informed us: "You are free. Go."

When we were out in the prison yard, the *yeshivah* student said to me: "You see, it helped. It has saved me thirteen times already."

He looked around the yard and found a piece of paper. "Here, I'll write it down for you. Keep it with you at all times. It will come in handy."

Waiting for me at the prison gate was my wife. When I told her the story about the young man and translated the prayer for her, she smiled, "Yes, prayer is a good thing, but in addition you must also give *tzedakah* [charity]."

In any case, I was free. Maybe the prayer worked, maybe the *tzedakah*, maybe a combination of both. The Polish woman was also freed, and she returned safely to her village.

On the Sabbath, for the tenth time since I had been in the Vilna ghetto, I went to *shul* to "*bentch gomel*."

APPENDIX

Translation 301/3605 J[15]
B.H. Kargastein

To the Main Office of the Jewish Historical Society:

When I learned from the newspapers that the above-mentioned organization intends to elaborate about the martyrdom of Jewish children during the German occupation, I decided to send this to the above-mentioned commission, to include by the largest court of the Soviet Lithuanian republic from May 10, 1945, from the town of Vilnius.

Before entering the Ghetto in Vilnius, my wife and I (who were escaping with others from Warsaw in 1941) were forced to give away our son of 13 months, Abrahama Henocha Fuksman), to his Polish nanny, Bronisława Kurpa. We gave her 90% of our possessions that we had at that time, furniture, clothing, bedding, and lots of money. In a word, everything we owned.

We went to the ghetto with what we had on our bodies. Not even a month went by from the time of our entering the ghetto when the same Mrs.

15 This document was apparently translated from Yiddish to Polish by Julia Jakubowska at the Jewish Historical Institute in Warsaw [Ed.]. The English translation is by the author. Copy of the Yiddish original can be found in Joseph Foxman's testimony at the Jewish Historical Institute, Yad Vashem Archives, M.49.E/3605, March 17, 1947.

Kurpa found out that we were working outside the ghetto in the Szuszkin hills in the suburbs of Snipiski in Vilna (Vilnius). She showed up unexpectedly demanding additional money, above the money she had already received from us. All my talking and begging didn't help, crying and telling her that we don't have anything, not even enough food to satisfy our hunger. And that's the way it was – and this is the truth.

Mrs. Kurpa threatened me that if I didn't give her the money she demanded, she would go the Gestapo and turn in our circumcised little boy. When I asked her to return my son, she refused to return him. Then I realized that the nanny, who is raising our baby, is blackmailing me. I couldn't find any way out. I risked my life every day in order to get the money that she demanded.

Anyhow, I paid her 5,000–8,000 rubles each month. By the end she forced my wife and I to put in writing with our signatures that we are giving her our baby forever to be her own. And also to date the letter a month earlier, before the Germans occupied Vilnius.

I agreed and did exactly what she demanded for the simple reason to save my baby, and also myself and my wife. If she would have taken the baby to the Gestapo office, not only would the baby's life be endangered, but also the whole family would have been in danger.

Mrs. Kurpa baptized our baby and named him Czesław Henryk Kurpa and registered him as her own born son from her marriage. (She was an old maid, about 40 years of age). Her blackmail lasted till the Red Army occupied Vilnius. Also, after the liberation, she blackmailed me in a different way, and I was many times stopped and arrested always with false accusations by Mrs. Kurpa. One time she accused me of being a thief and having stolen from the factory when I was in charge of the Dajwa chemical factory in Vilnius, on Małej Stefanskiej Street 23. The second time she accused me before the authorities that I had hidden 5,000 rubles and gold. The third time, that I beat her up. The fourth time, that I have a gun. The fifth time, that I attacked her in her apartment during the night with other Jews dressed in police uniforms and that we ransacked her apartment in that particular attack, so she claimed. The sixth time, she accused me before the authorities, that I was a counterrevolutionary in 1941. They were going to arrest me, but I was able to hide out.

The court and the authorities were fed up with us. Mrs. Kurpa and my face were known in the Russian institutions in the city of Vilnius and also the police stations, and especially in the main administration in the city of Vilnius, in the NKVD, NKGB, in the public prosecutor's office. Everywhere I was known famously as a man who had been blackmailed, and everywhere she presented herself as the injured party because she was the nanny of our child.

In the Lithuanian papers, she was known as a housekeeper and that we took advantage of her and were not grateful that Mrs. Kurpa saved our baby. We can't understand that the years cannot be reversed. With all that, the truth triumphed. Twice the court after listening to tens of witnesses from her side, and then listening to my wife's side, at the end they awarded the baby to us.

ORIGINAL YIDDISH MANUSCRIPT

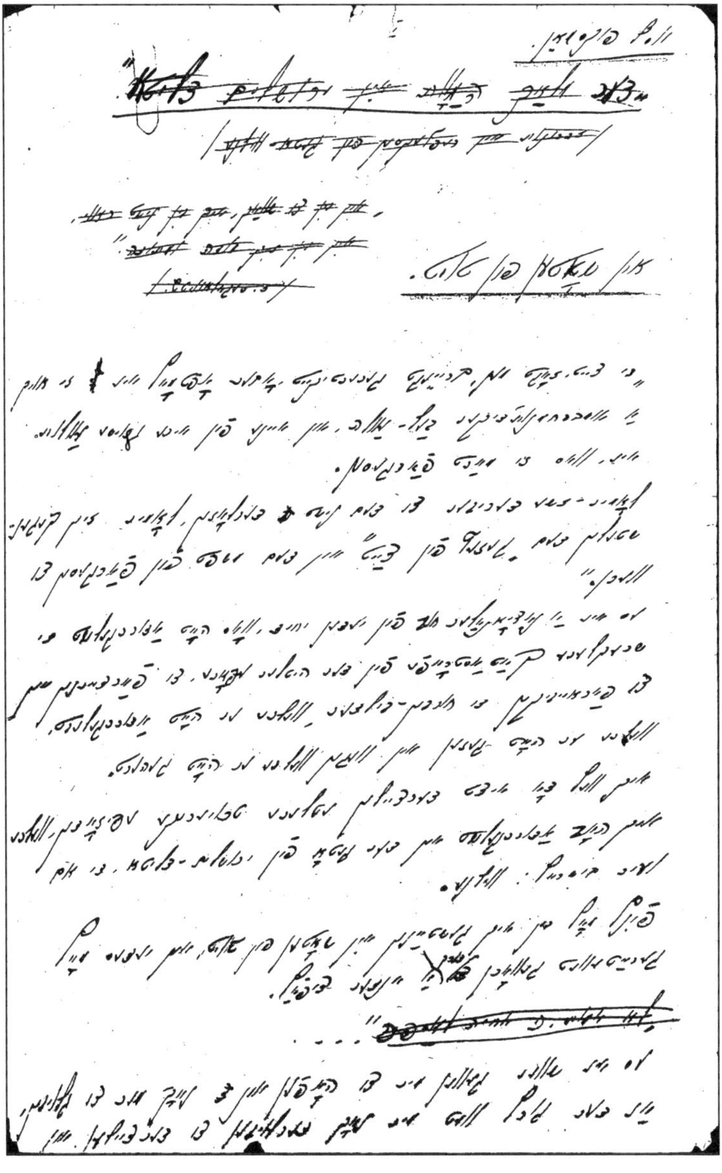

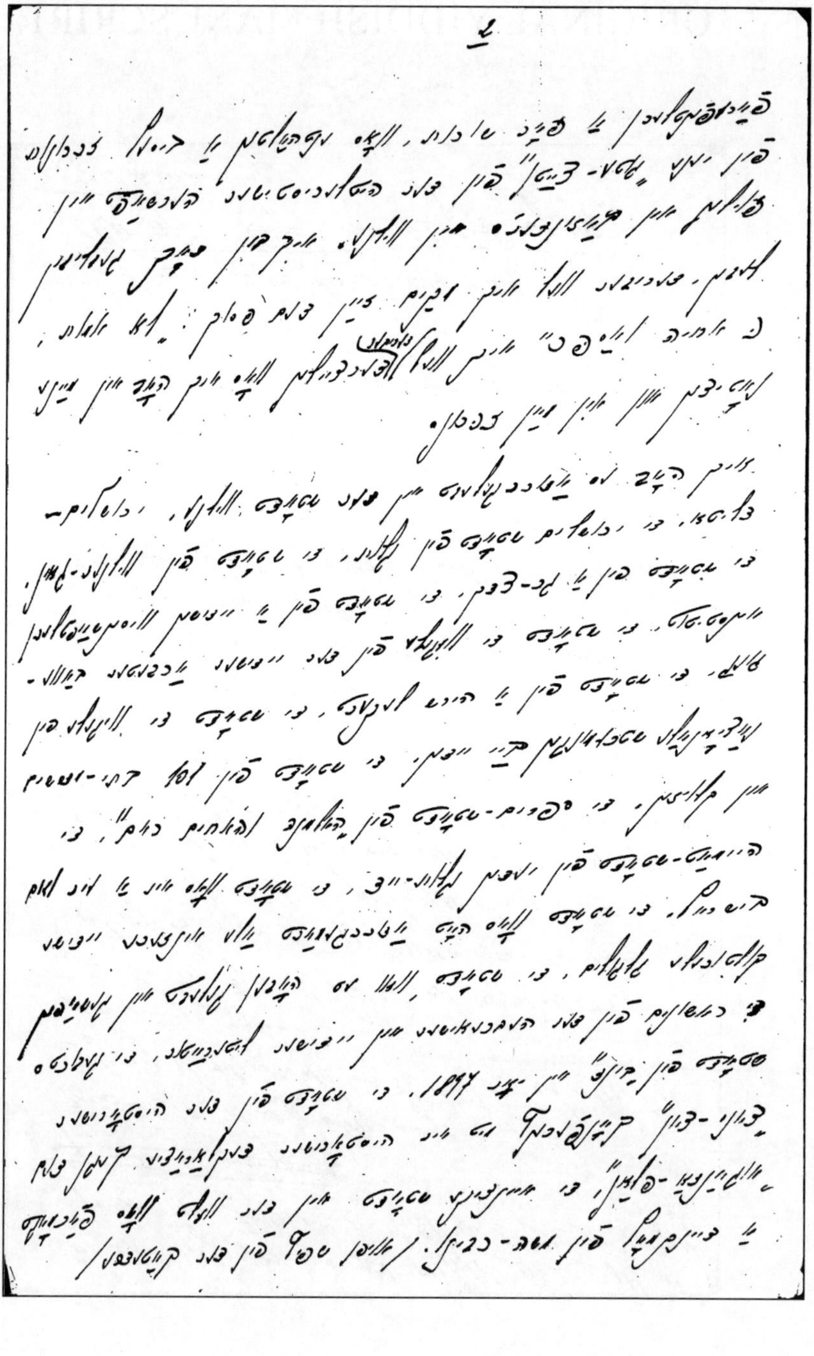

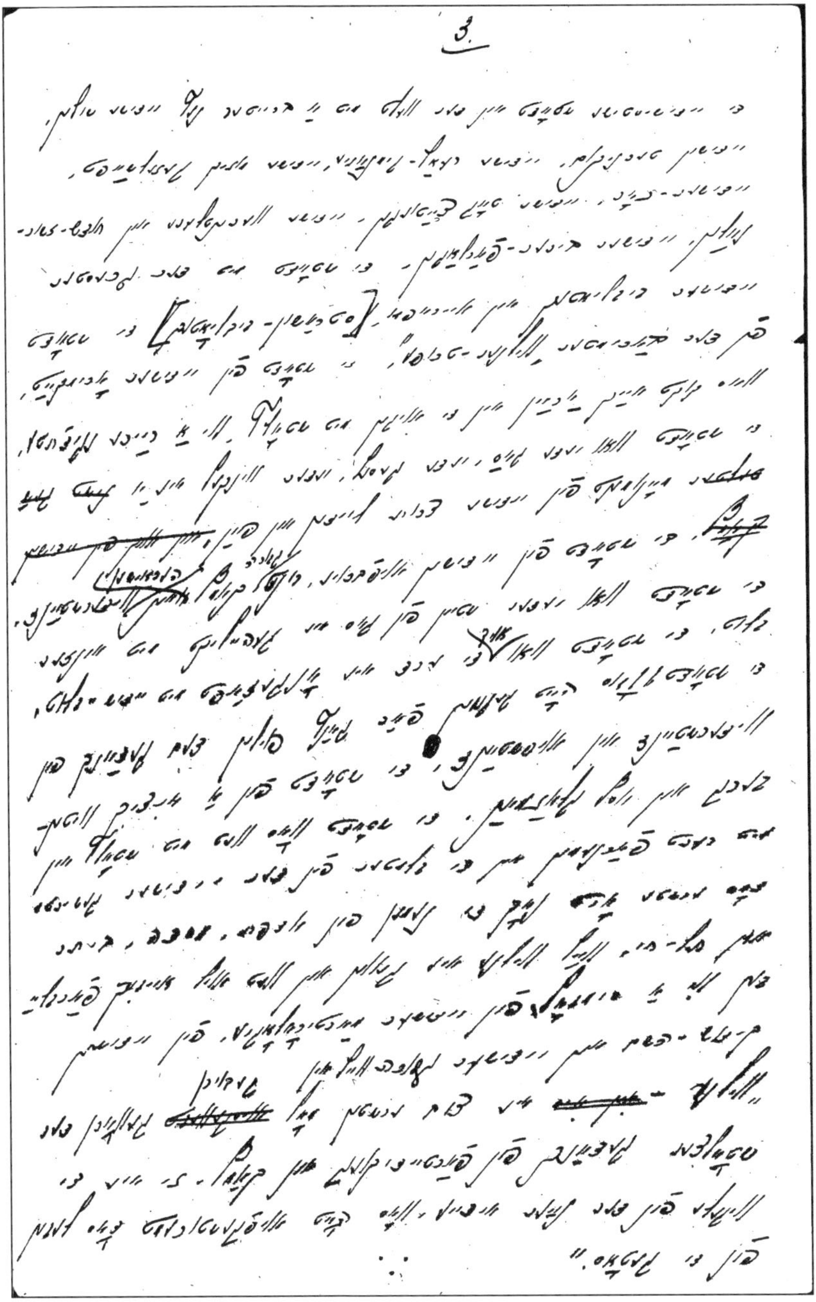
3.

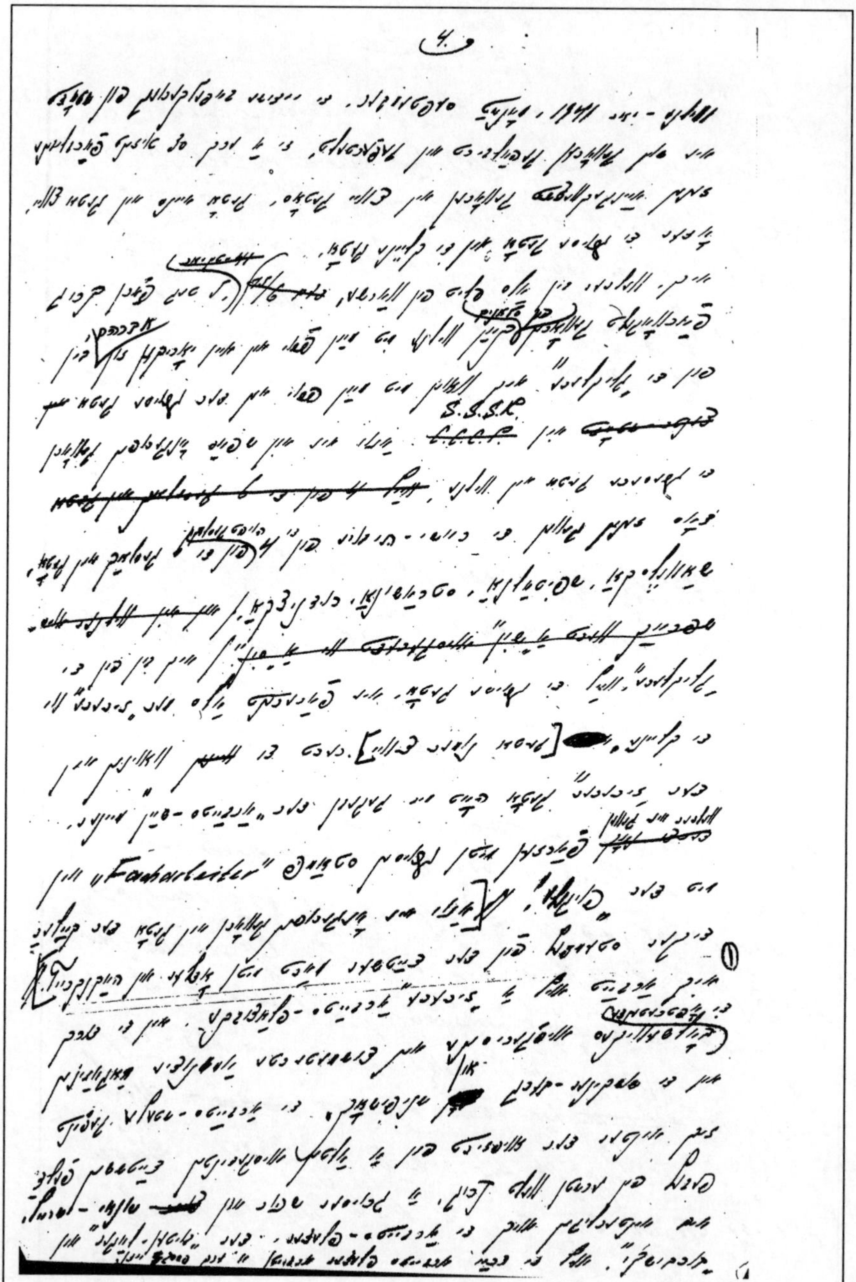
S.S.S.K.

Facharbeiter

(6)

אונזערע [illegible] אַבֿרהם, [illegible] האָט אַ יאָר מיט [illegible]

[illegible], האָבן זיי [illegible] אין דער [illegible]

[illegible], "COLONIA MAGISTRACKA" בײַ

זײַן ווײַב, אַ פּוילישע קאַטוילישע קריסטין בראָ-

ניסלאַווא קורפּי BRONISLAWA KURPI.

מיר האָבן זיי [illegible] אין אונזער דירה, מיט

[illegible] אין [illegible], וואָס זיי געהאַט אין [illegible].

און [illegible] האָבן זיי געהאַט, אַז דער [illegible] וואָס

[illegible] [illegible] [illegible] [illegible] אין זיי [illegible] [illegible]

ווידער זײַן [illegible].

[illegible]

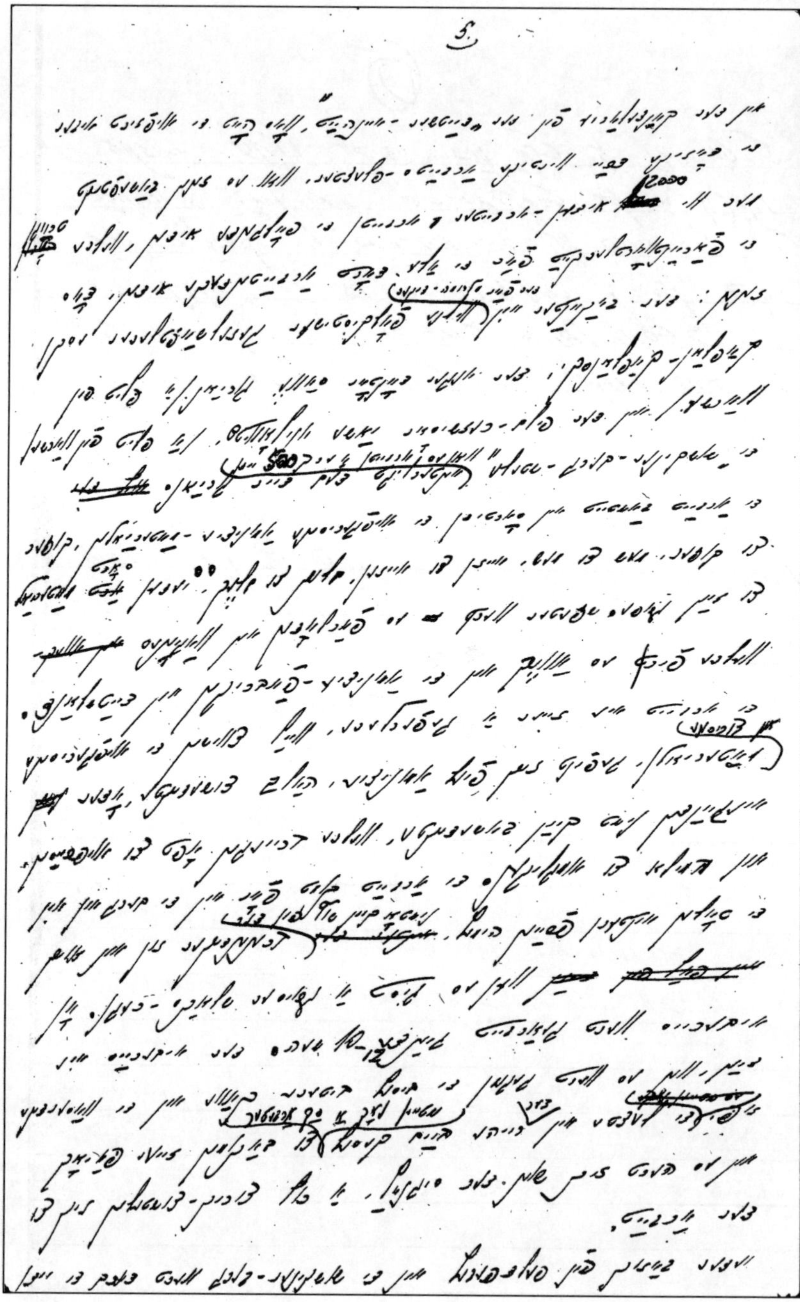

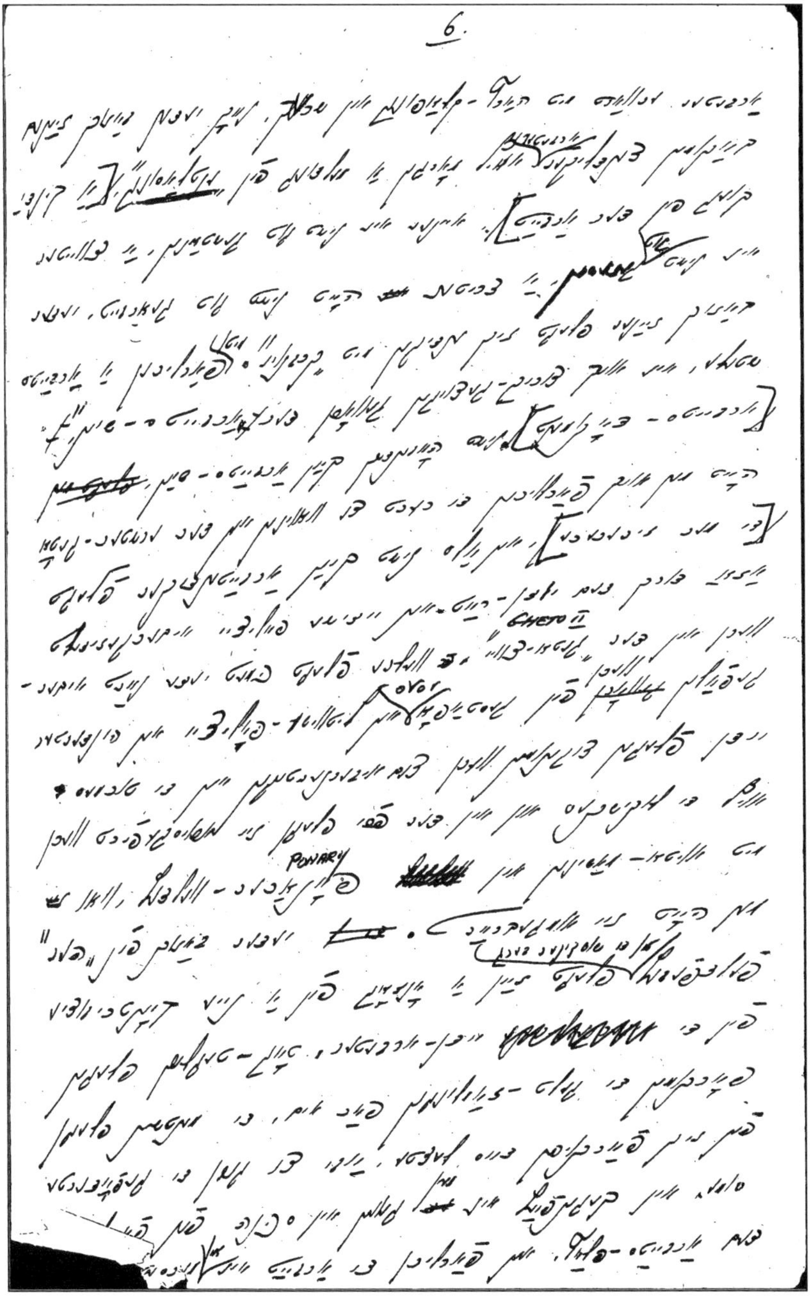
6.
GHETTO II
PONARY

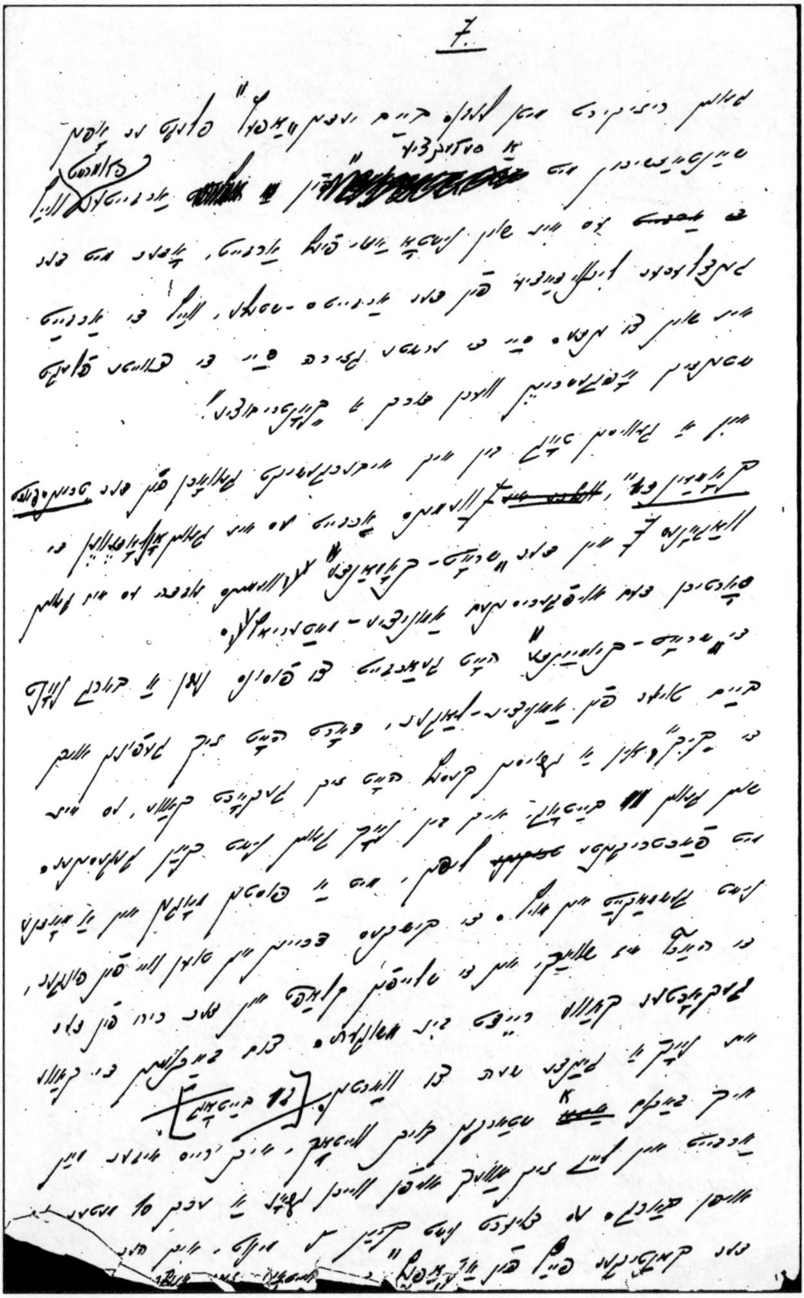

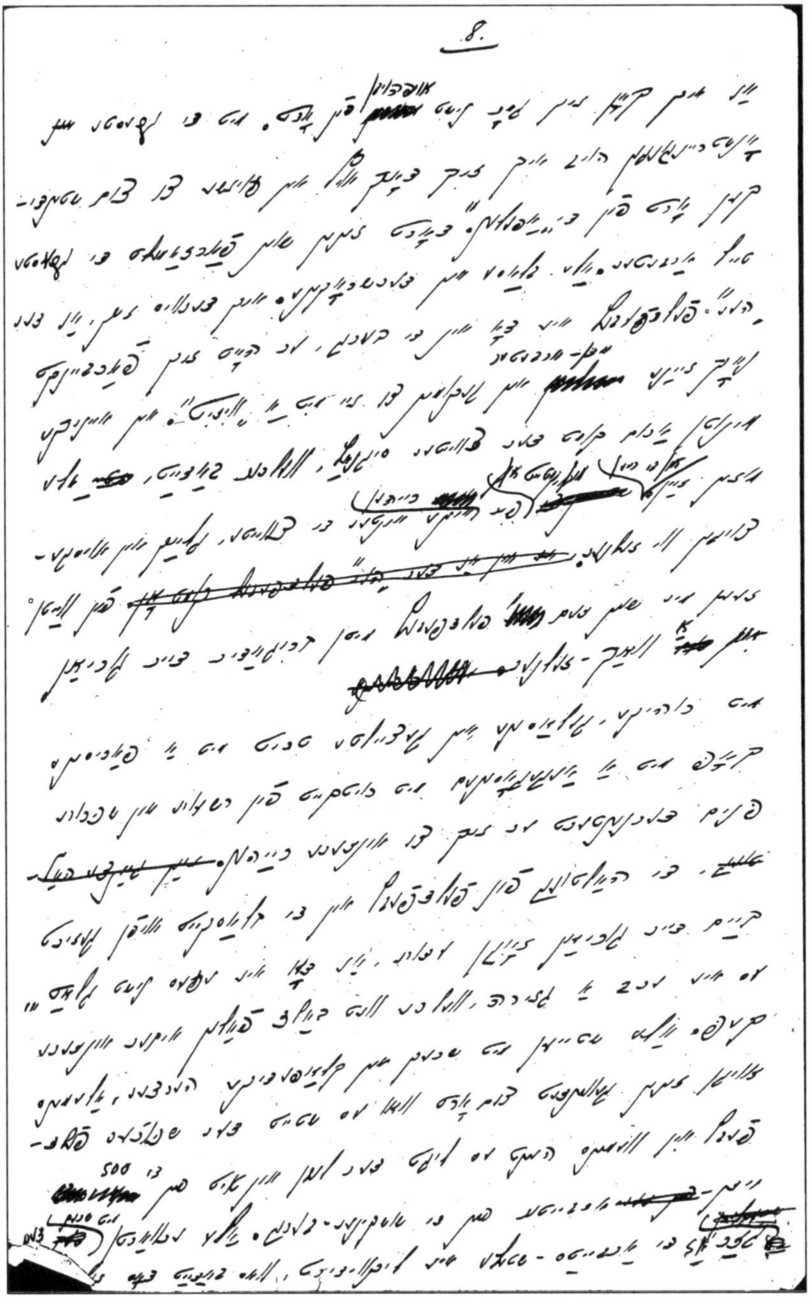
8.

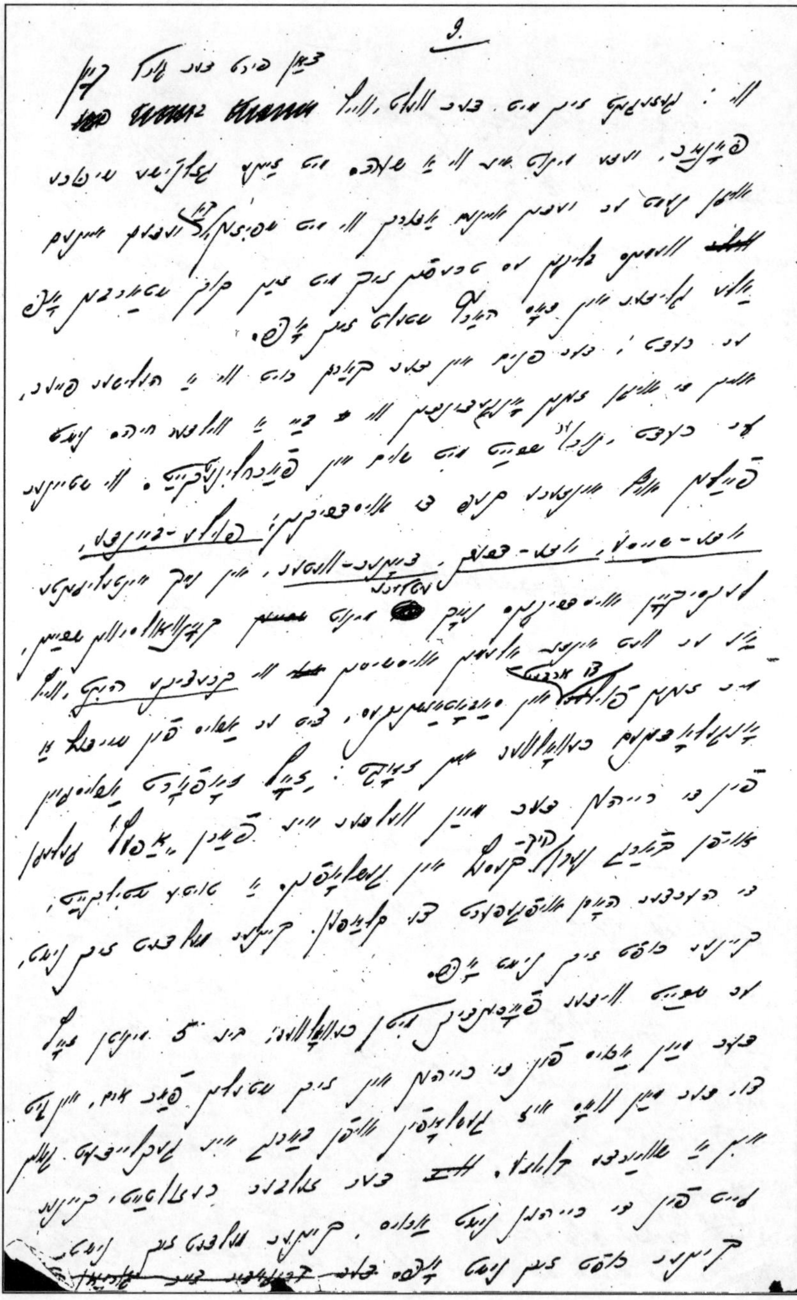
9.

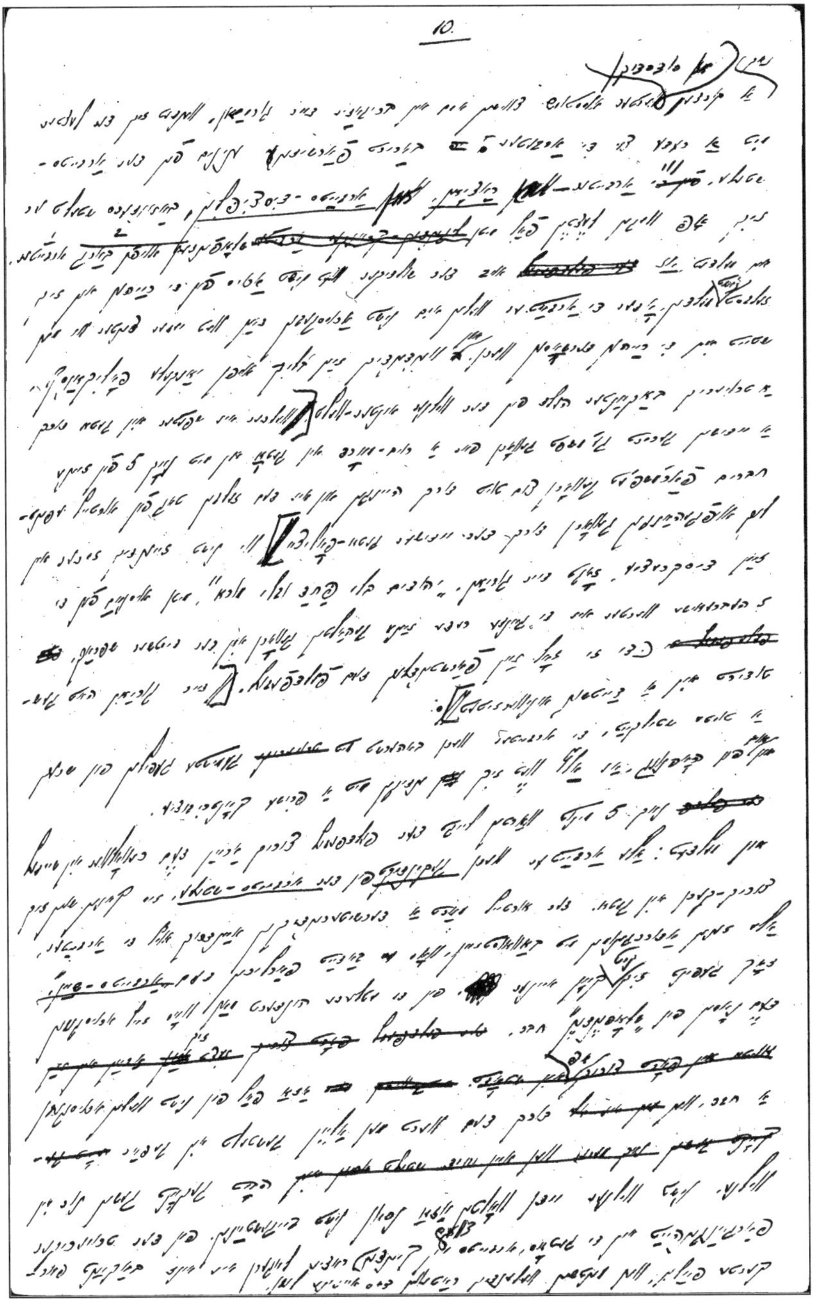
10.

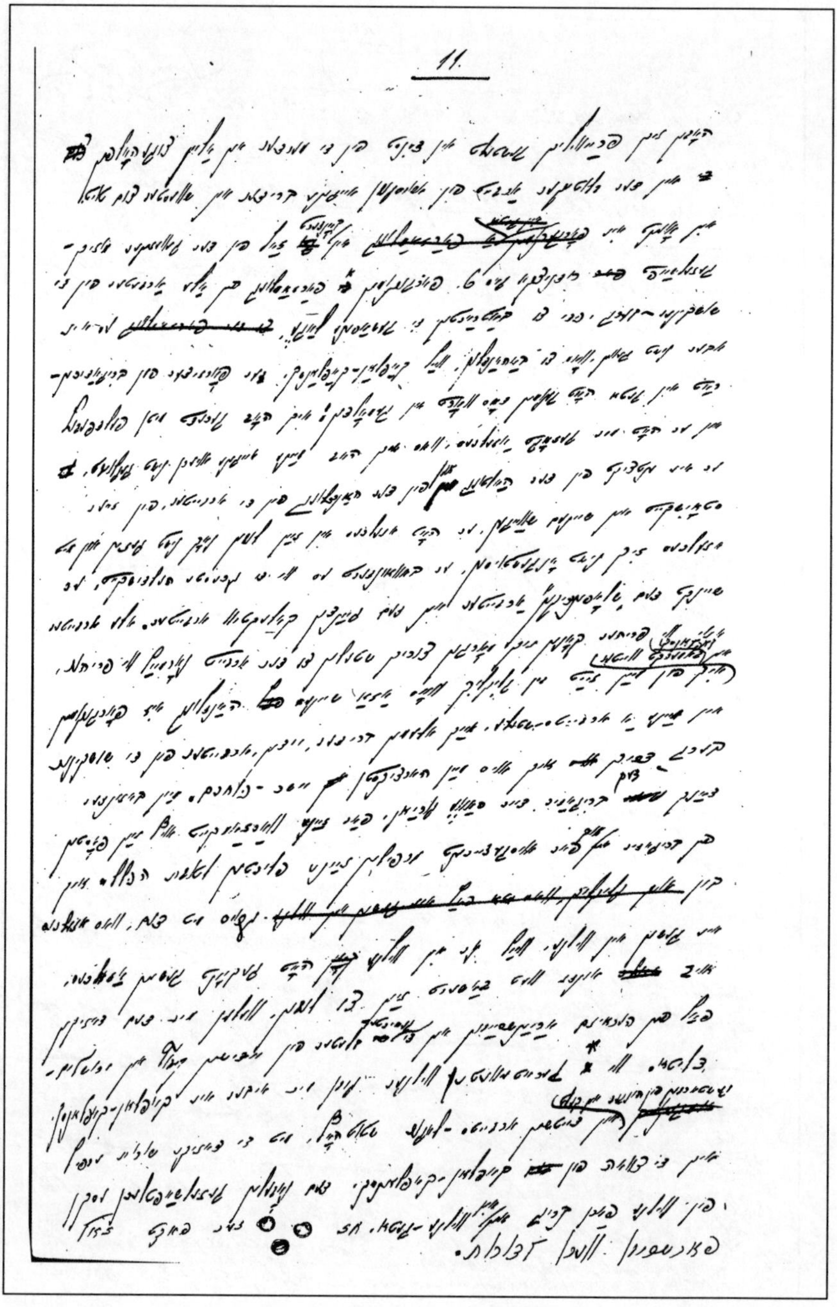
11.

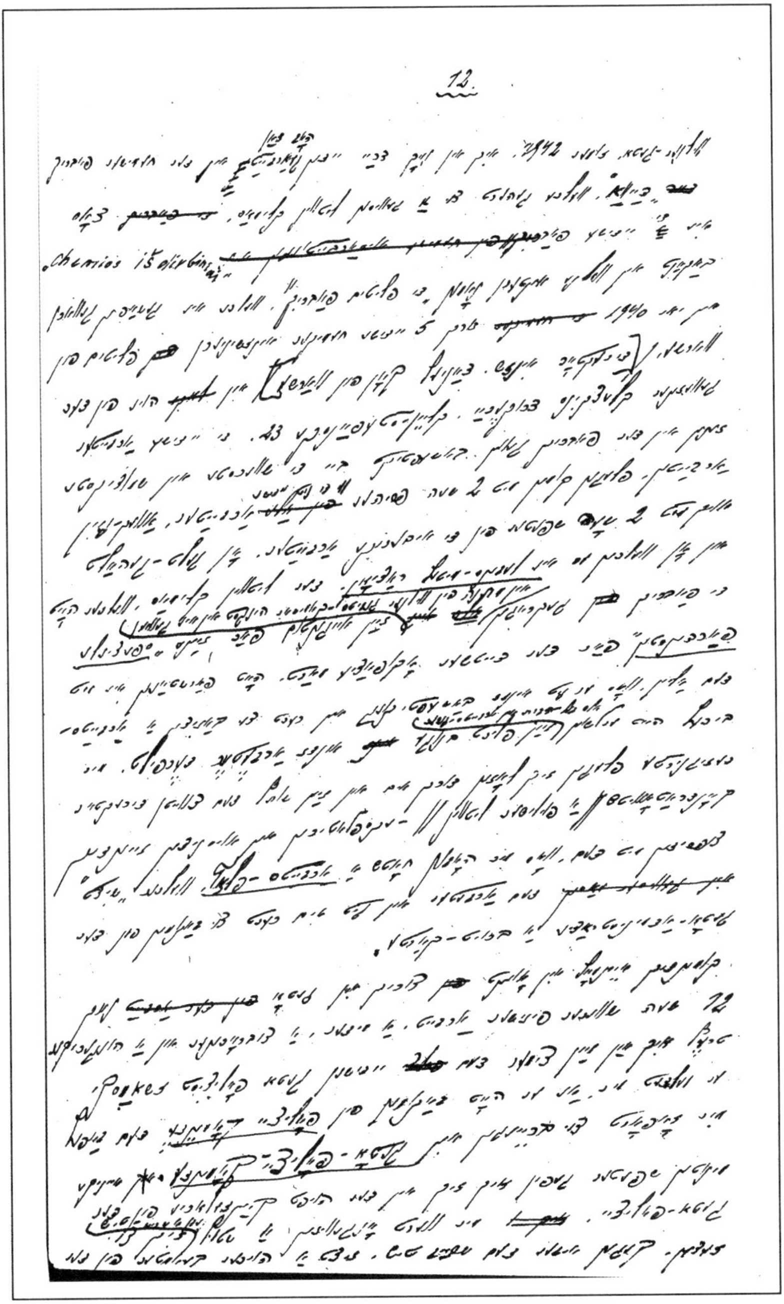

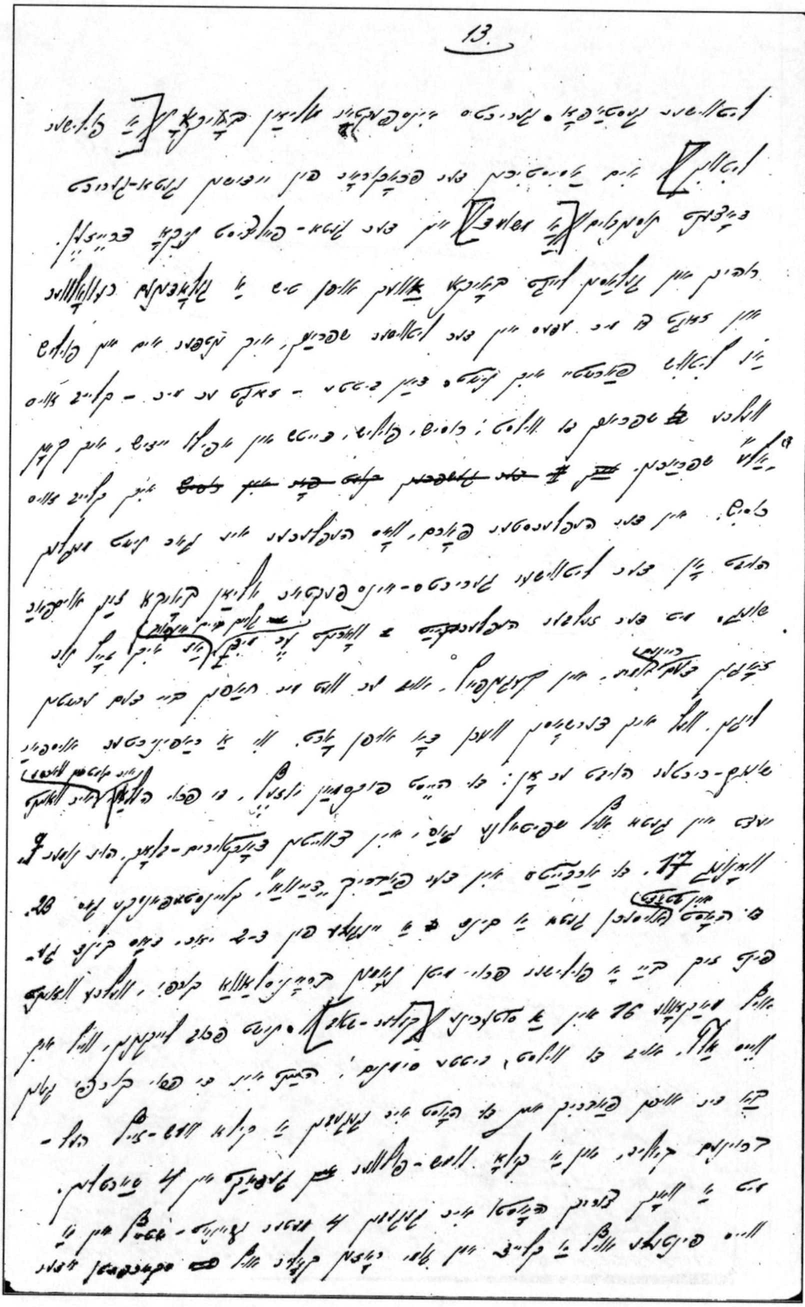

13.

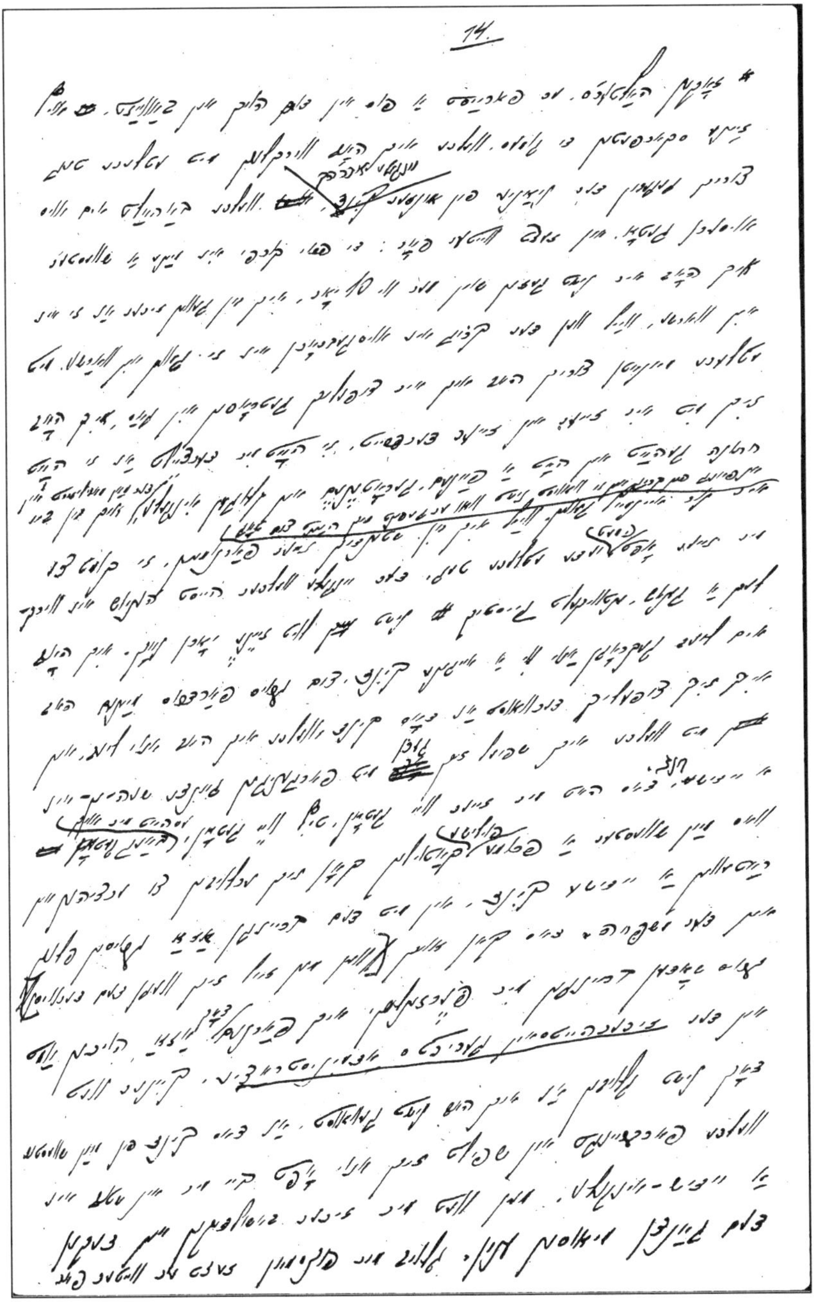

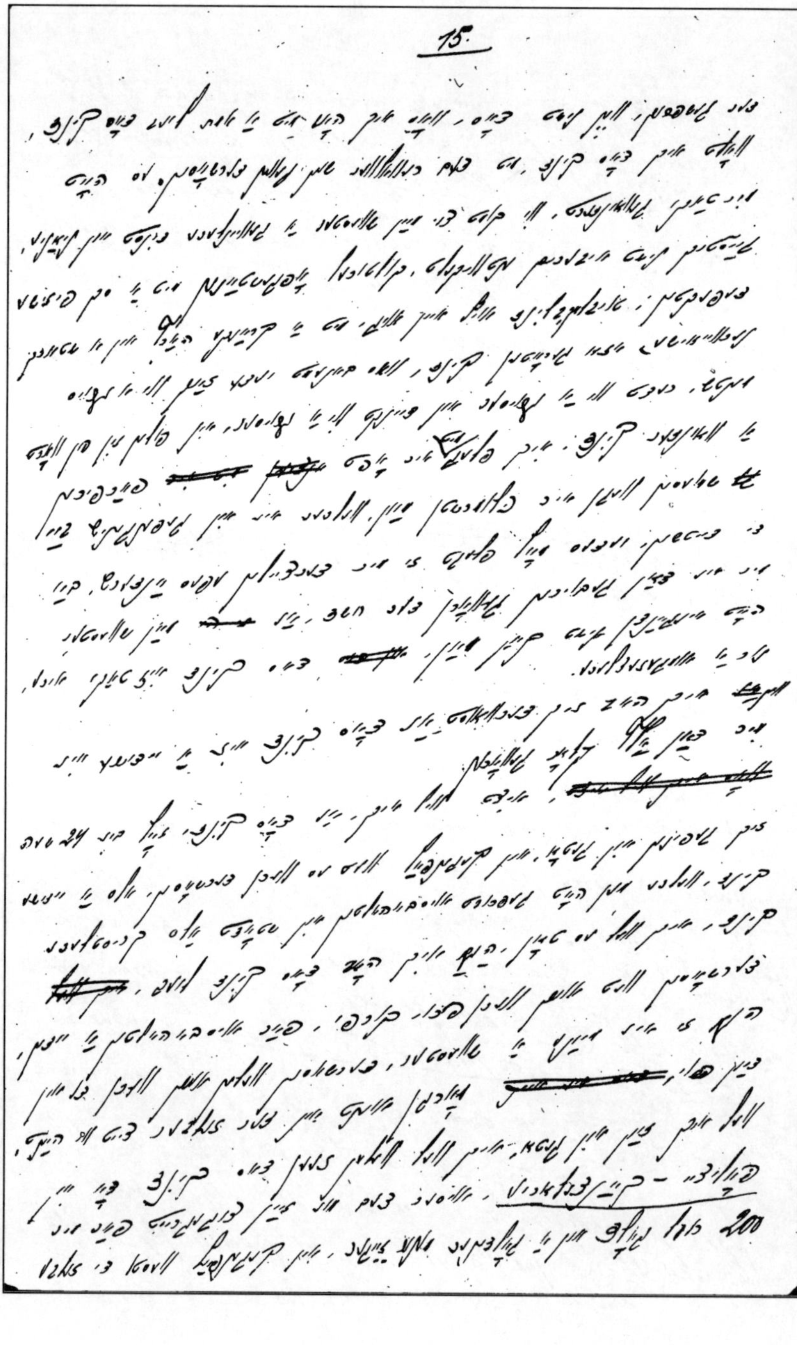

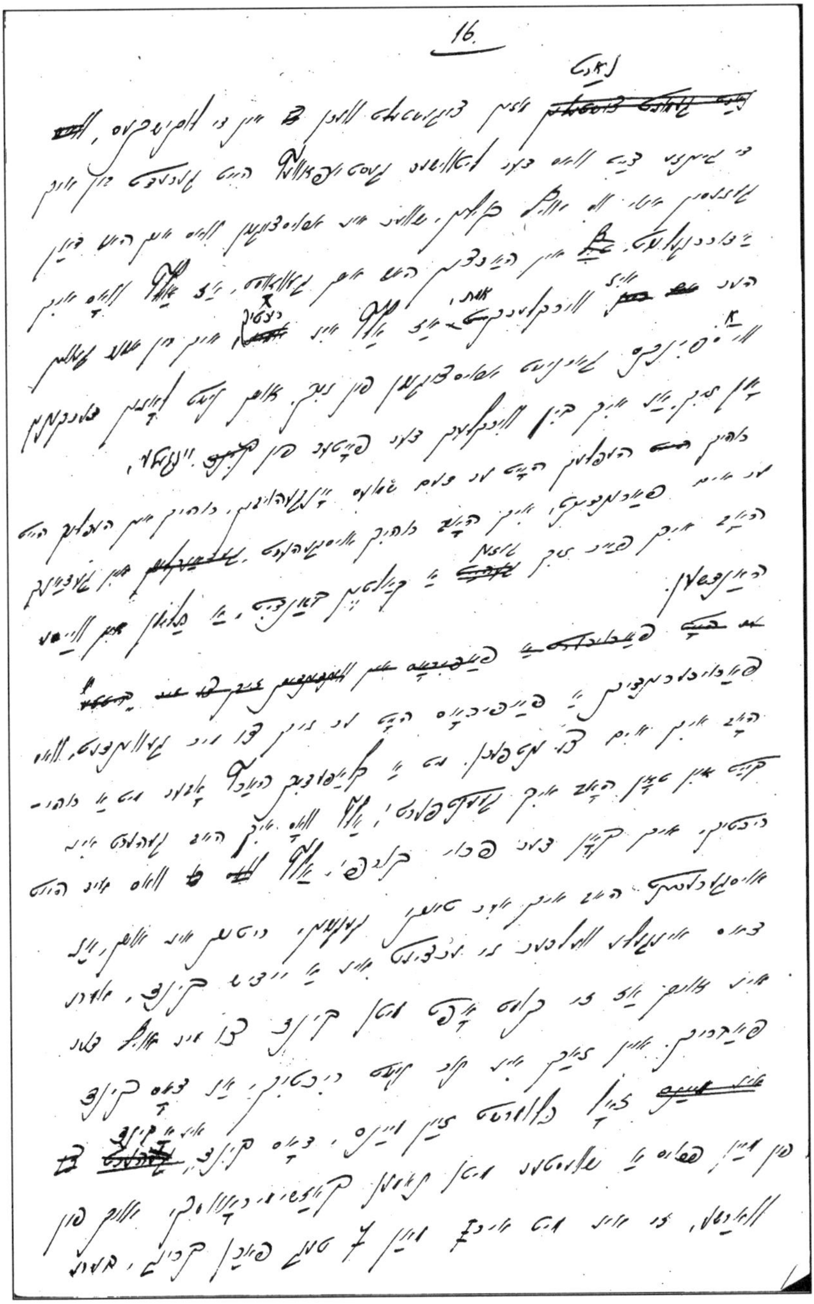
16.

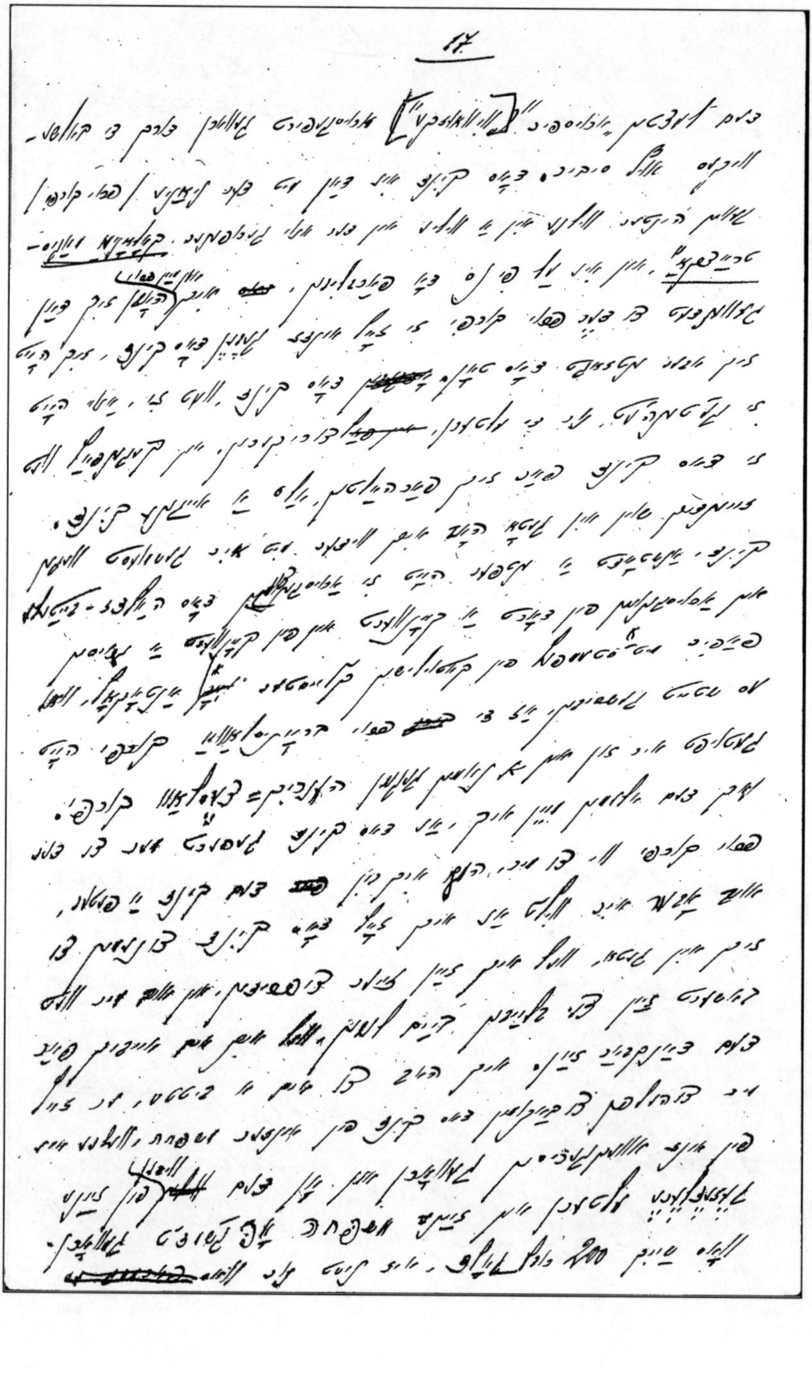

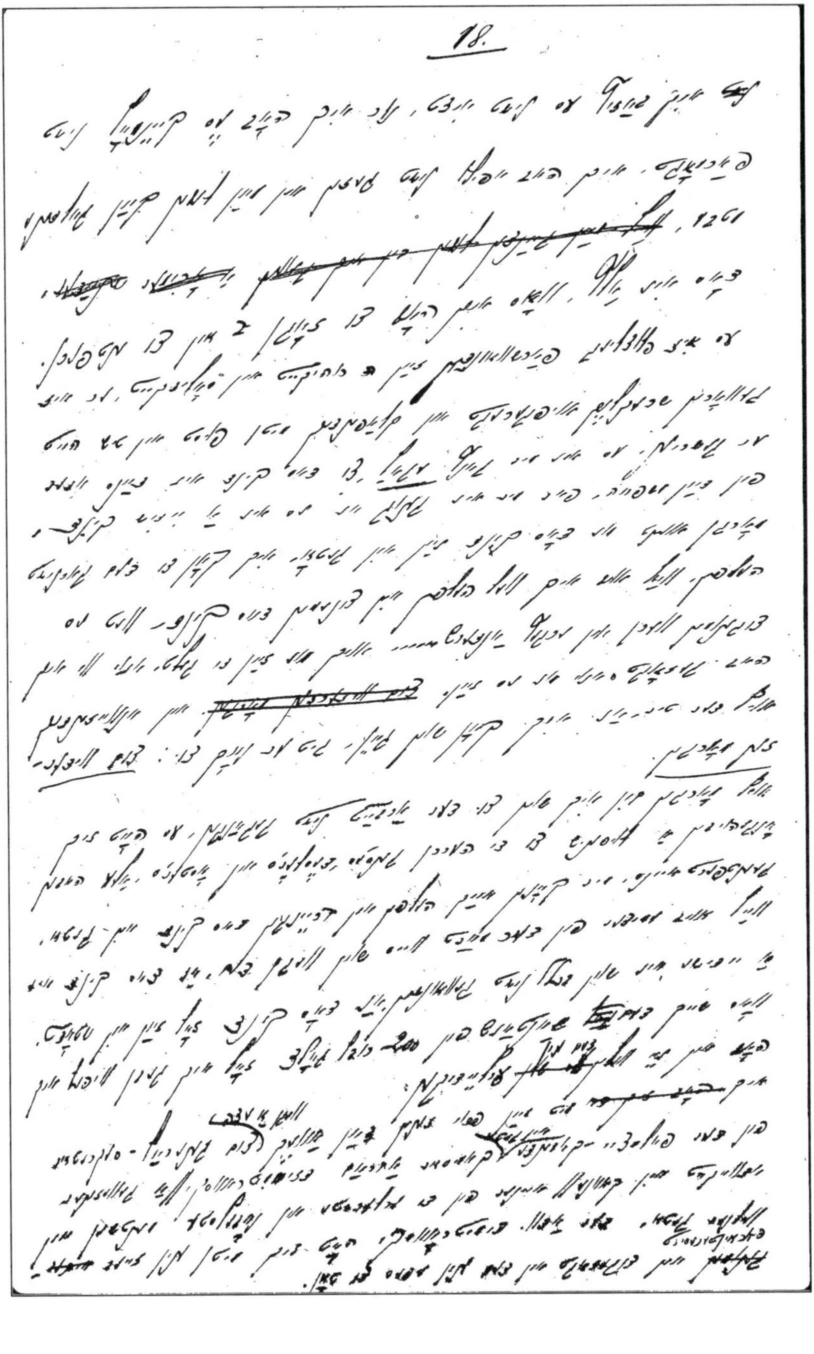
18.

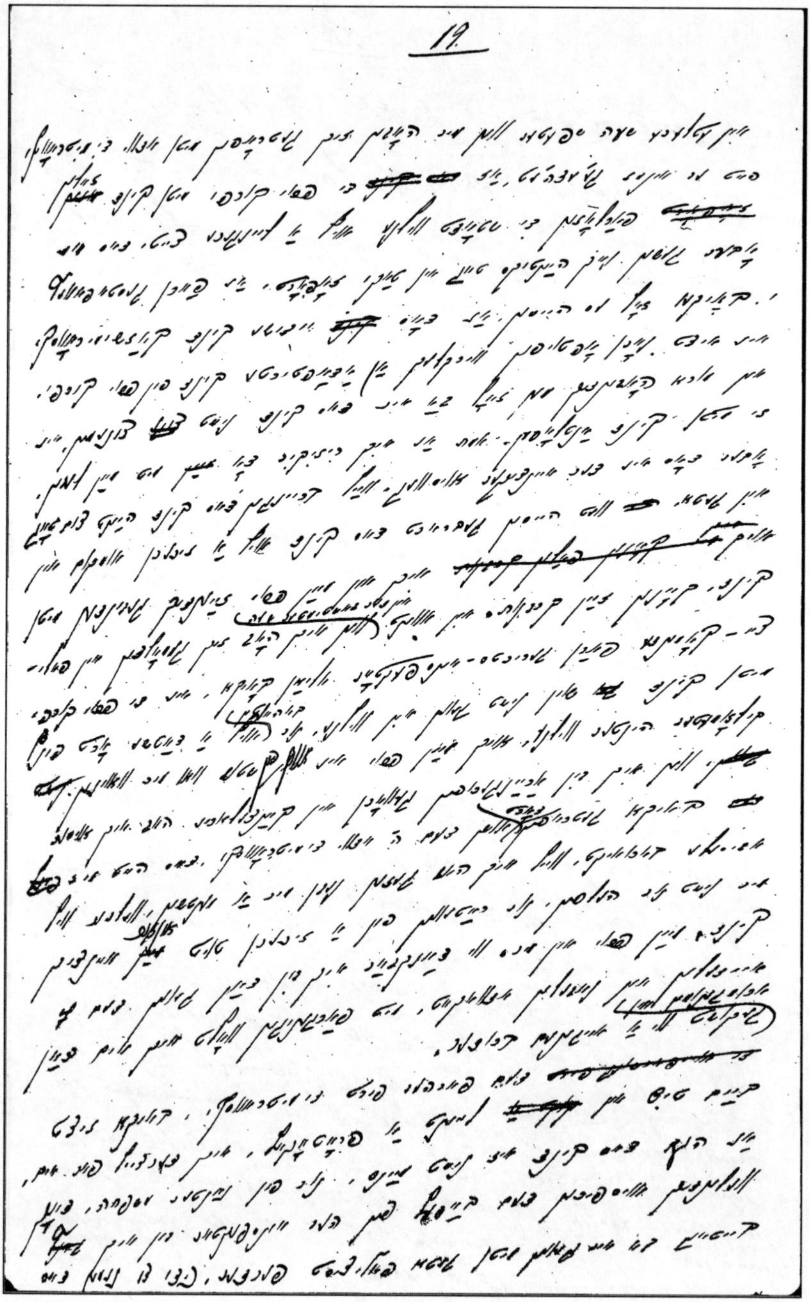
19.

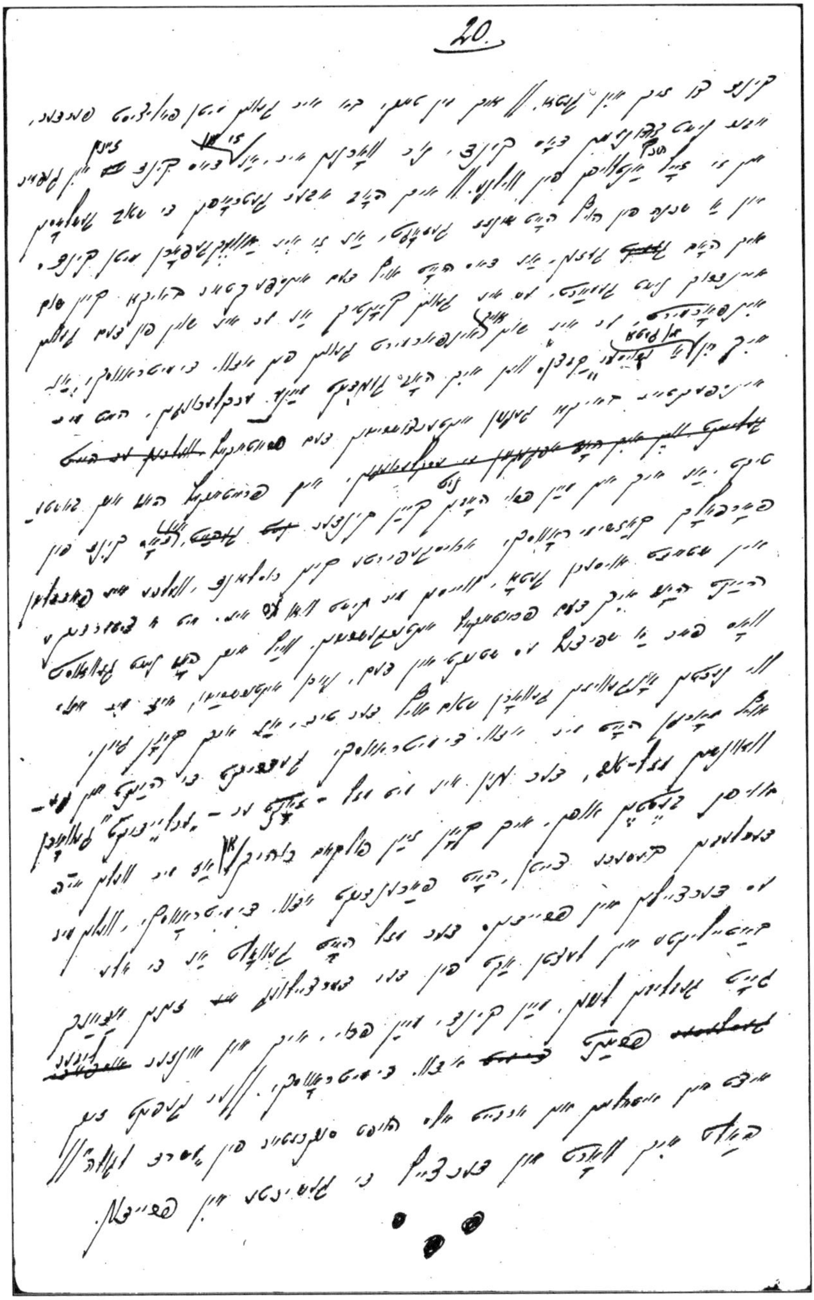
20.

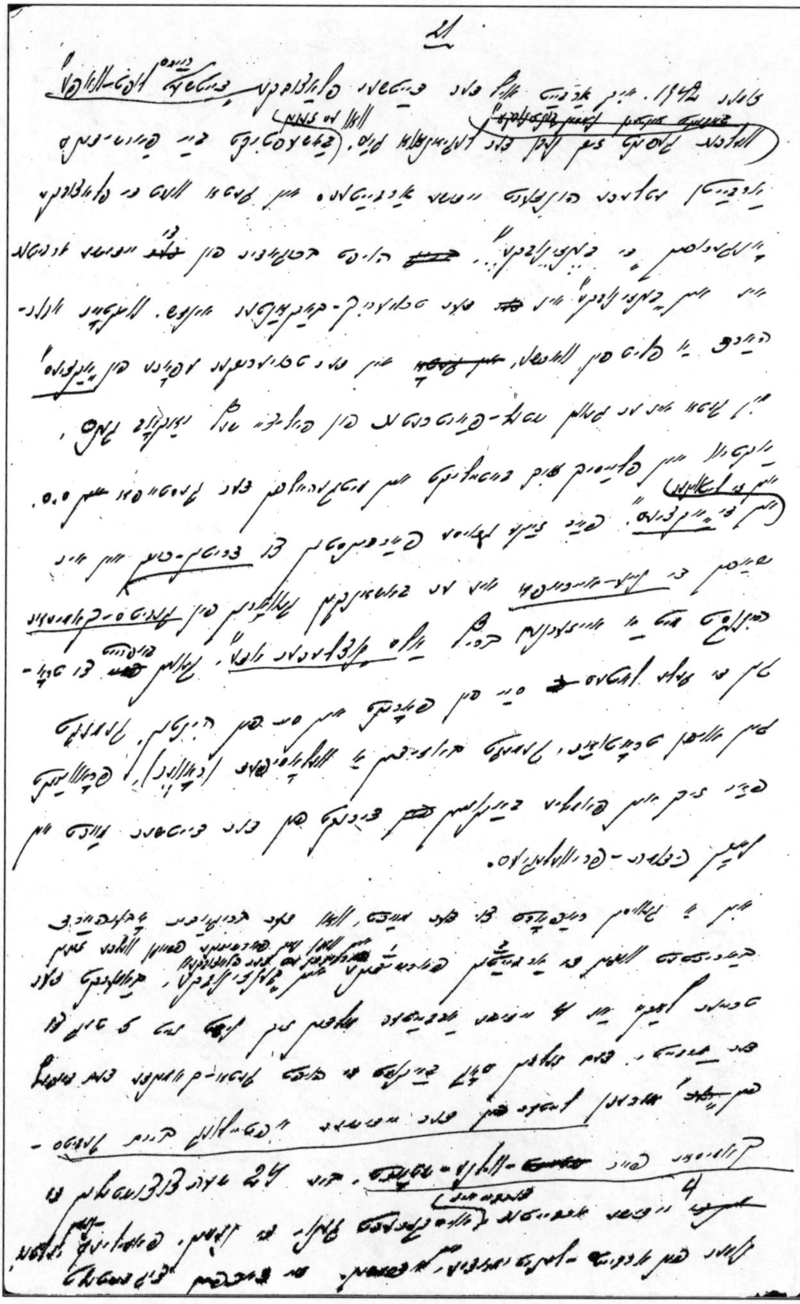

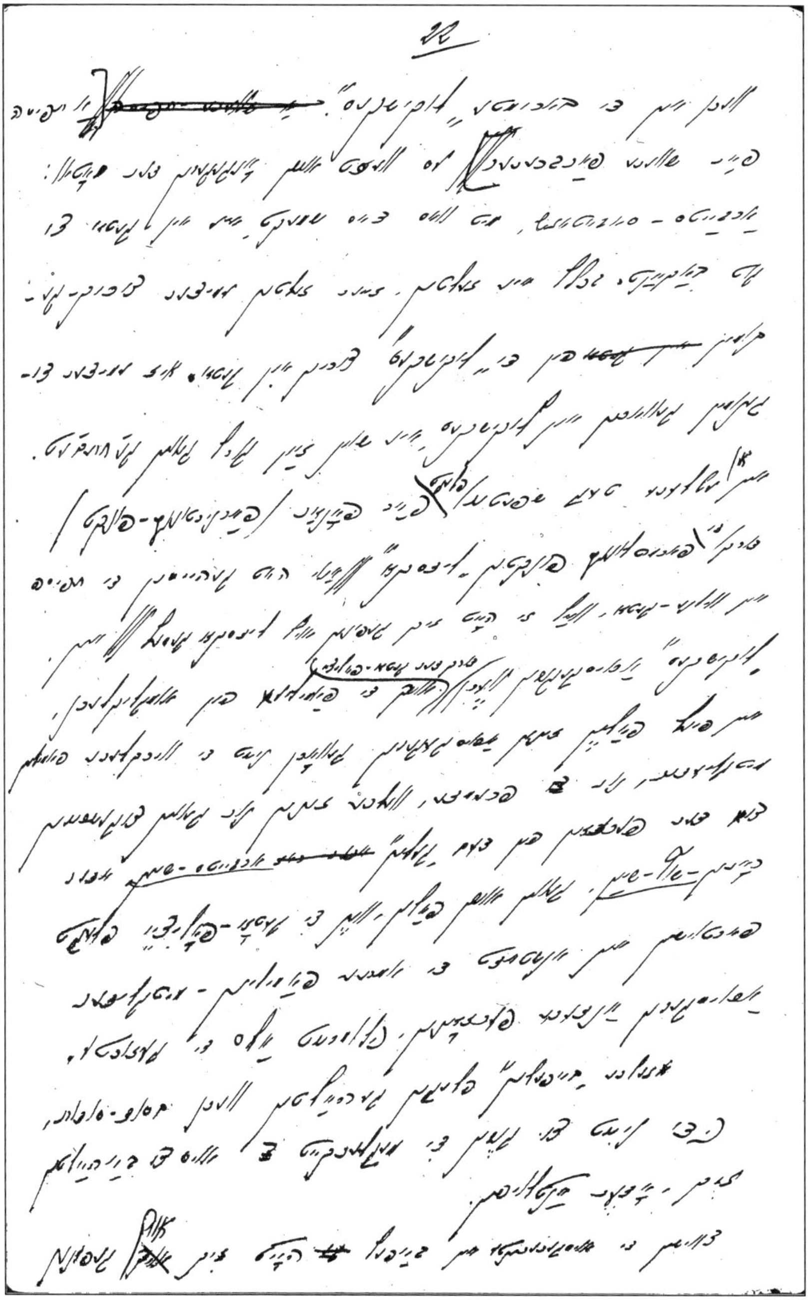

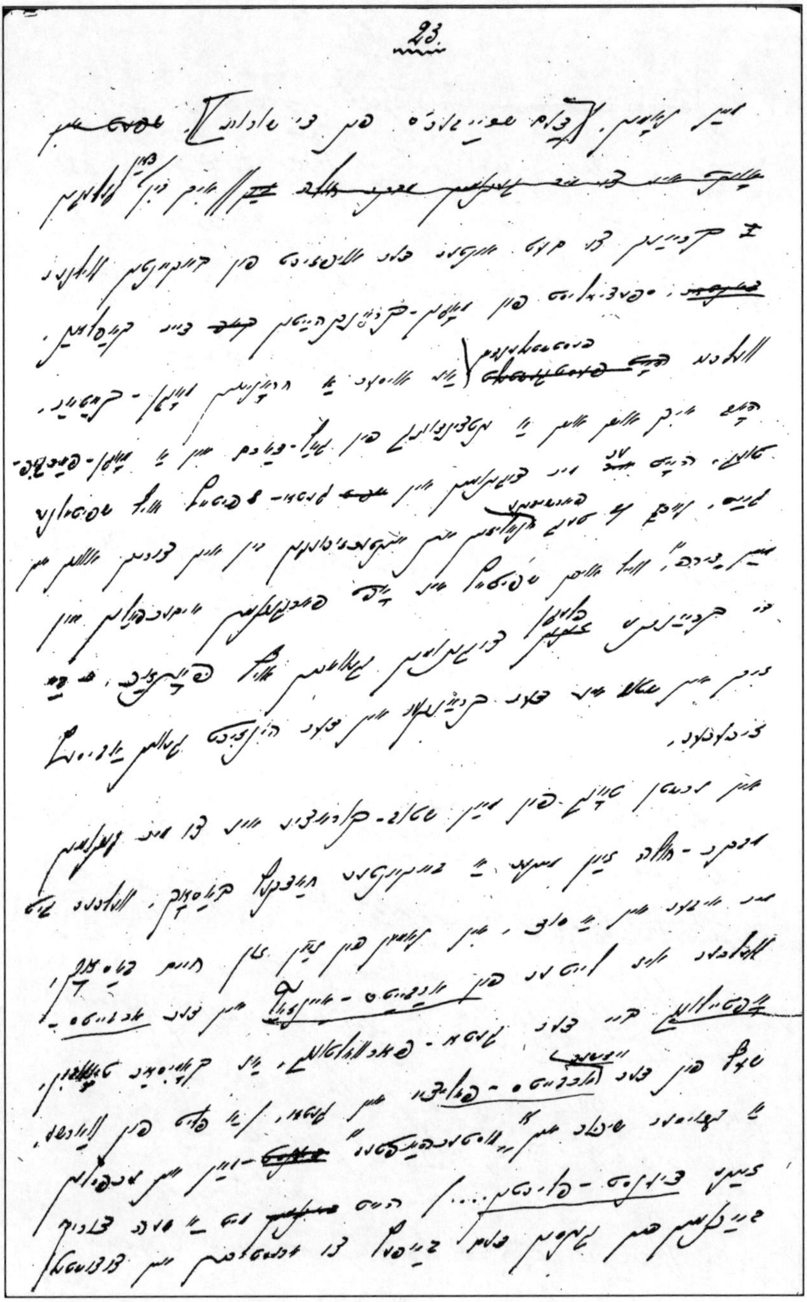

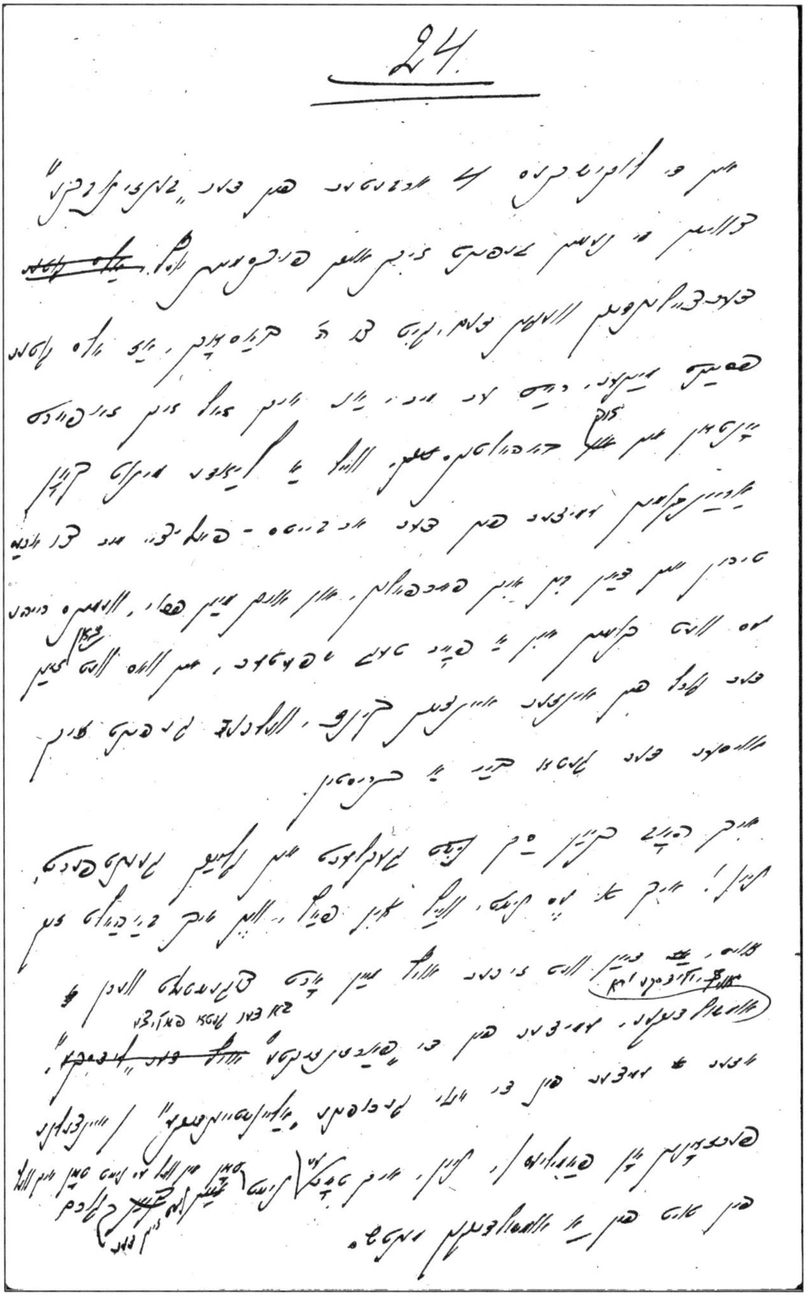

24.

[illegible]

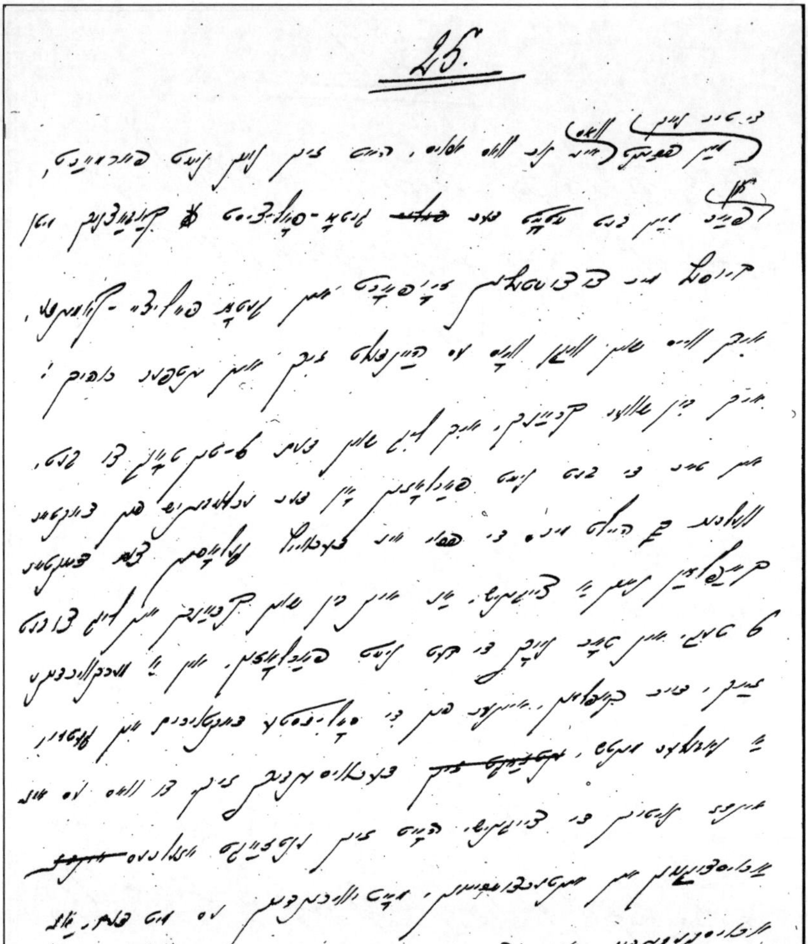
25.

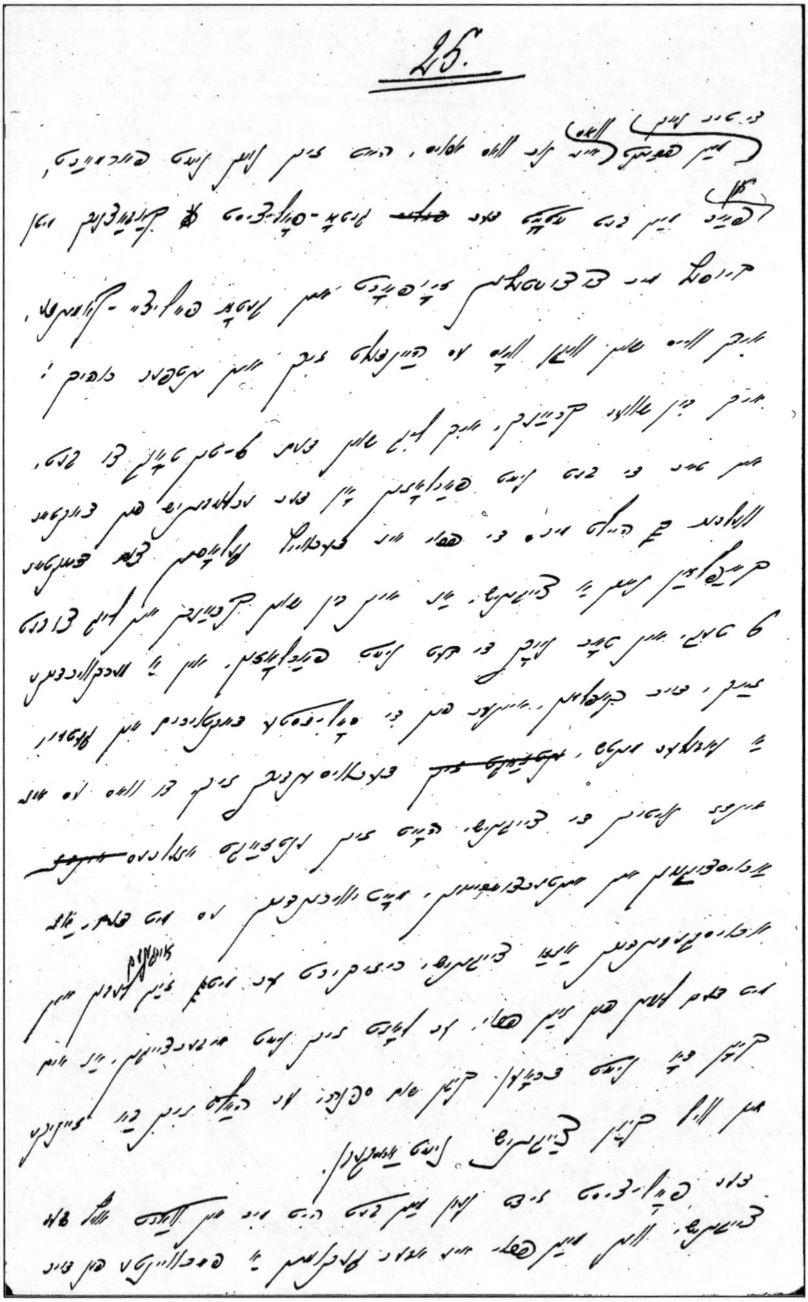

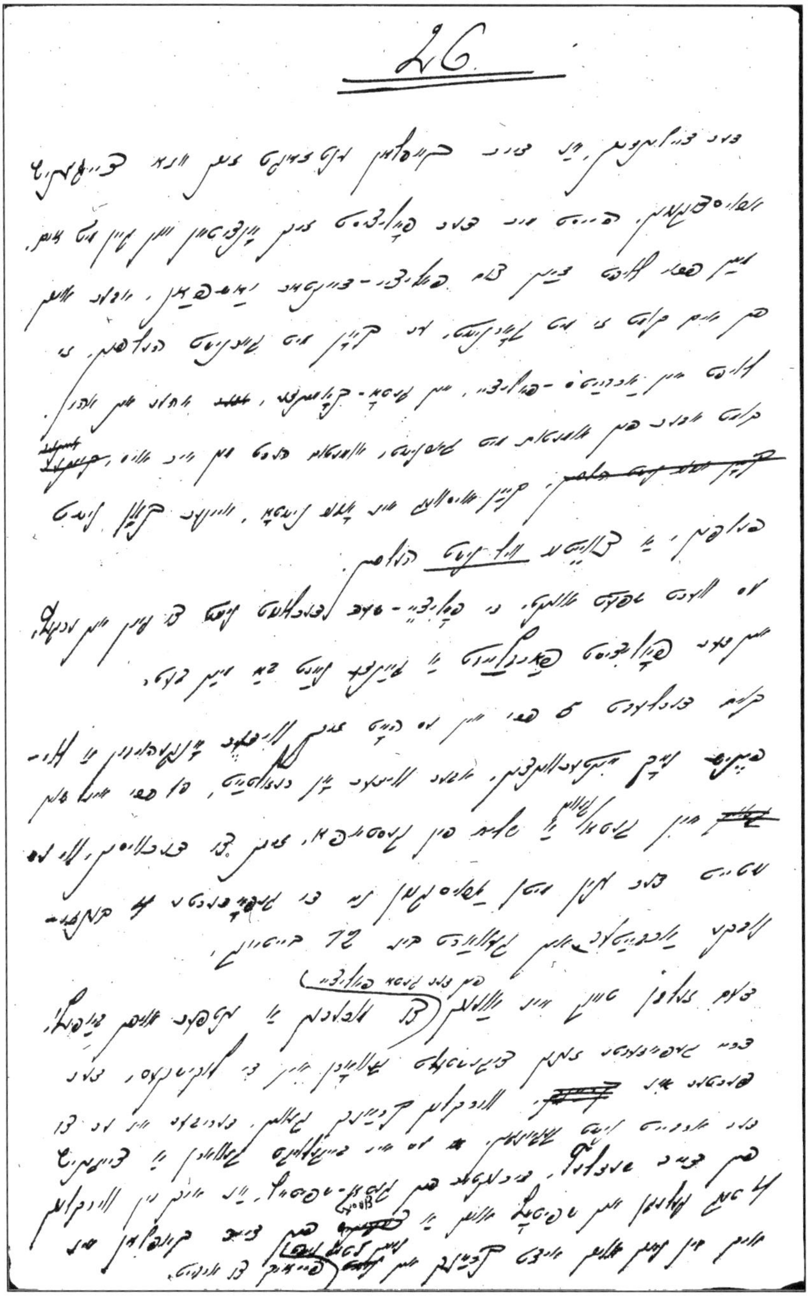
26.

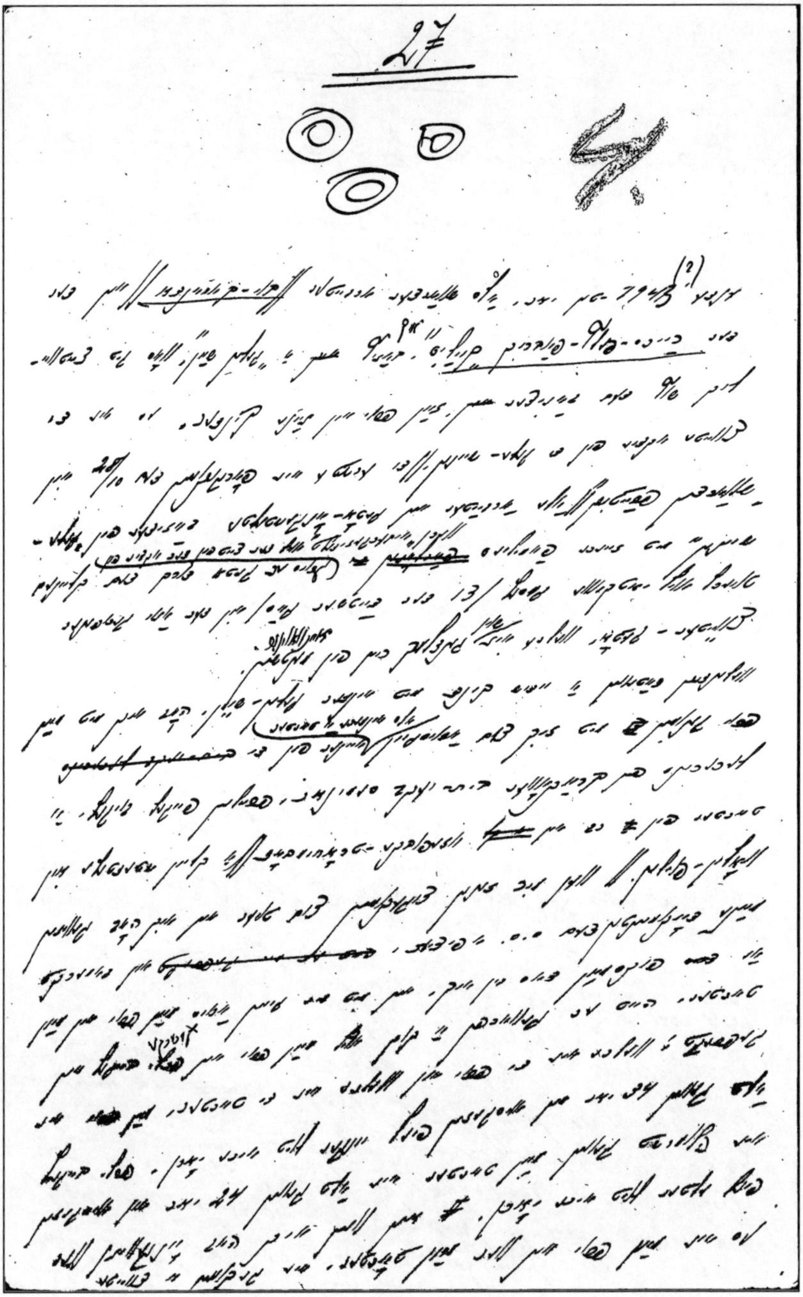

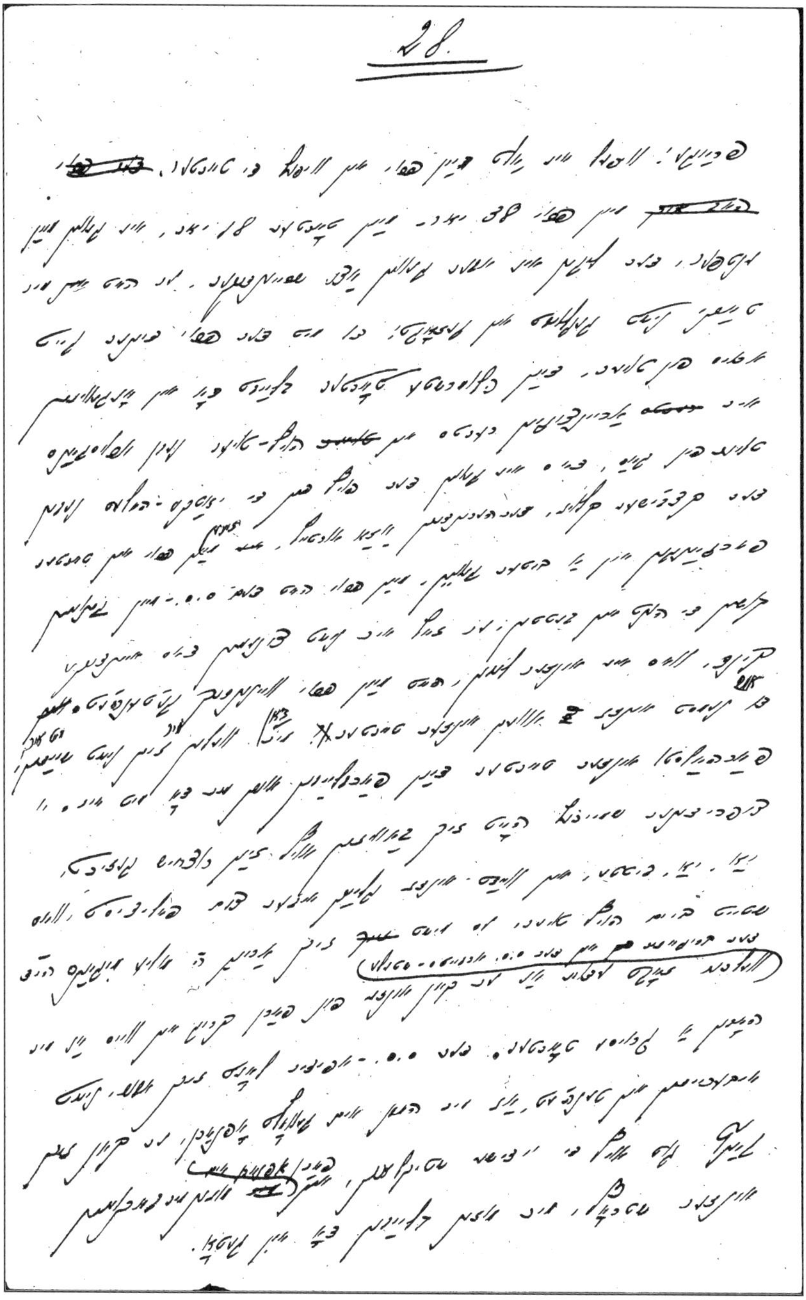

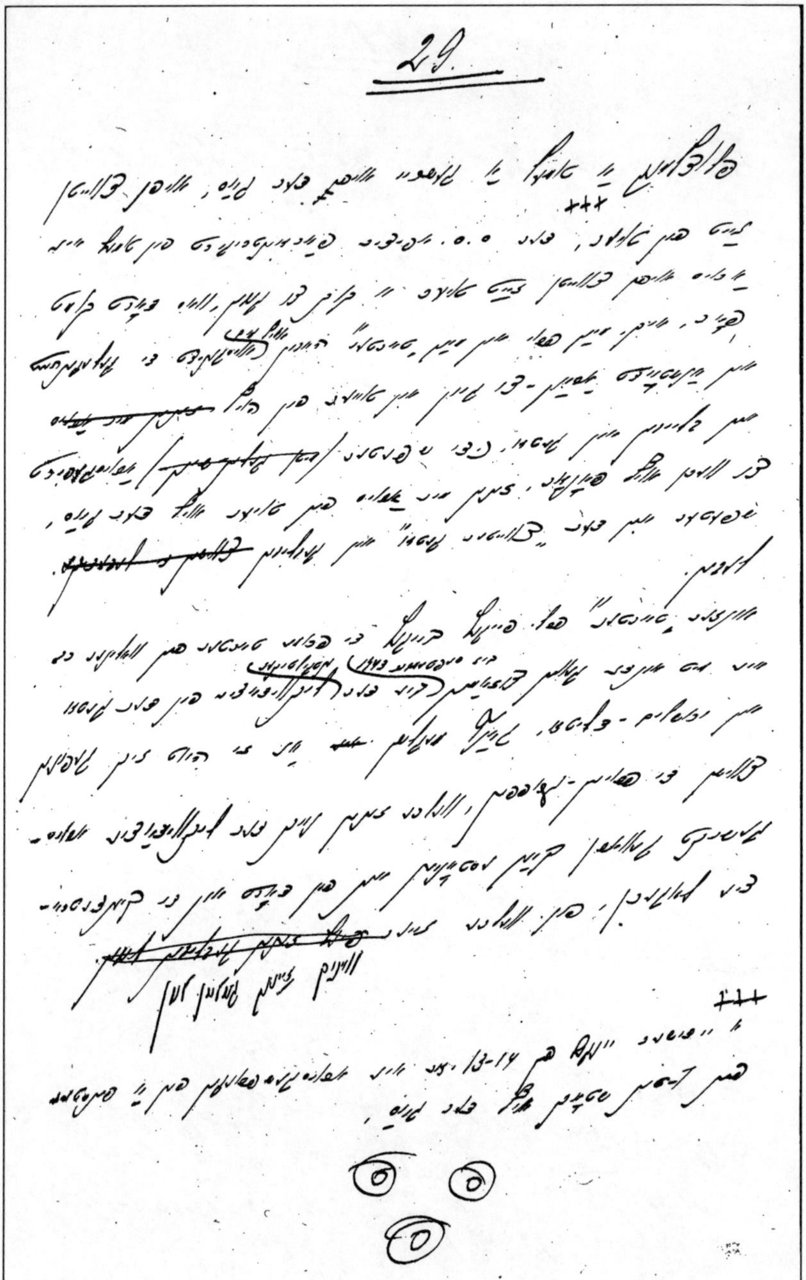
29.

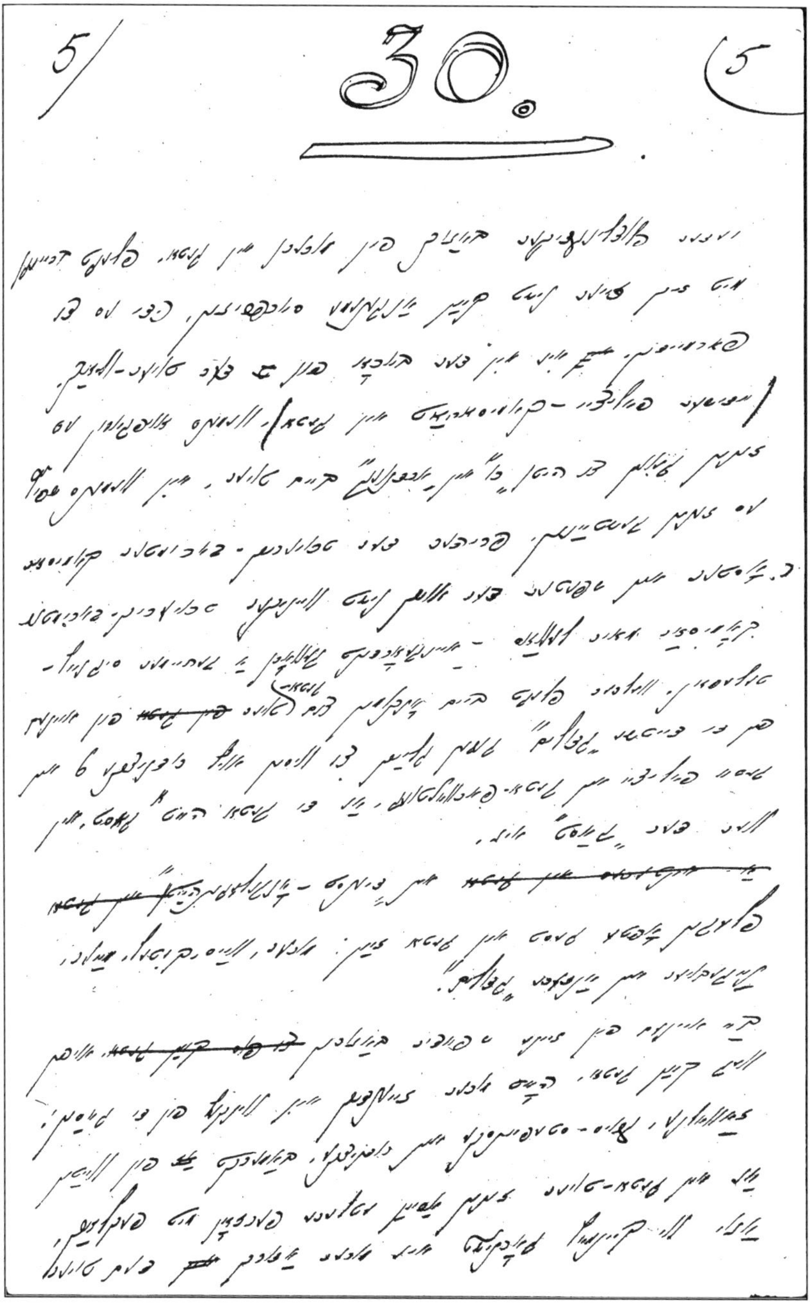
5/
30.
(5

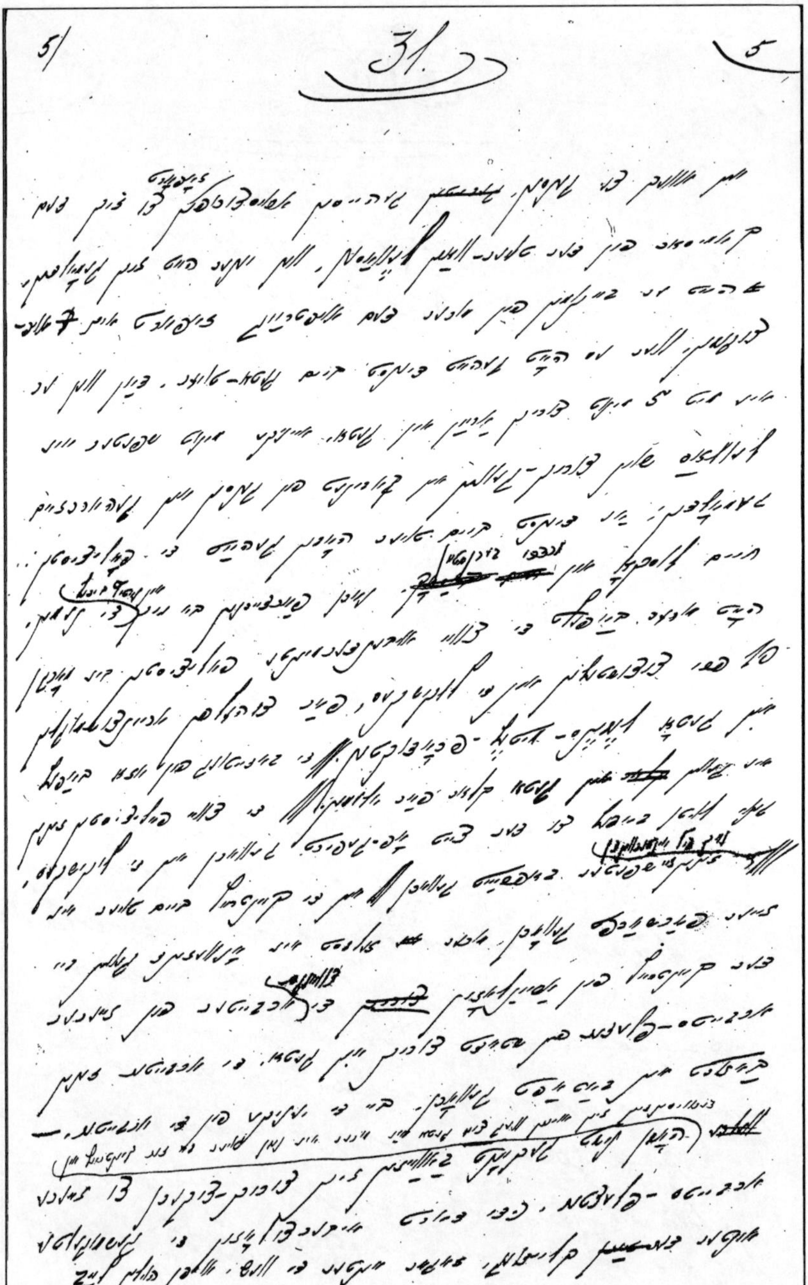

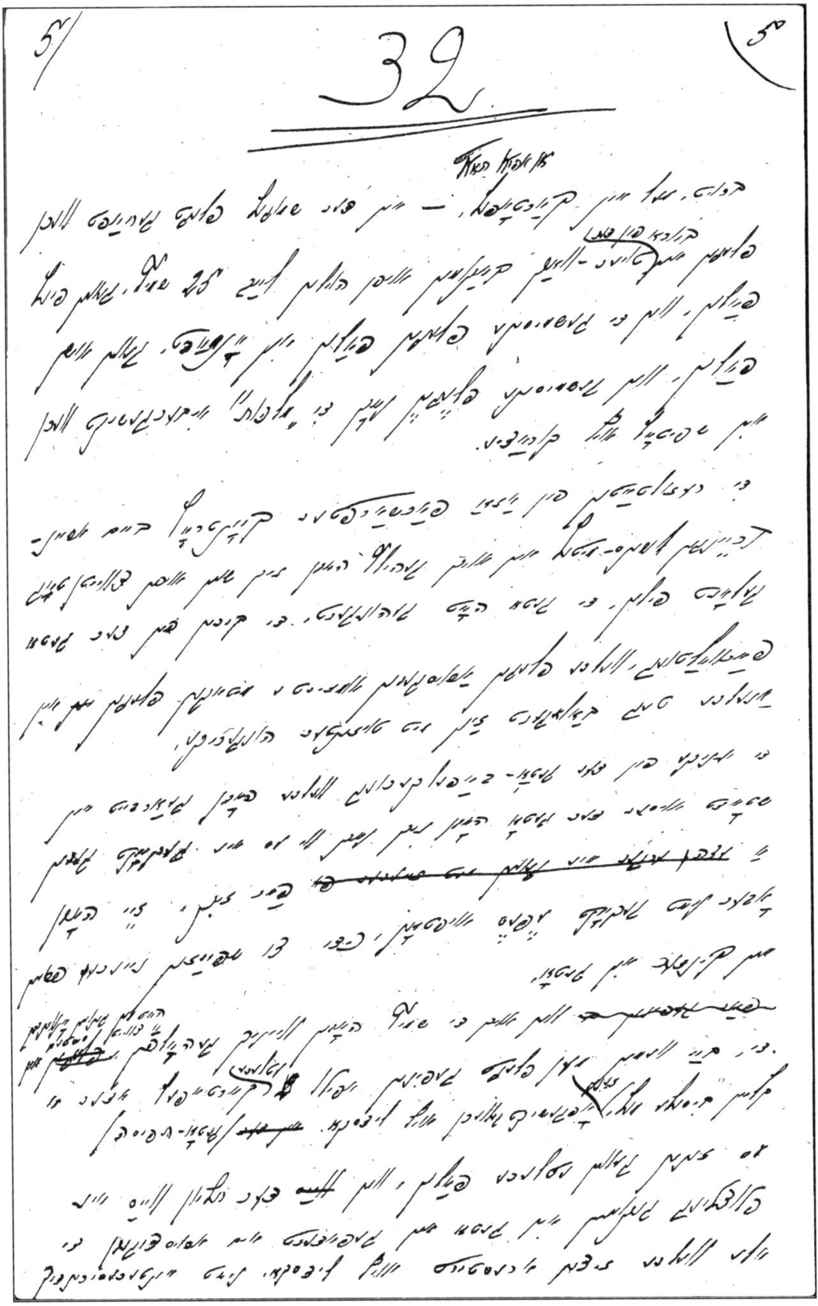

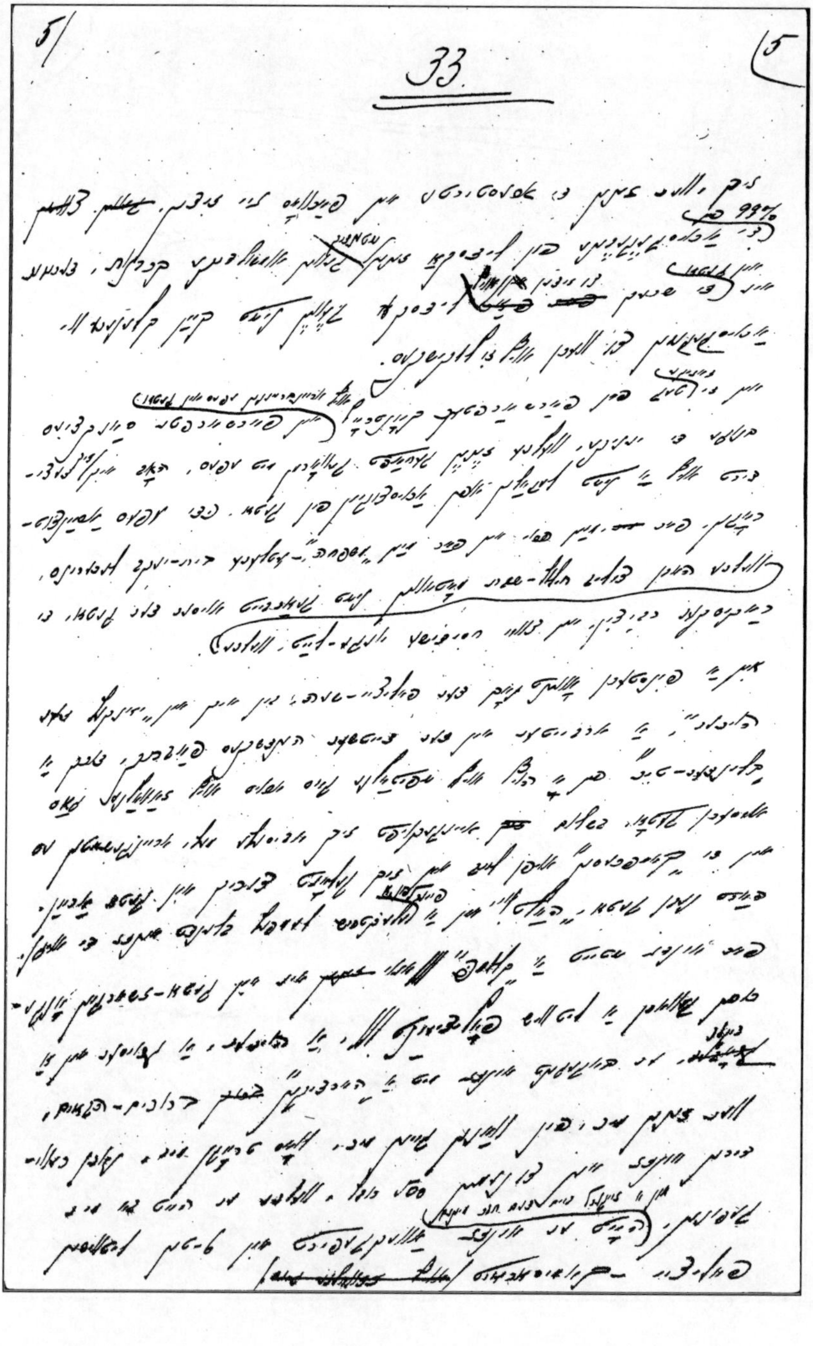

33.

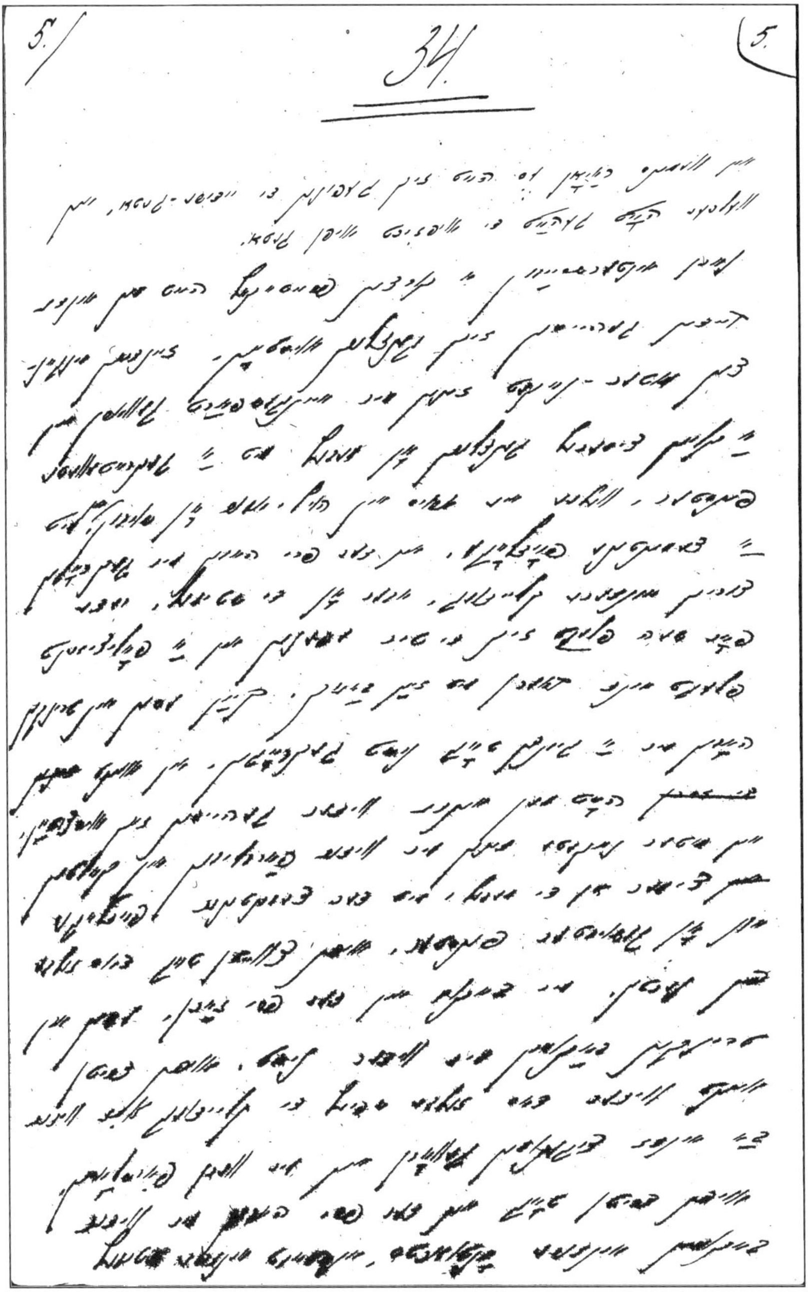
5.
34.
5.

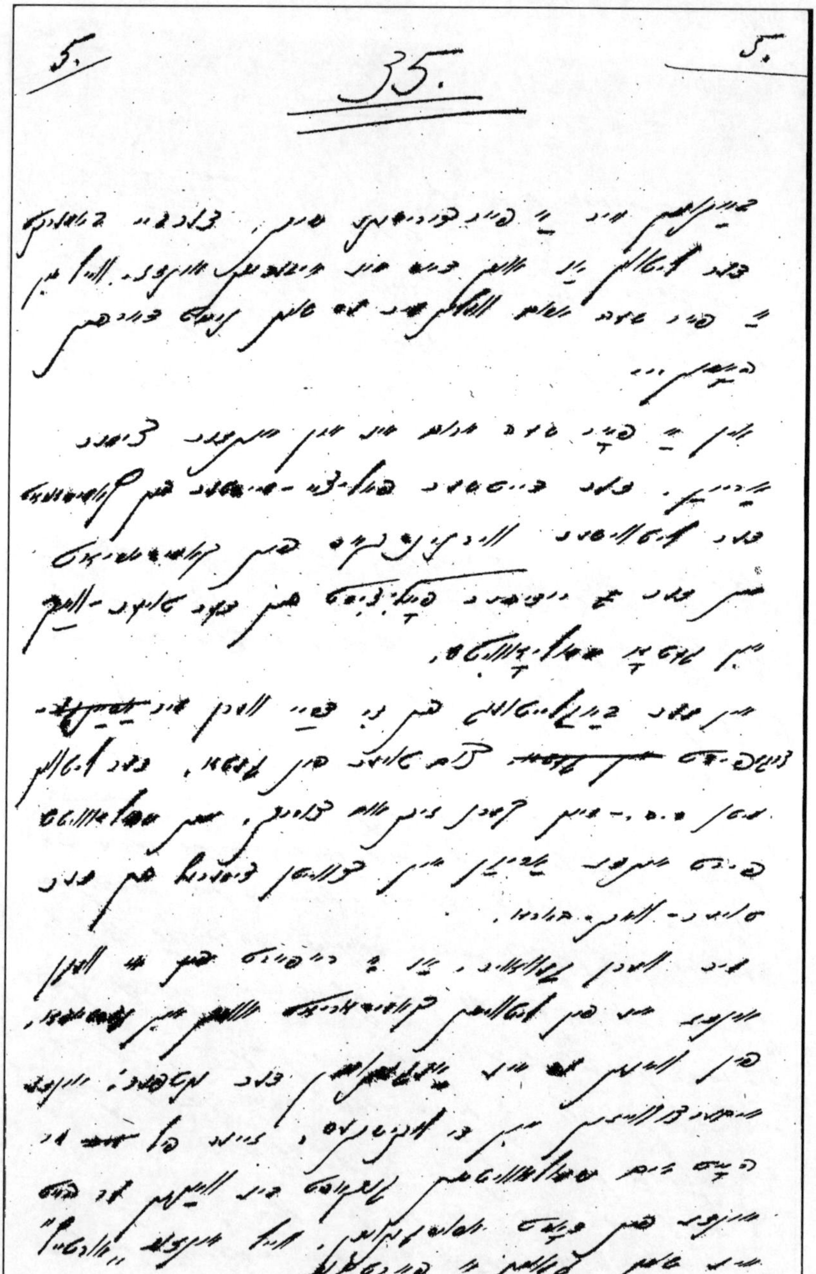
5.

35.

5.

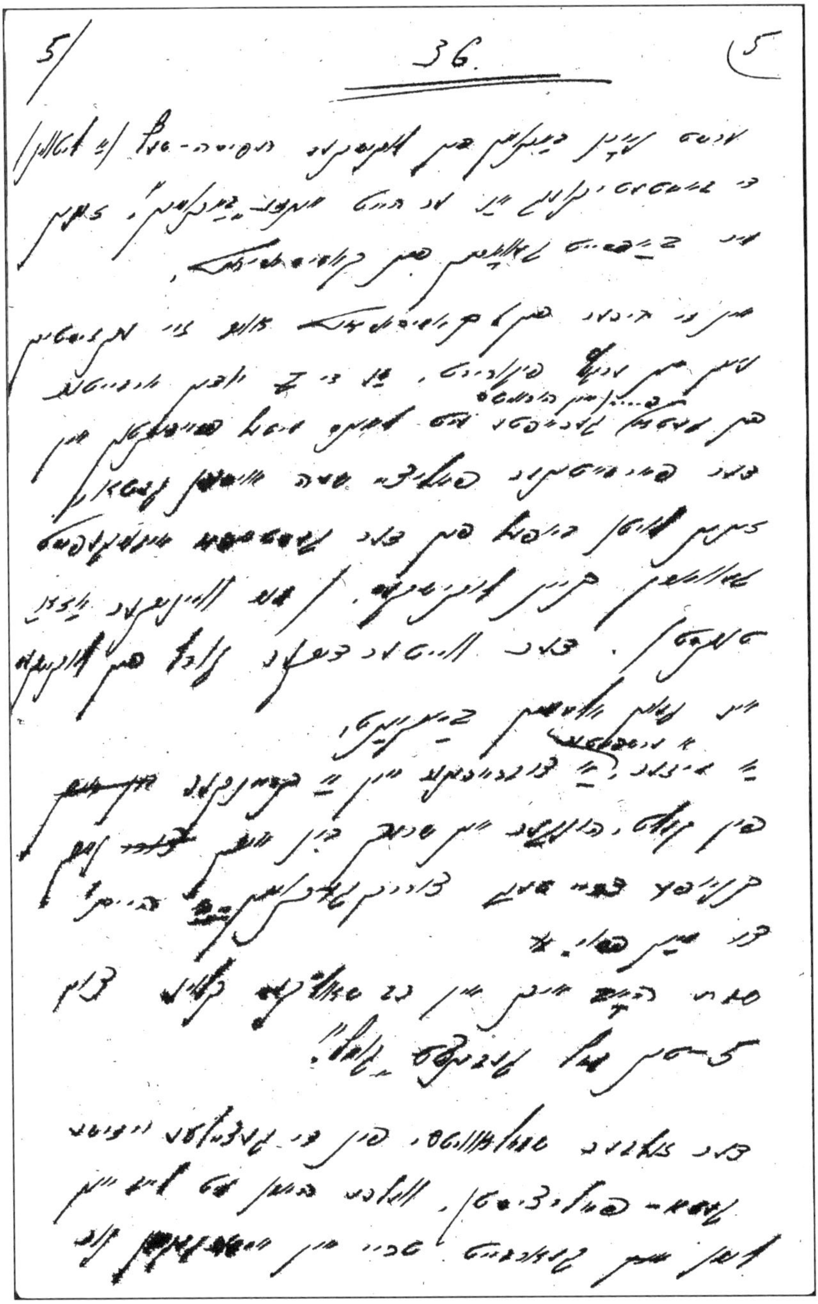

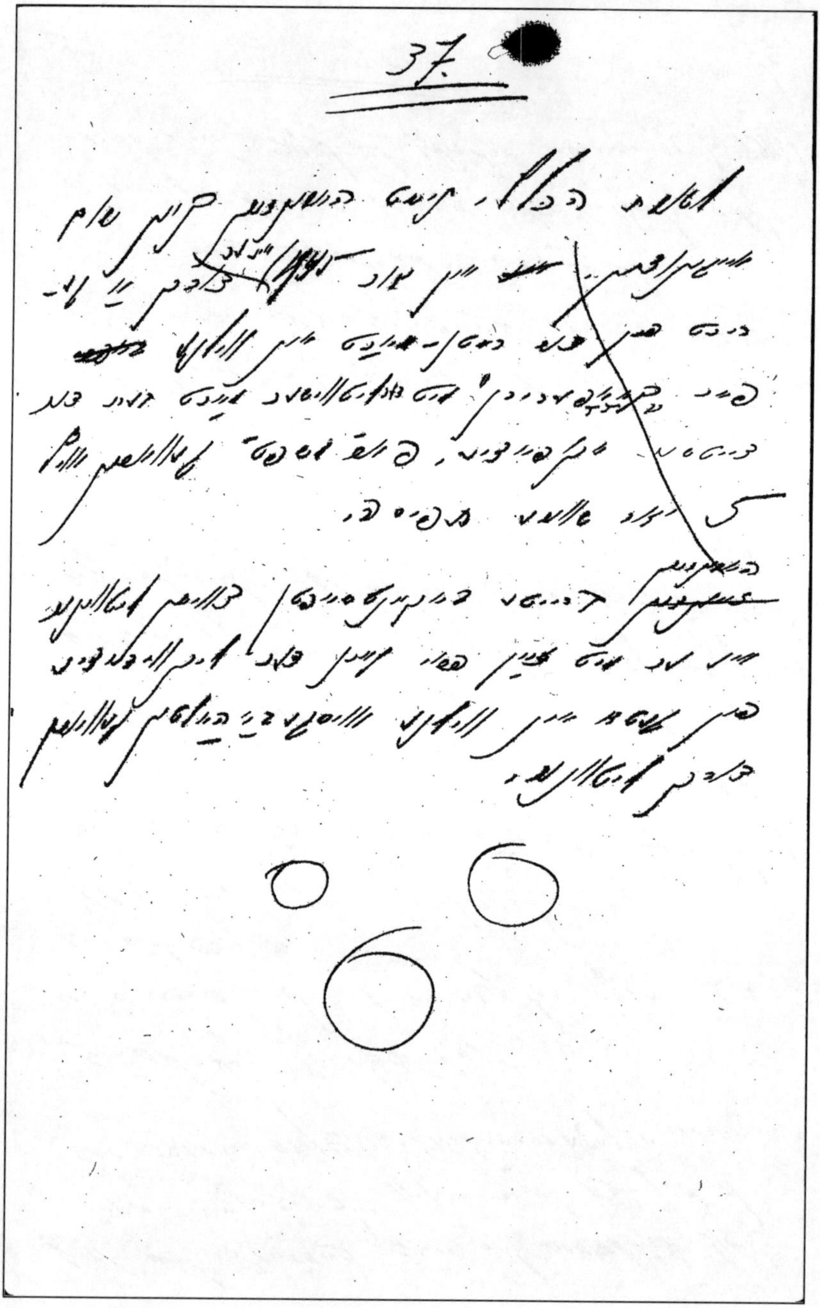

37.

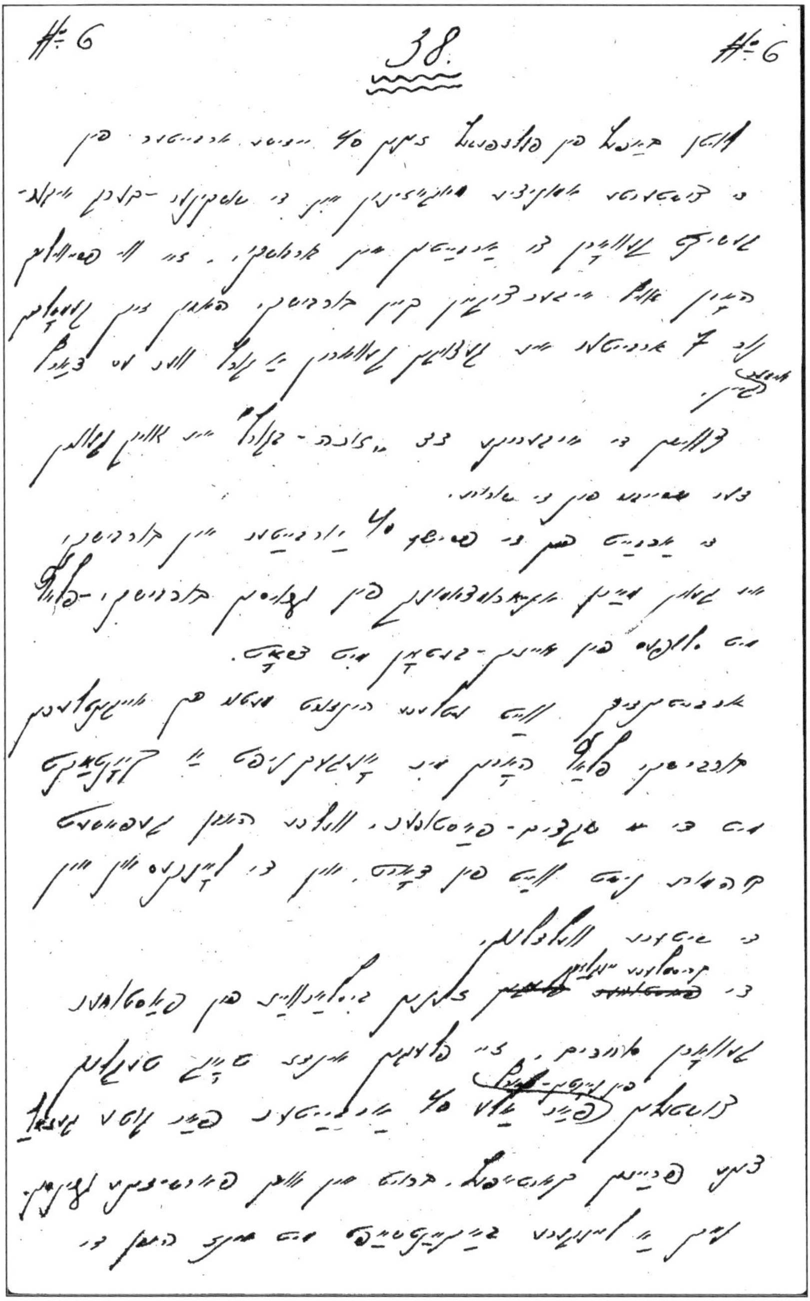

#6 38. #6

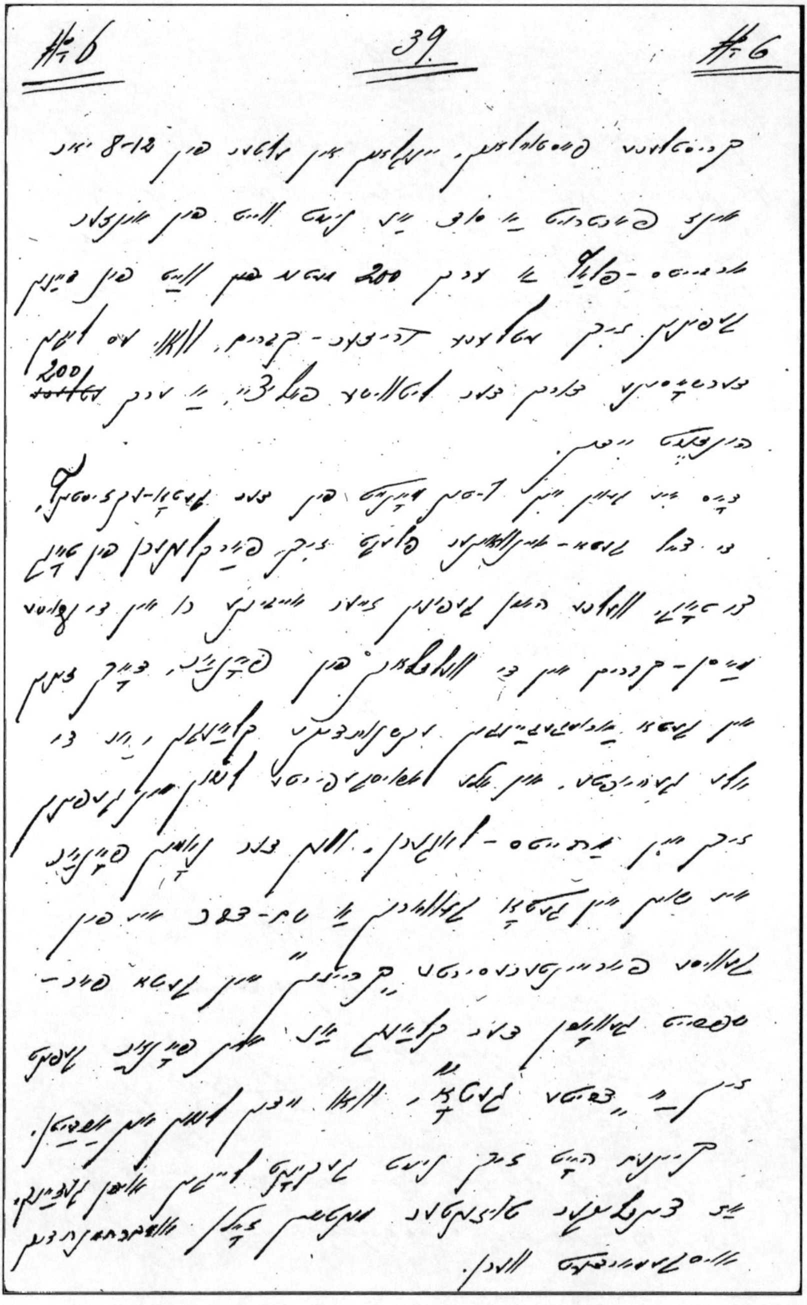

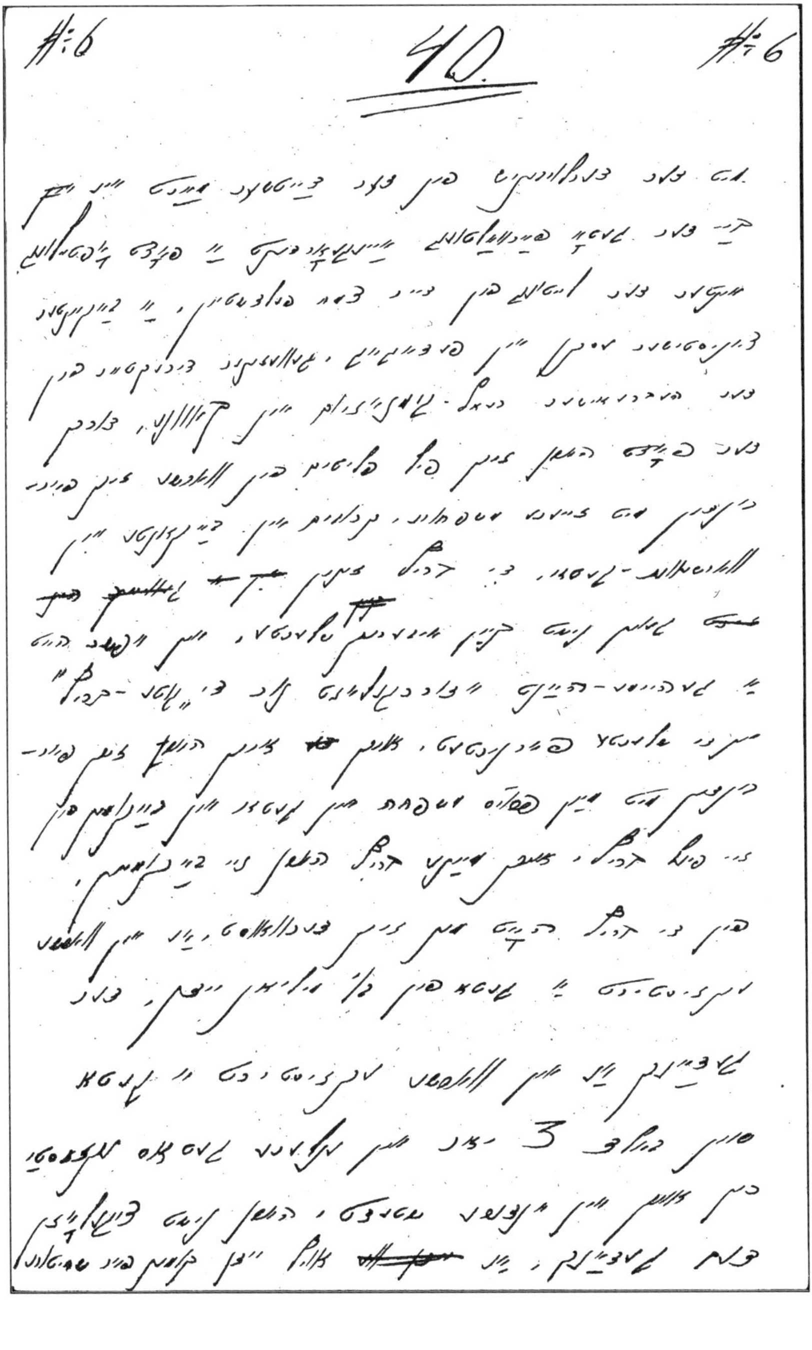

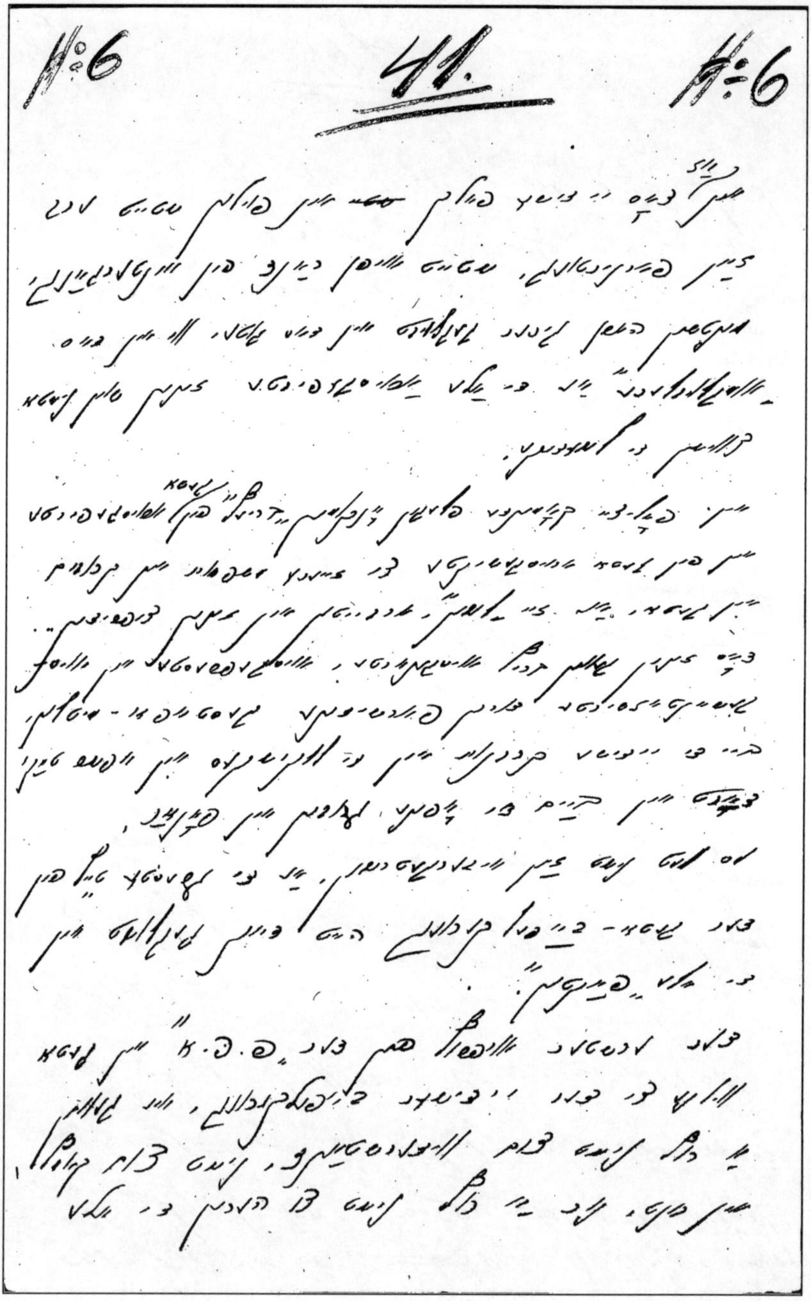
№6
41.
№6

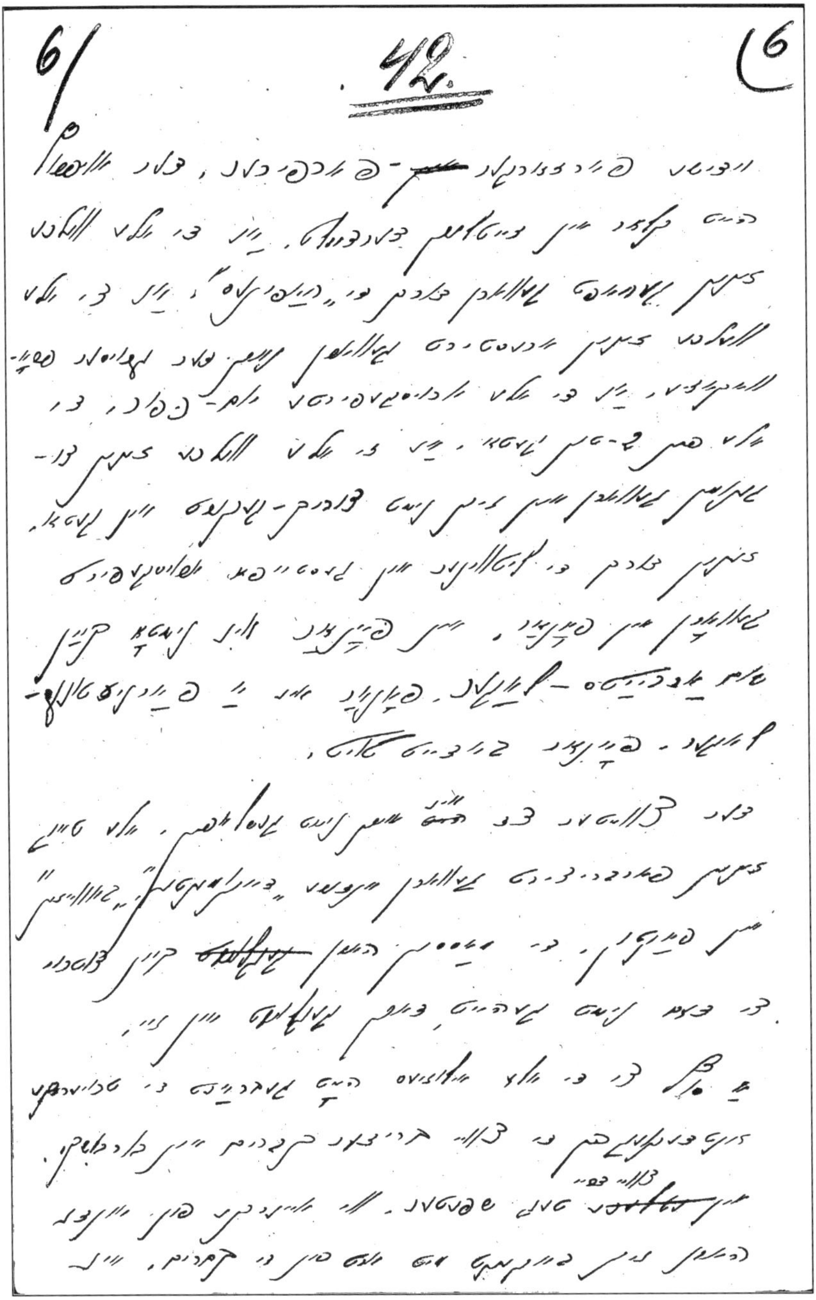

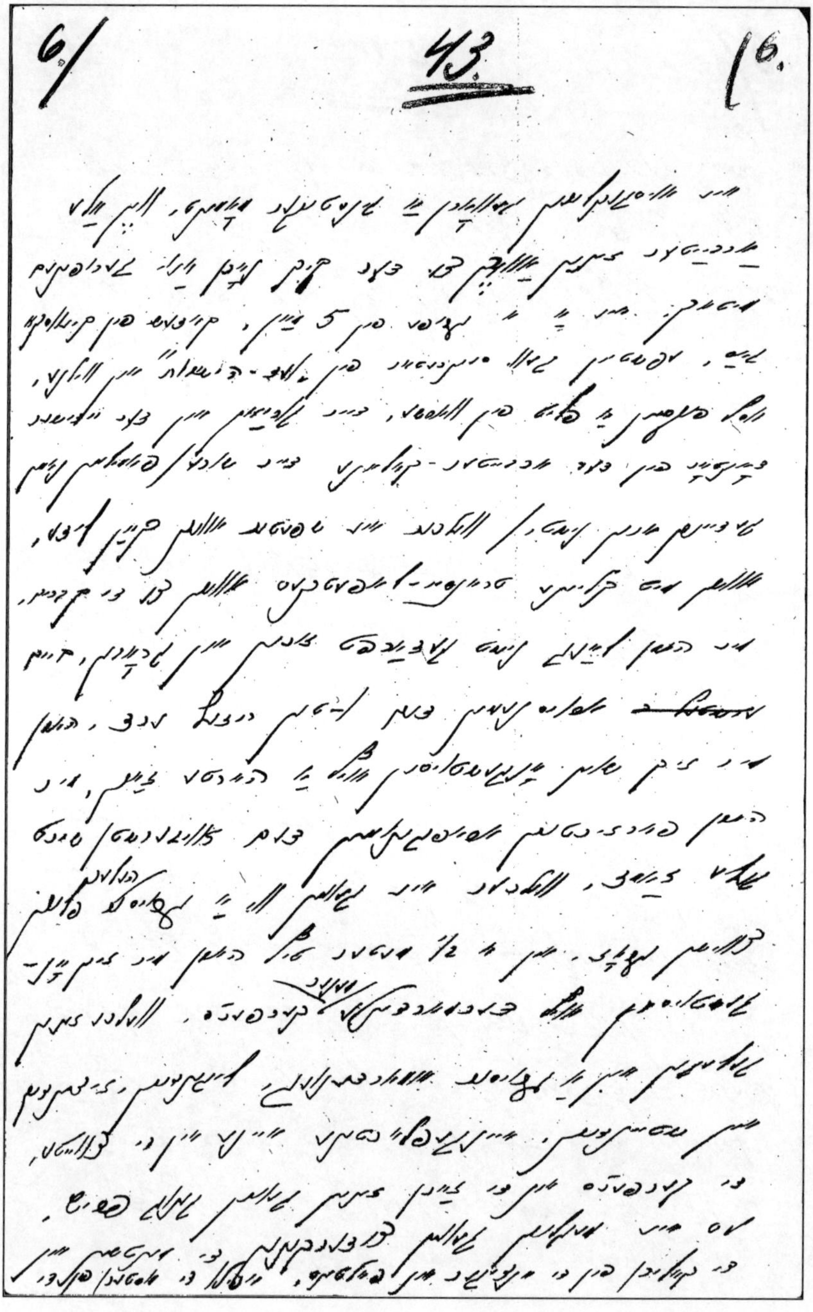

6/ 43. 16.

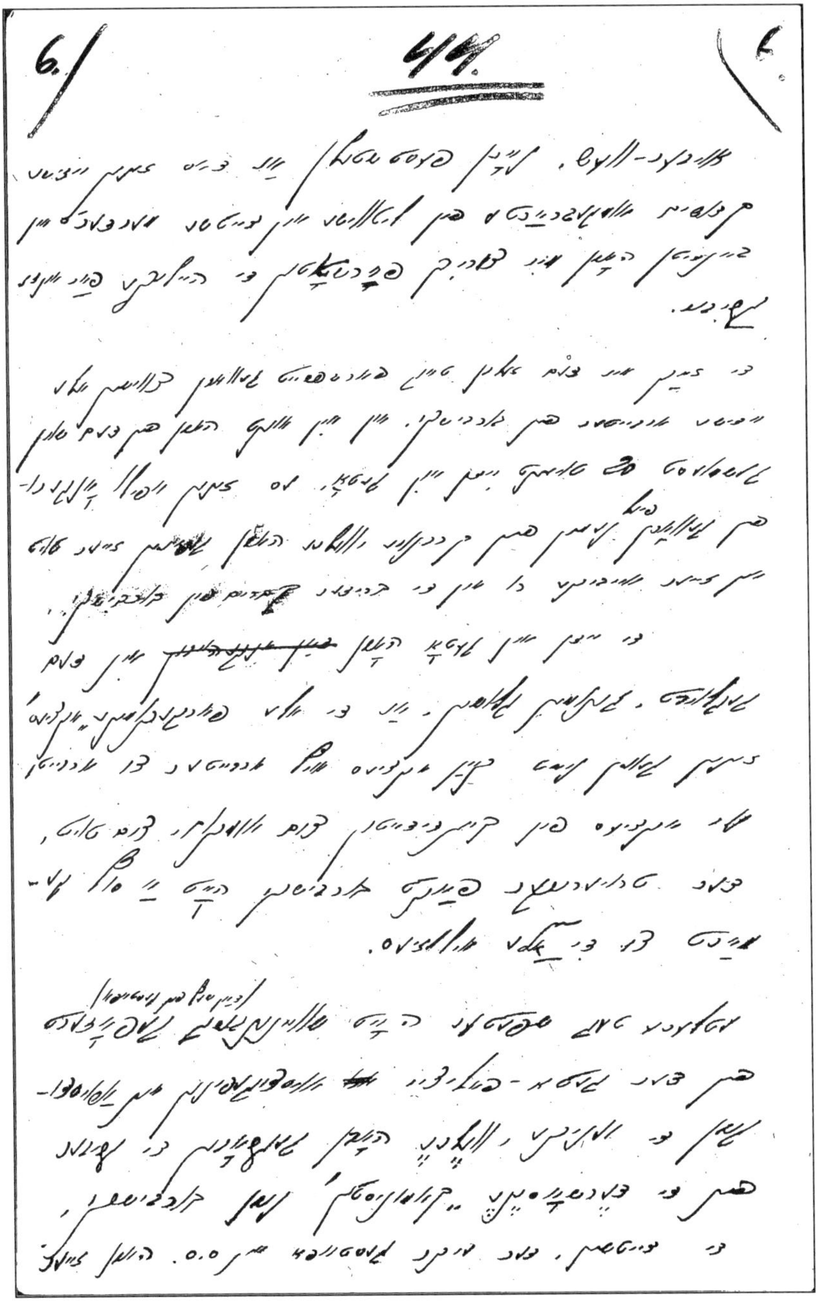

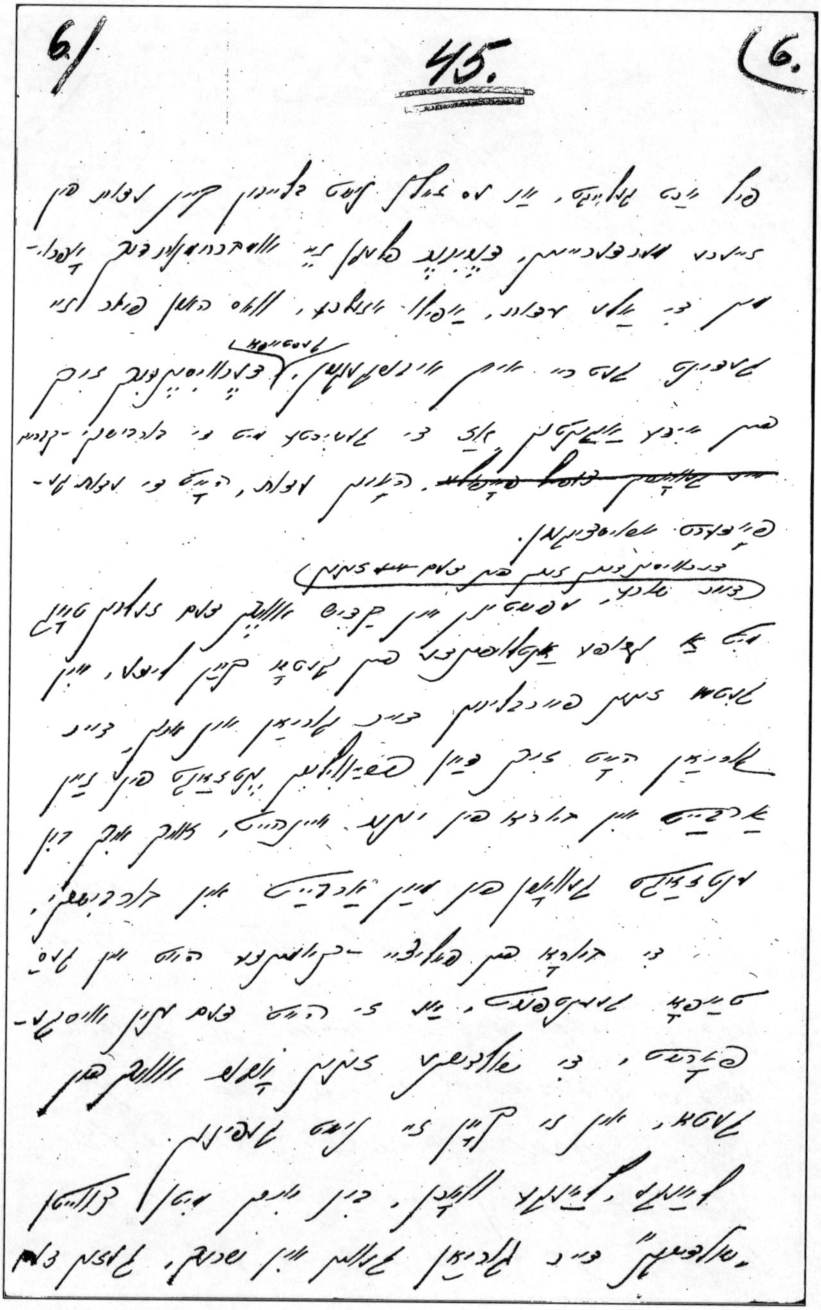
6/
45.
6.

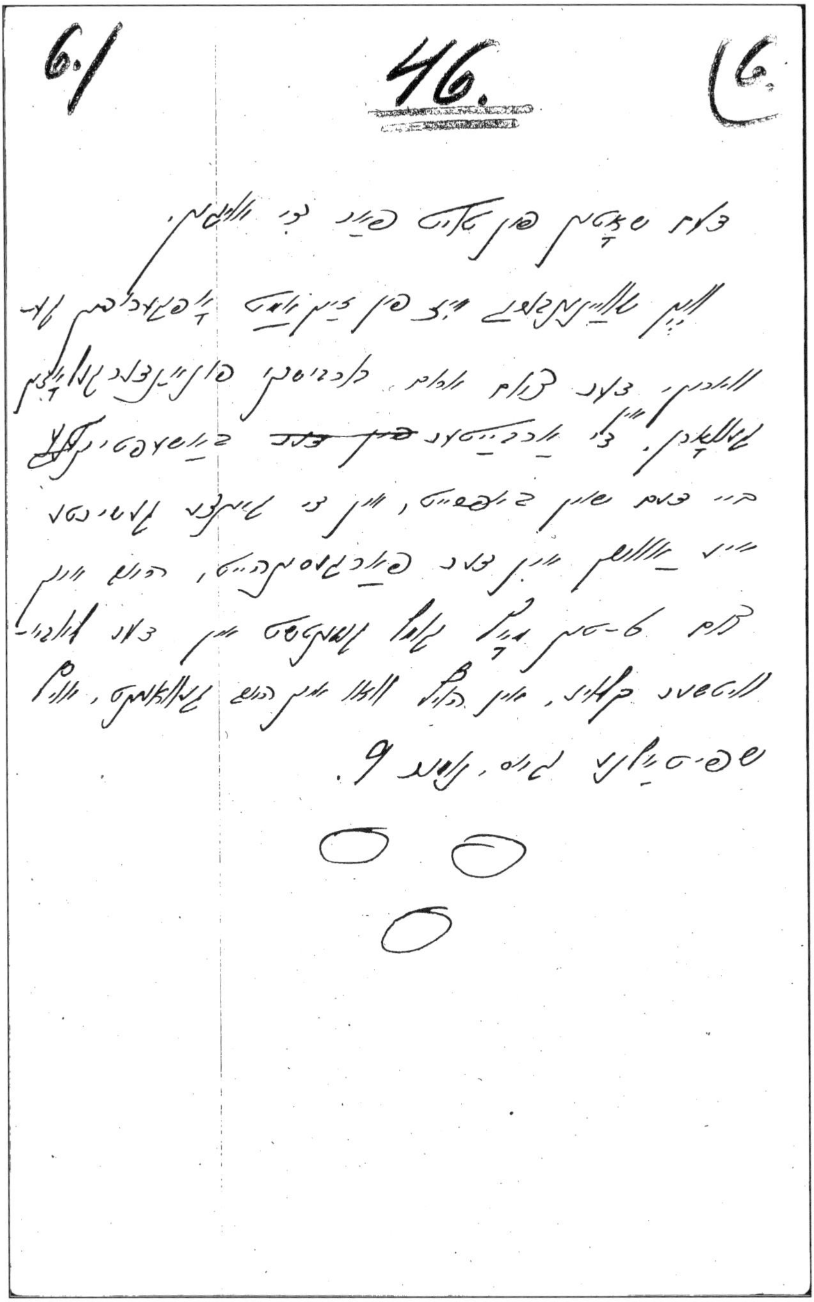

6./

46.

6.

דער שפּאַציר פֿון טאַטע פֿאַר די וואָלקן

ווען [illegible] ביז פֿון זײַן וועלט [illegible]

[illegible] דער גרויס וועלט. [illegible]

[illegible] די [illegible] ~~[illegible]~~ [illegible]

ביי דעם שיין [illegible], און די [illegible]

[illegible]

[illegible] דער [illegible]

[illegible]

[illegible] 9.

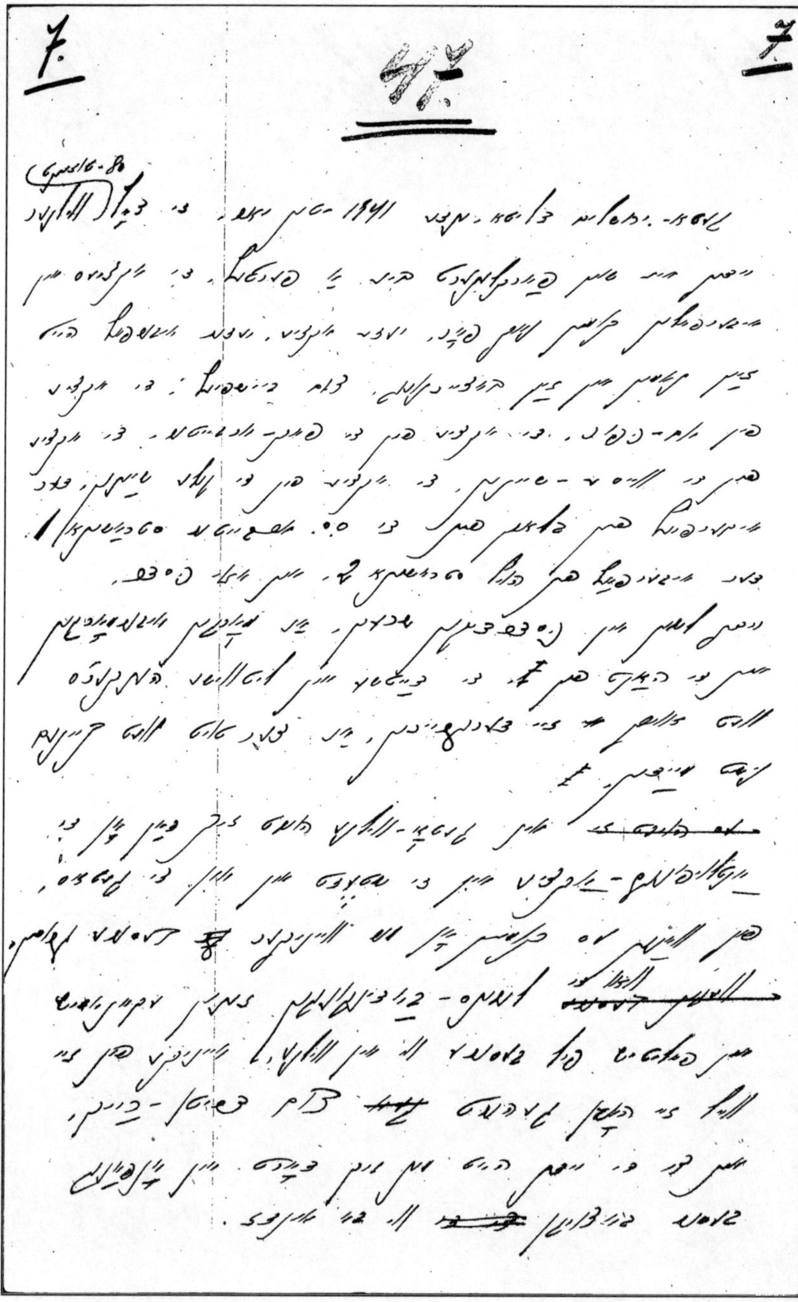

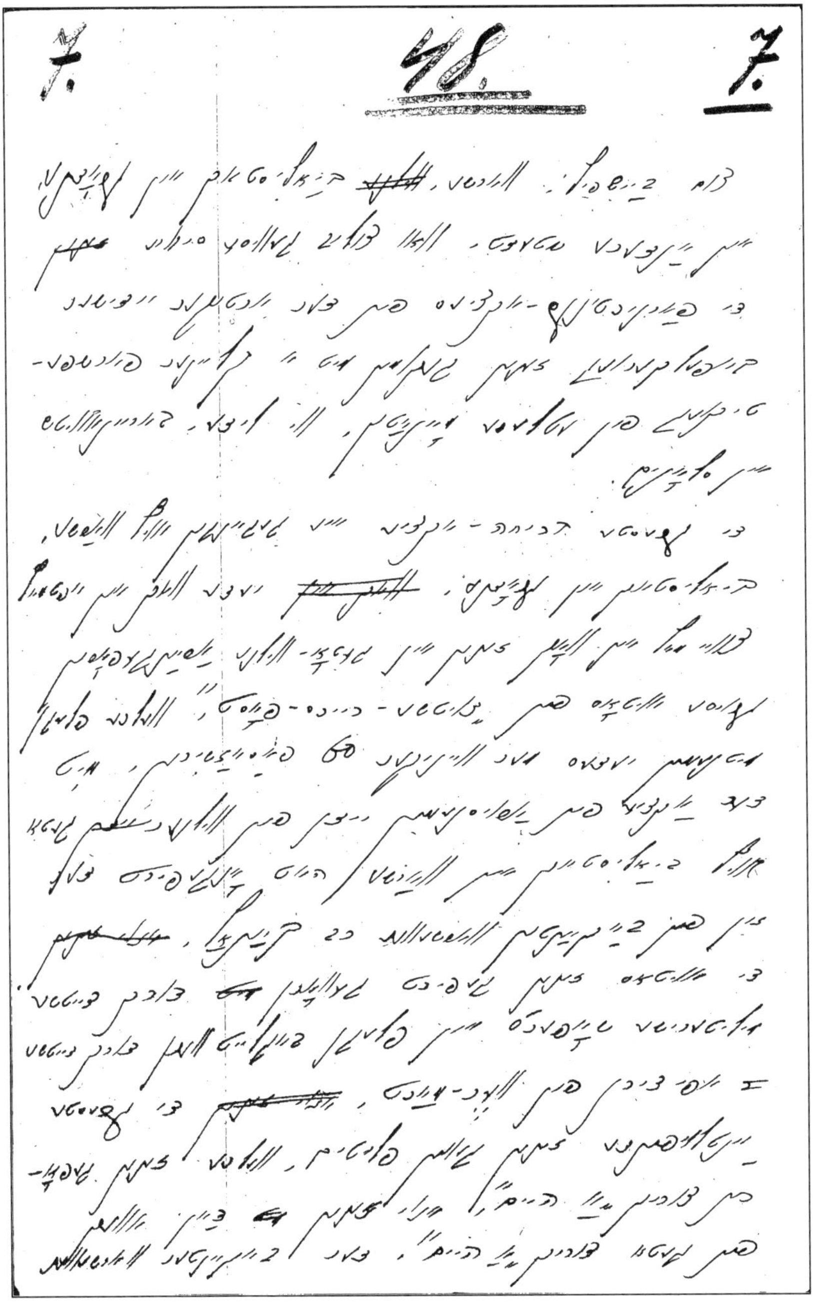

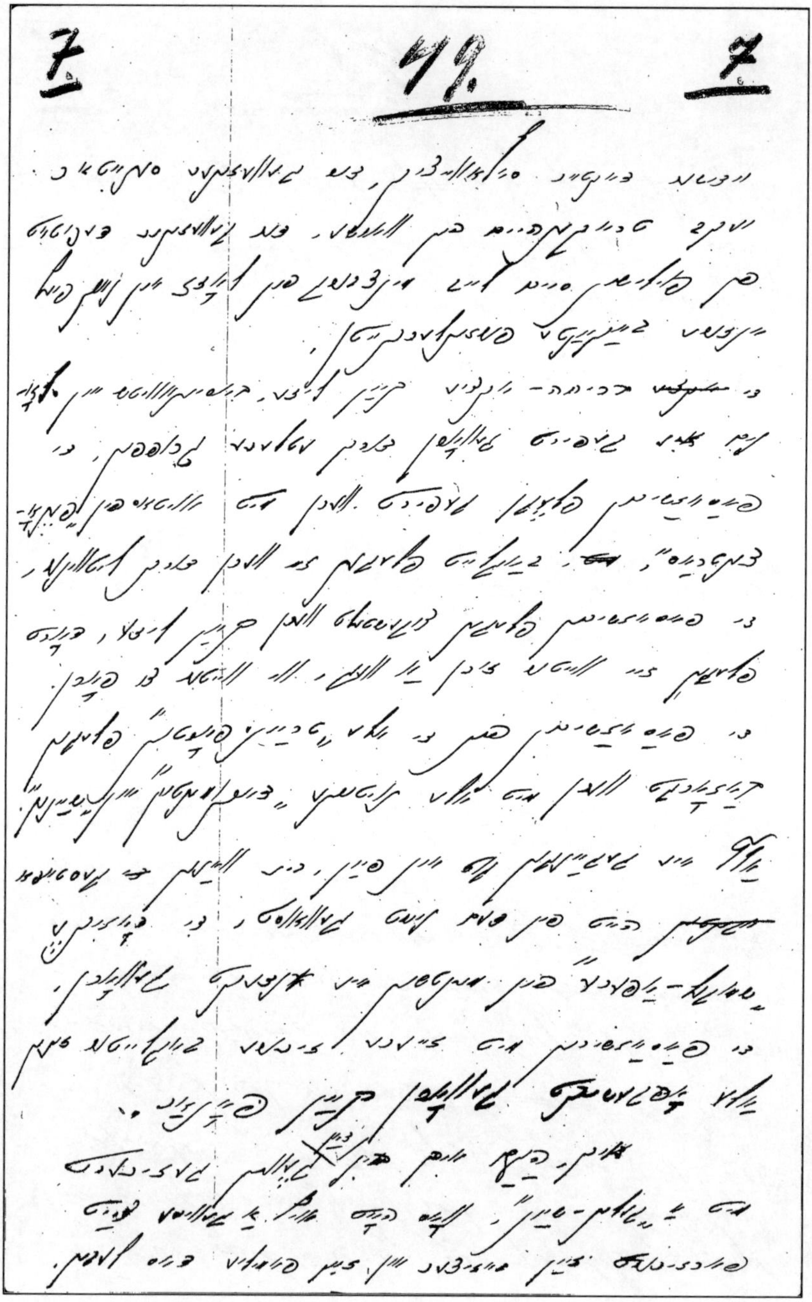

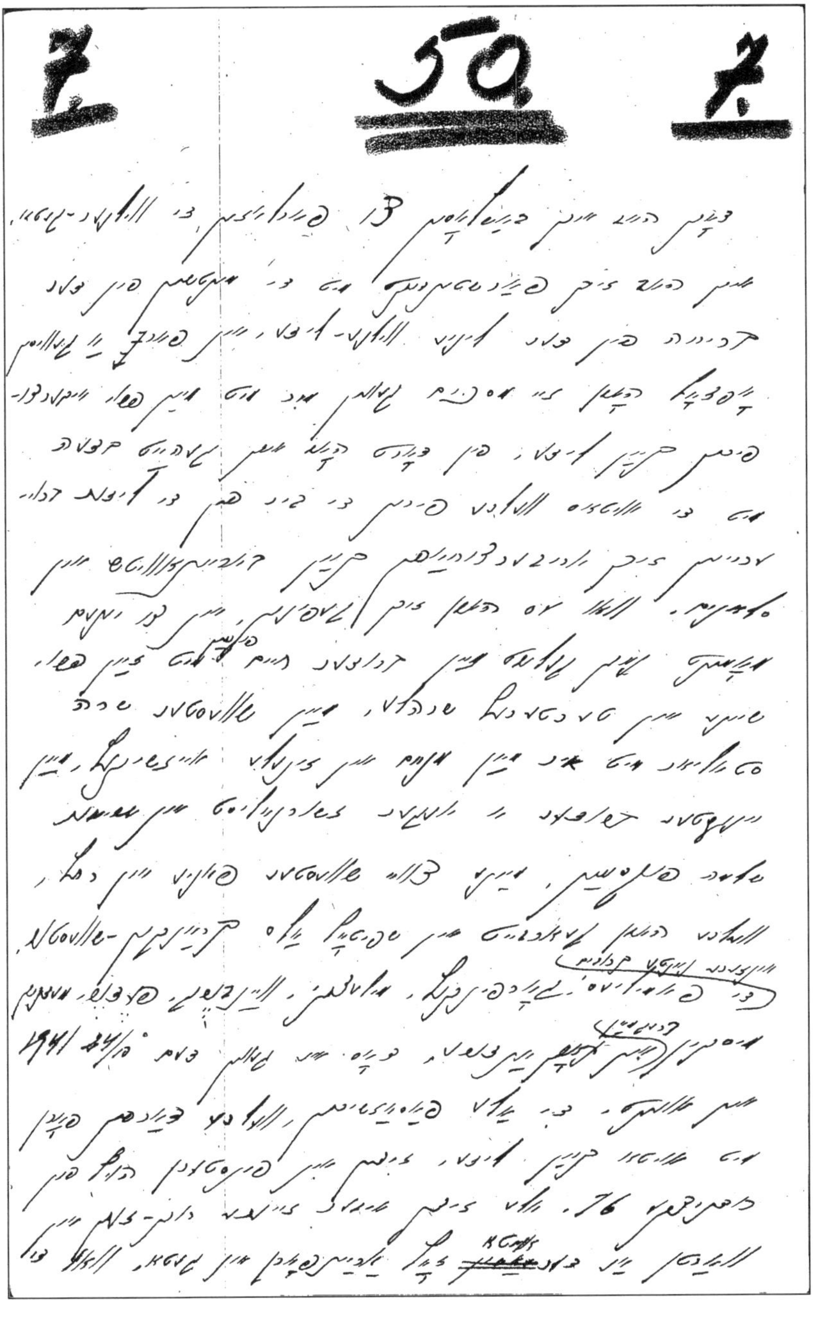

[illegible]

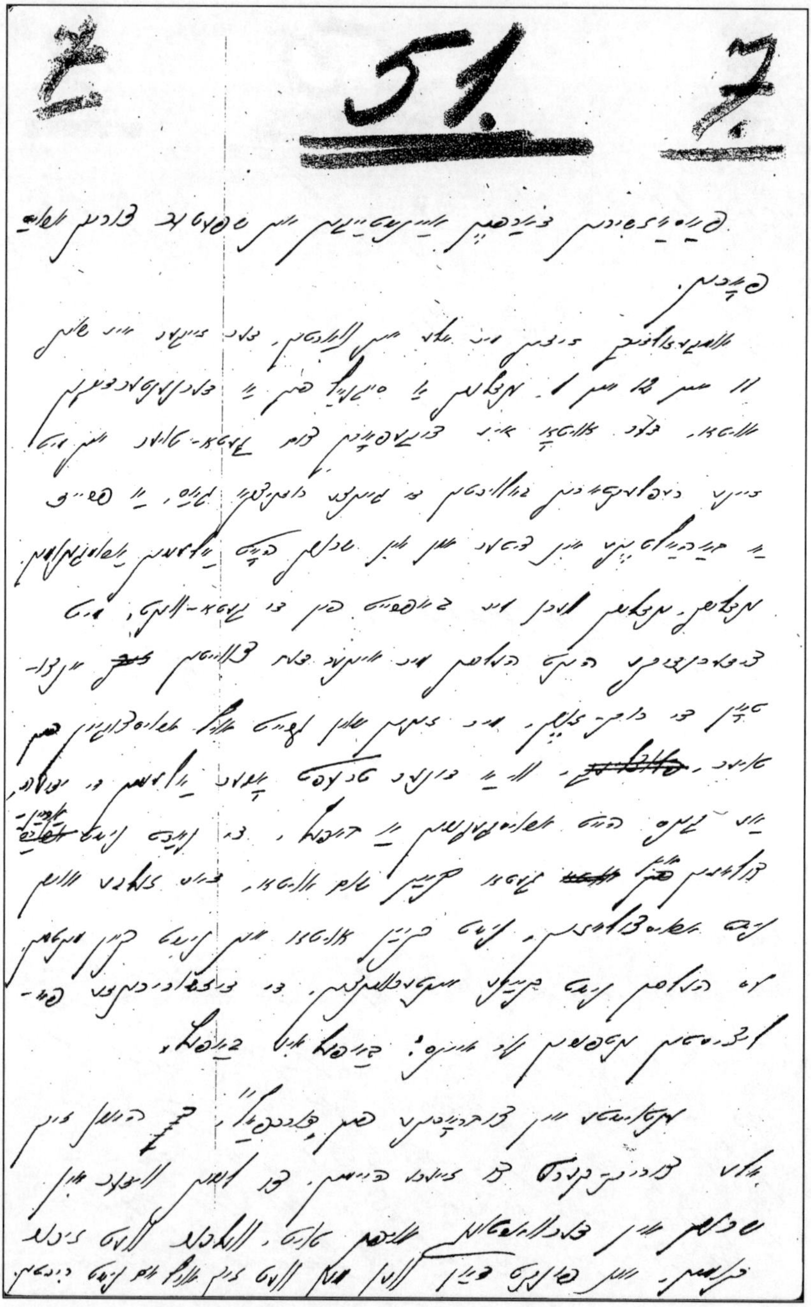

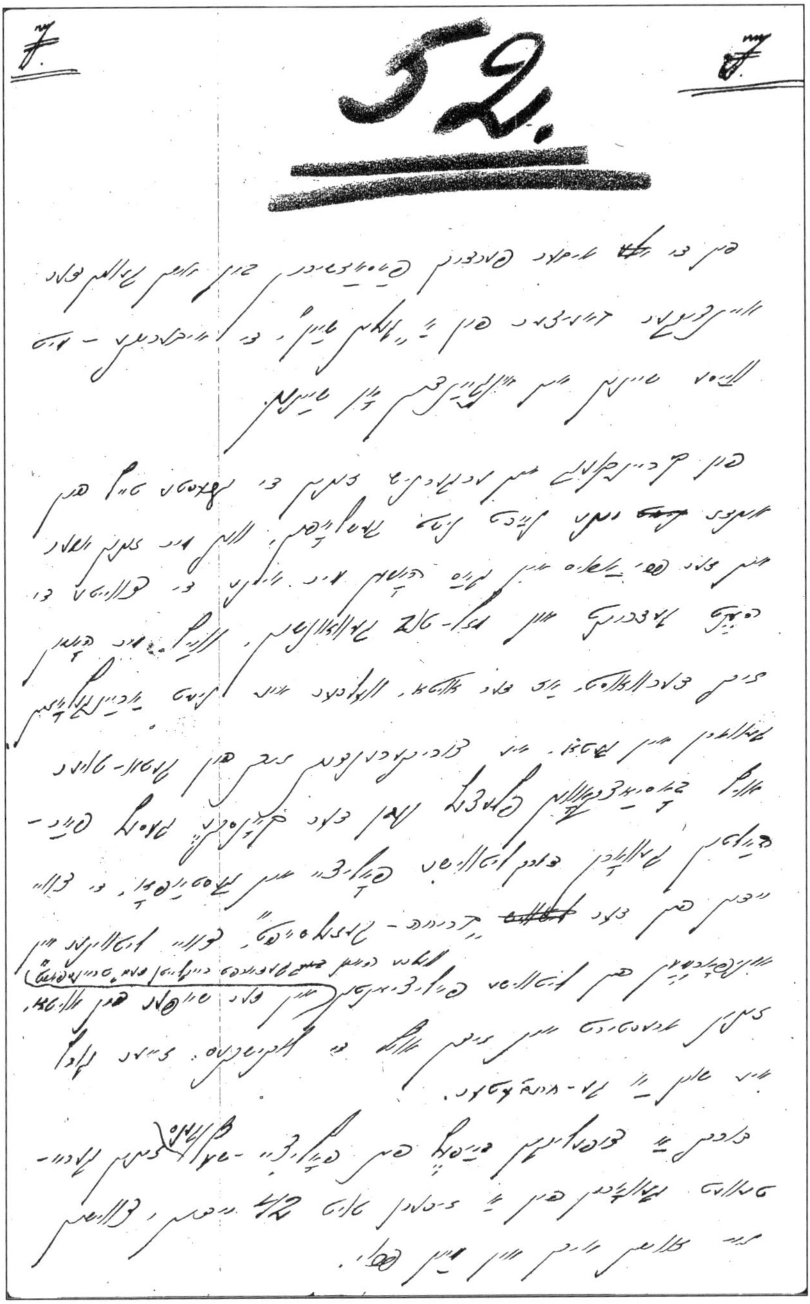
7

52

7

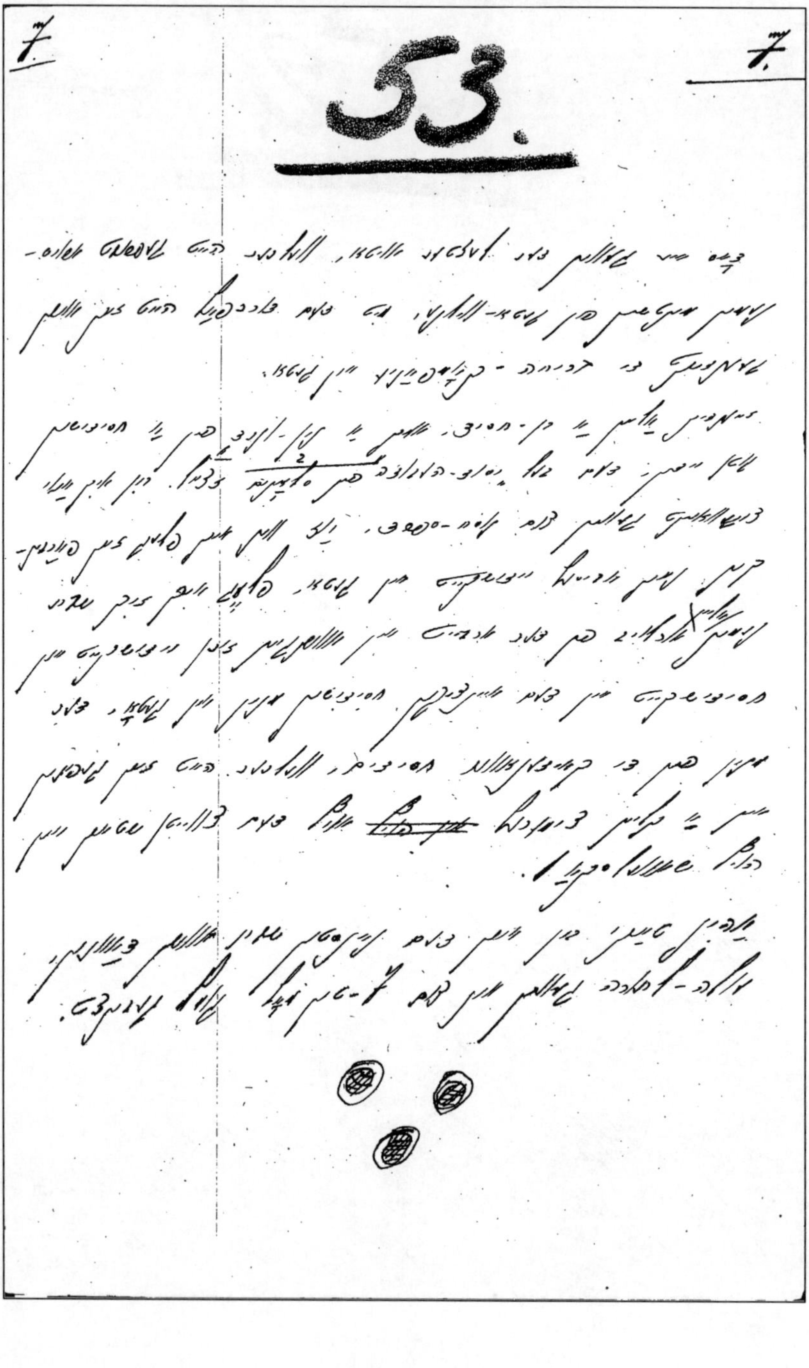

7. 53. 7.

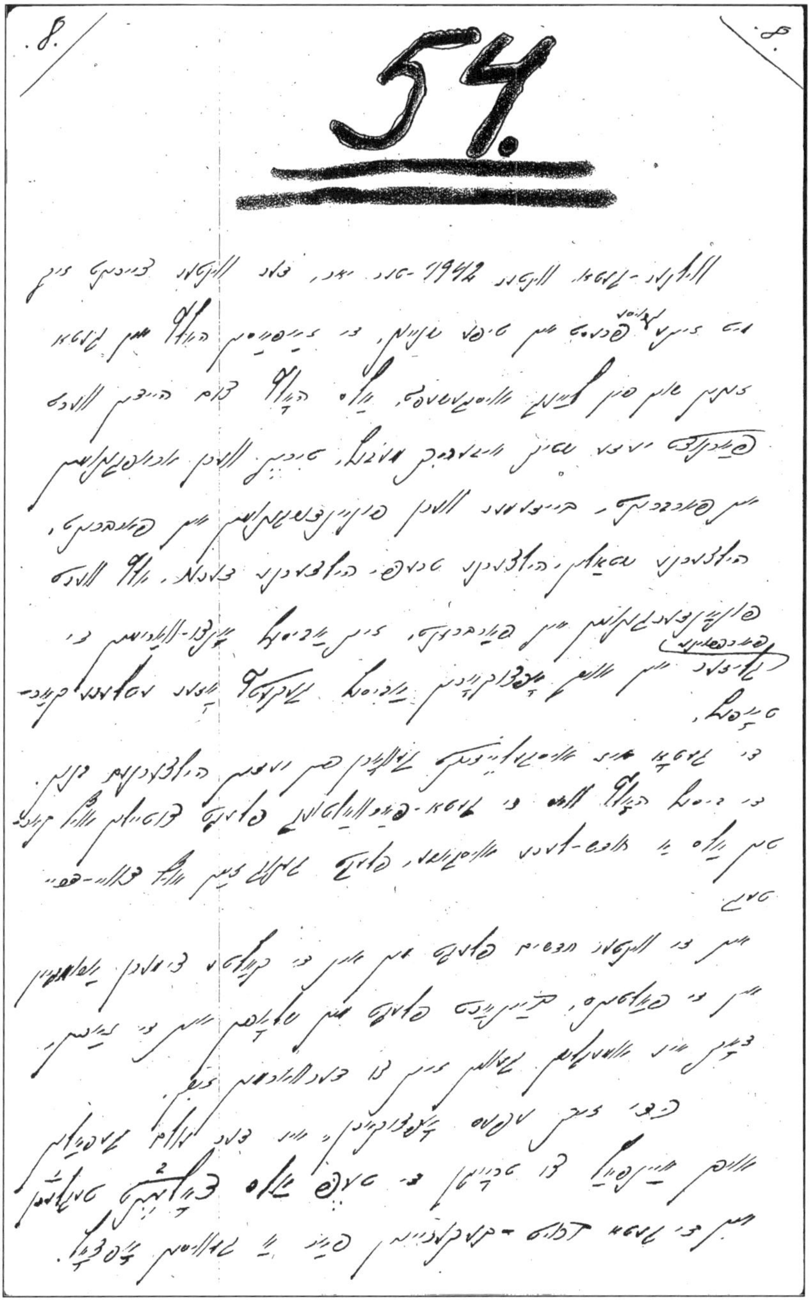

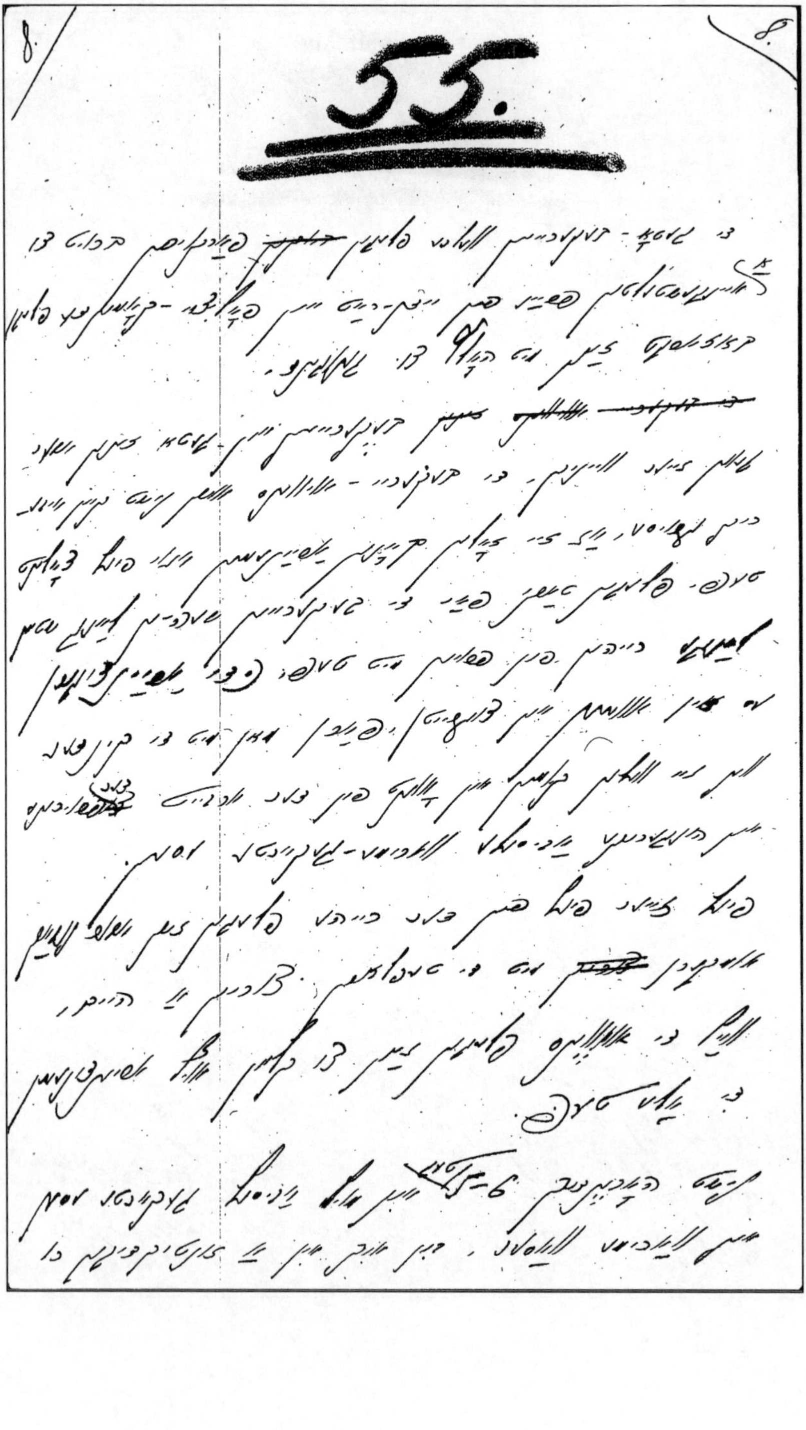
8.

8.

55.

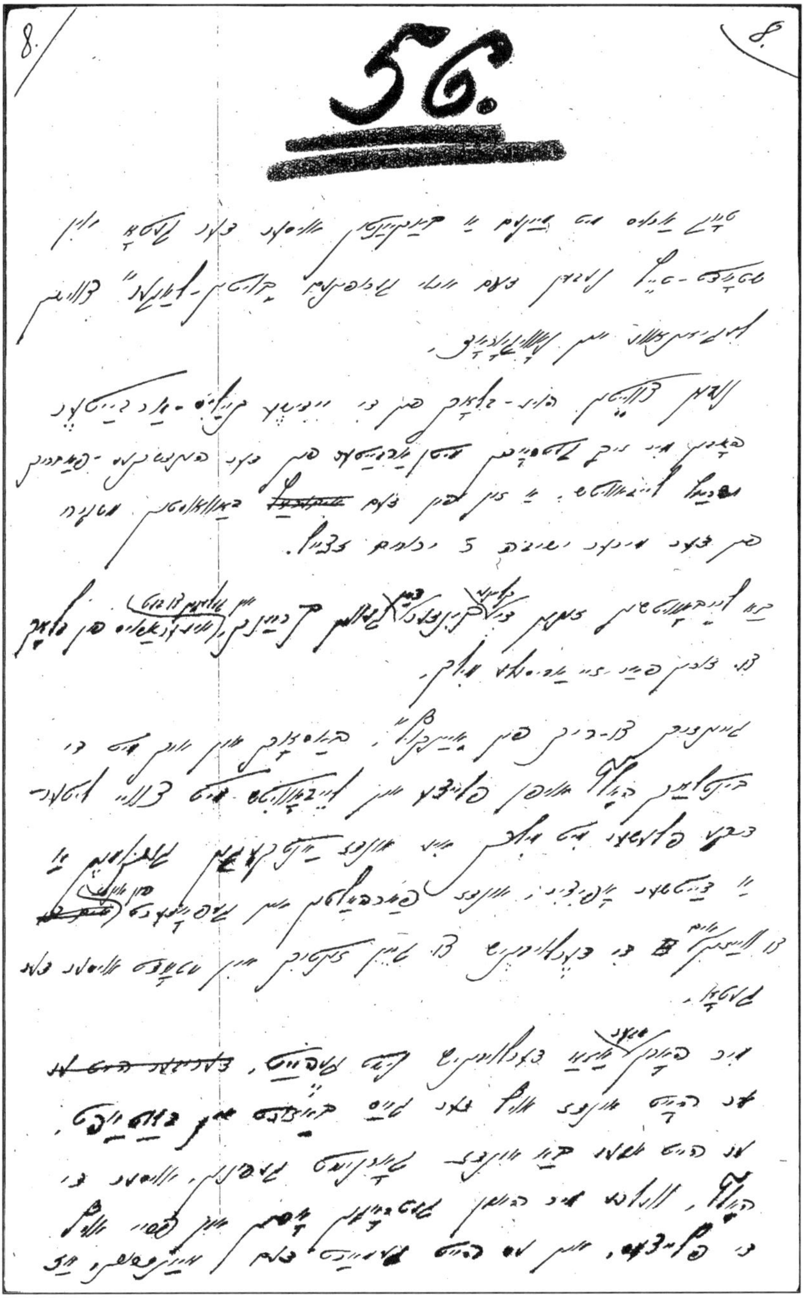

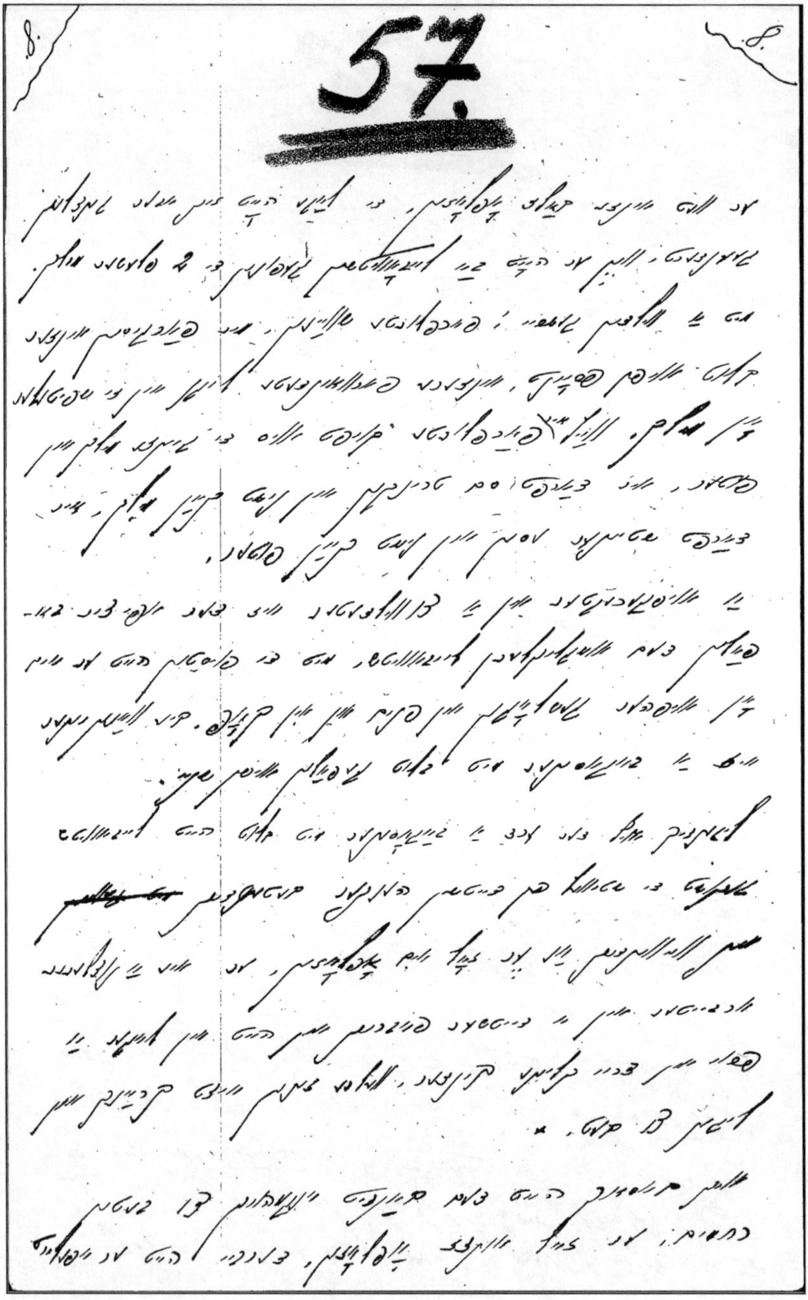

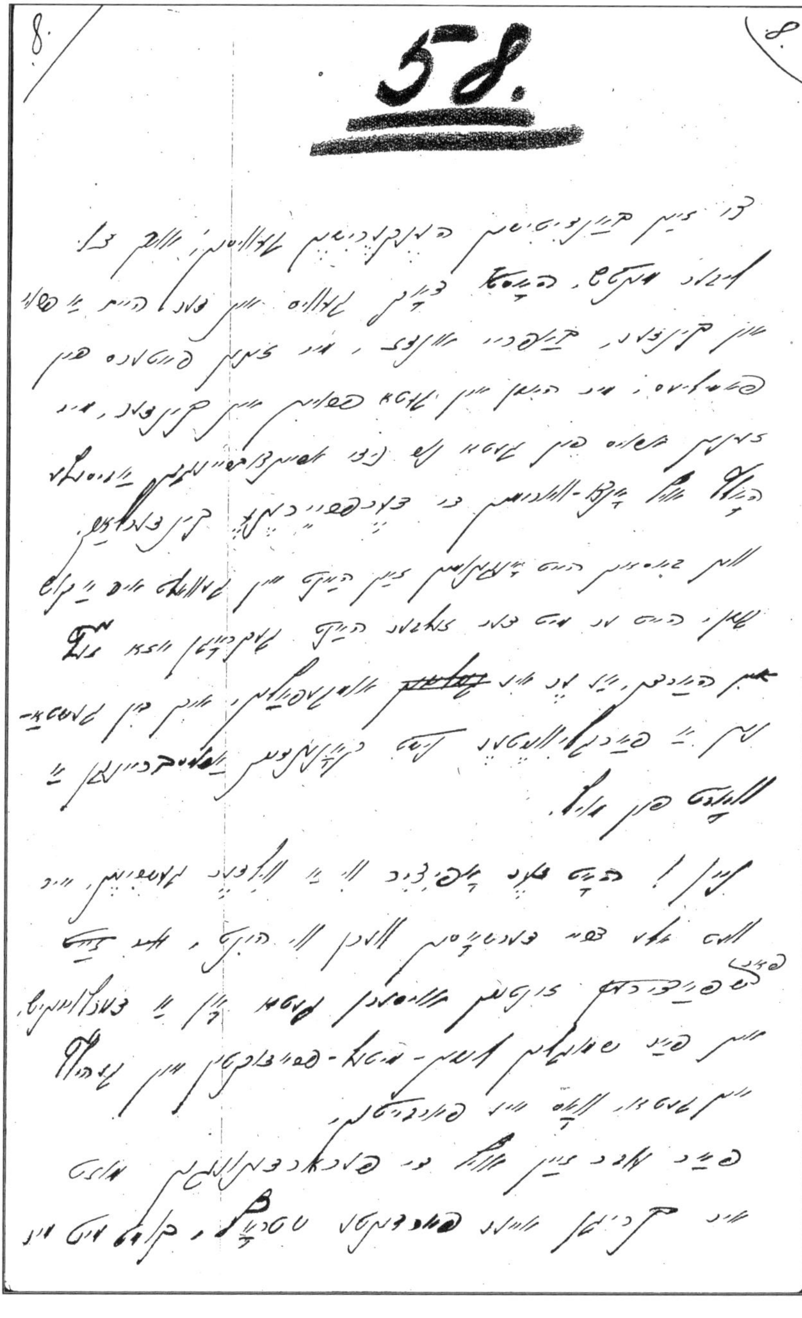
58.

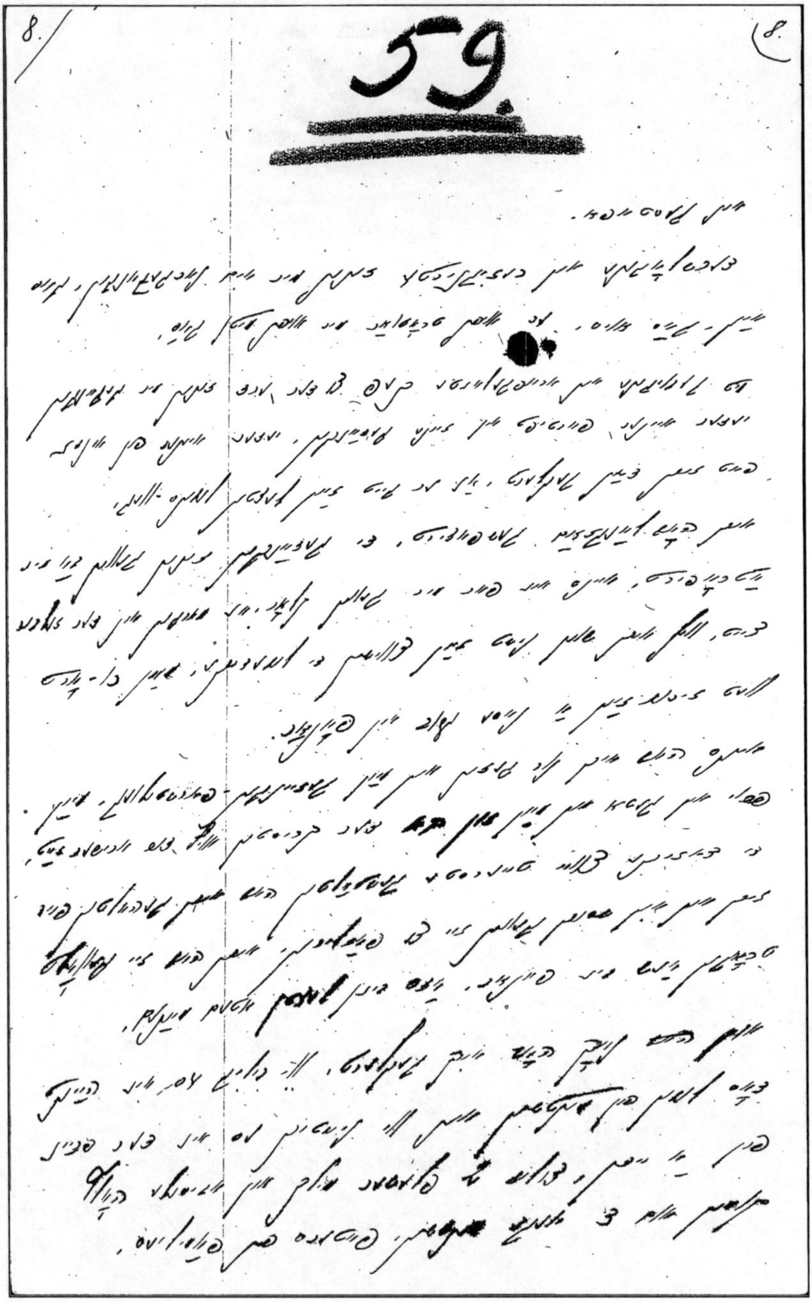
8.

59

(8.

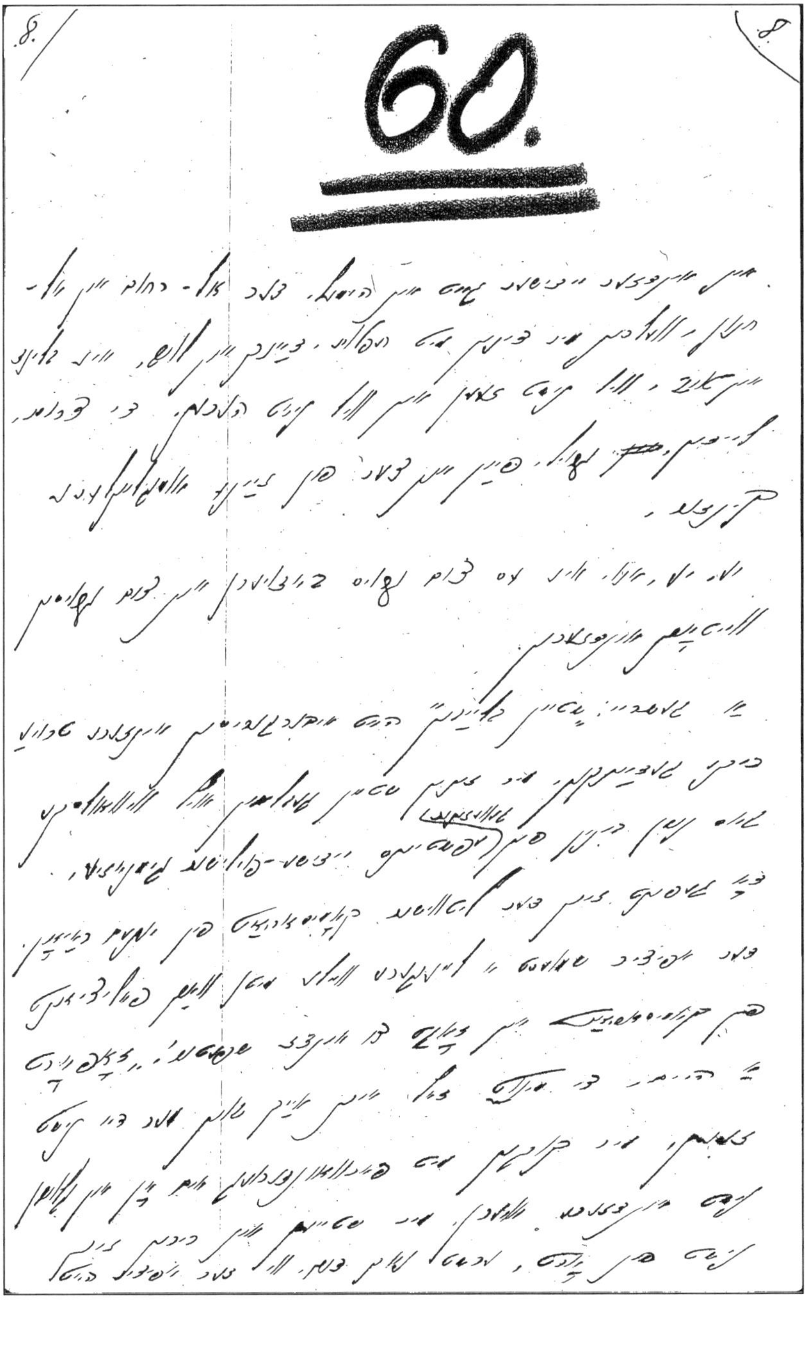

60.

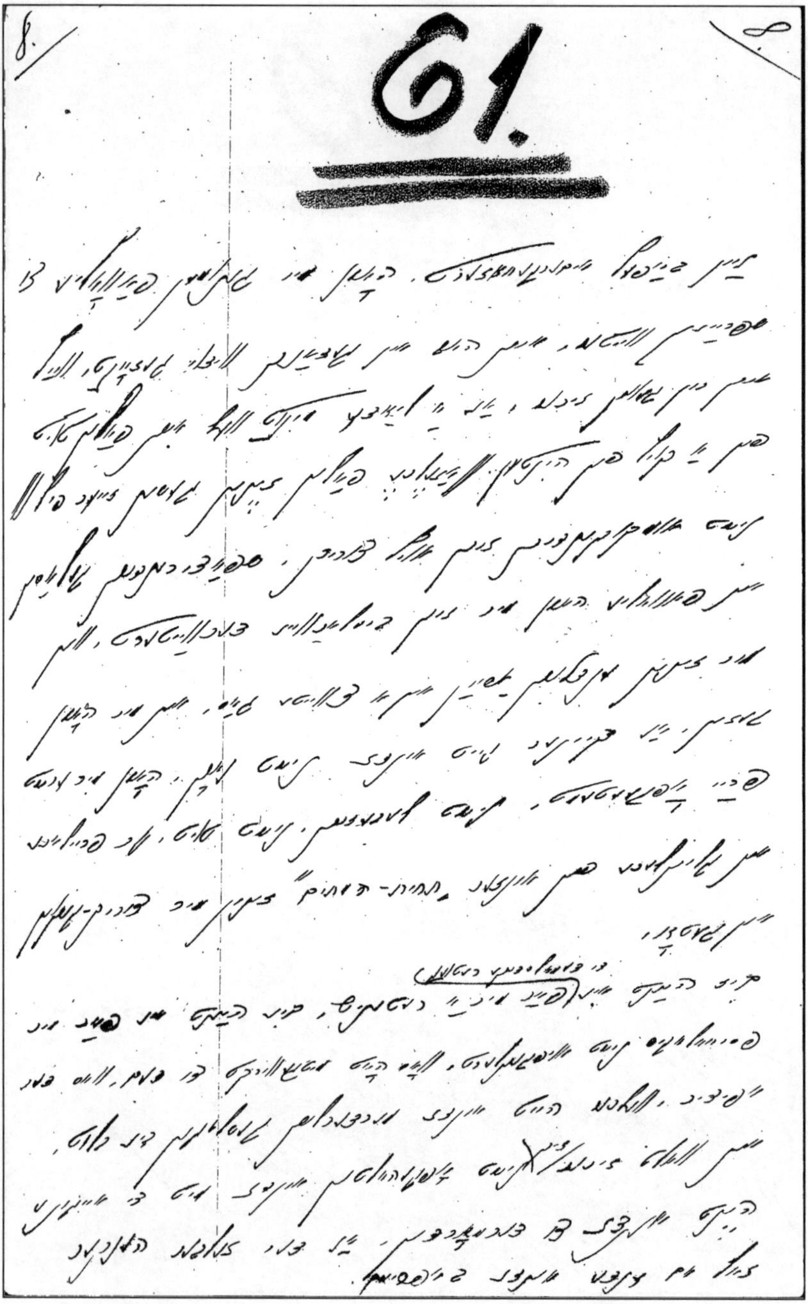

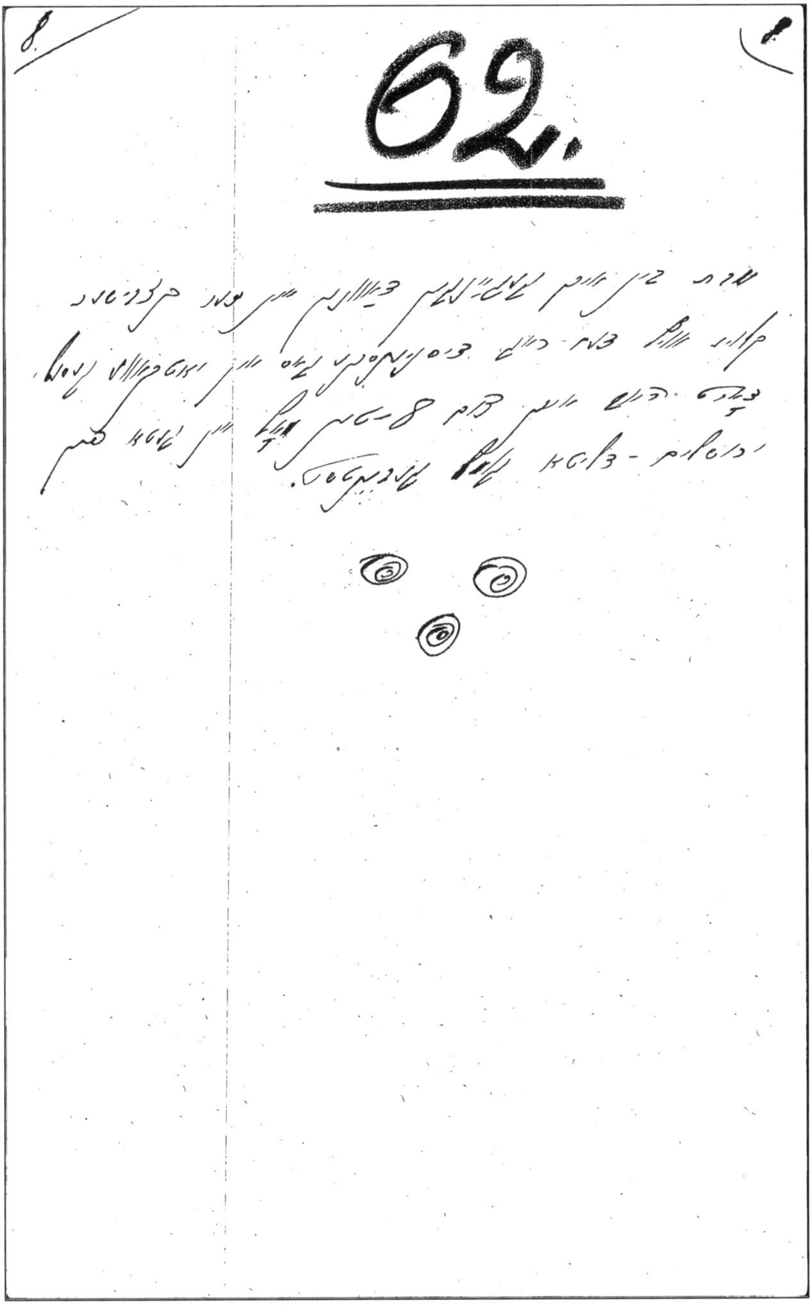
8.

62.

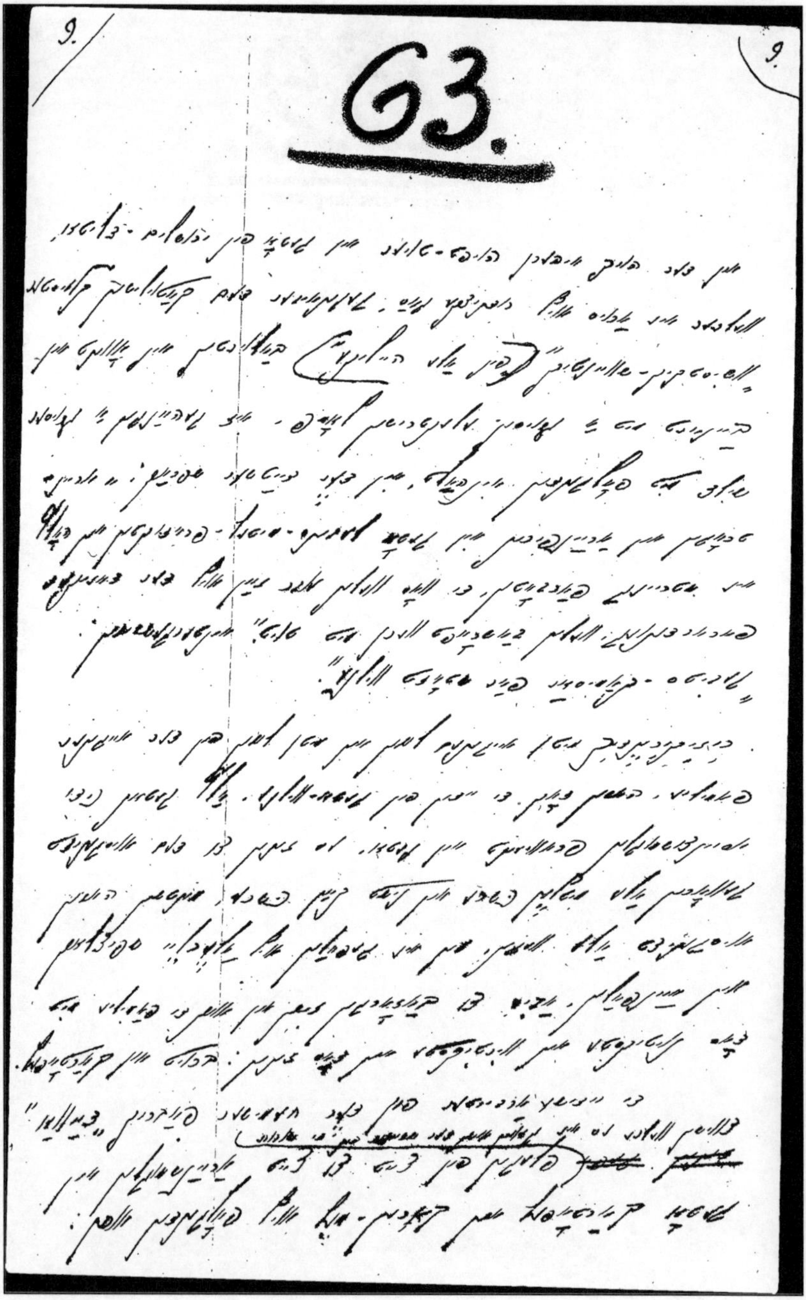
9.
9.
63.

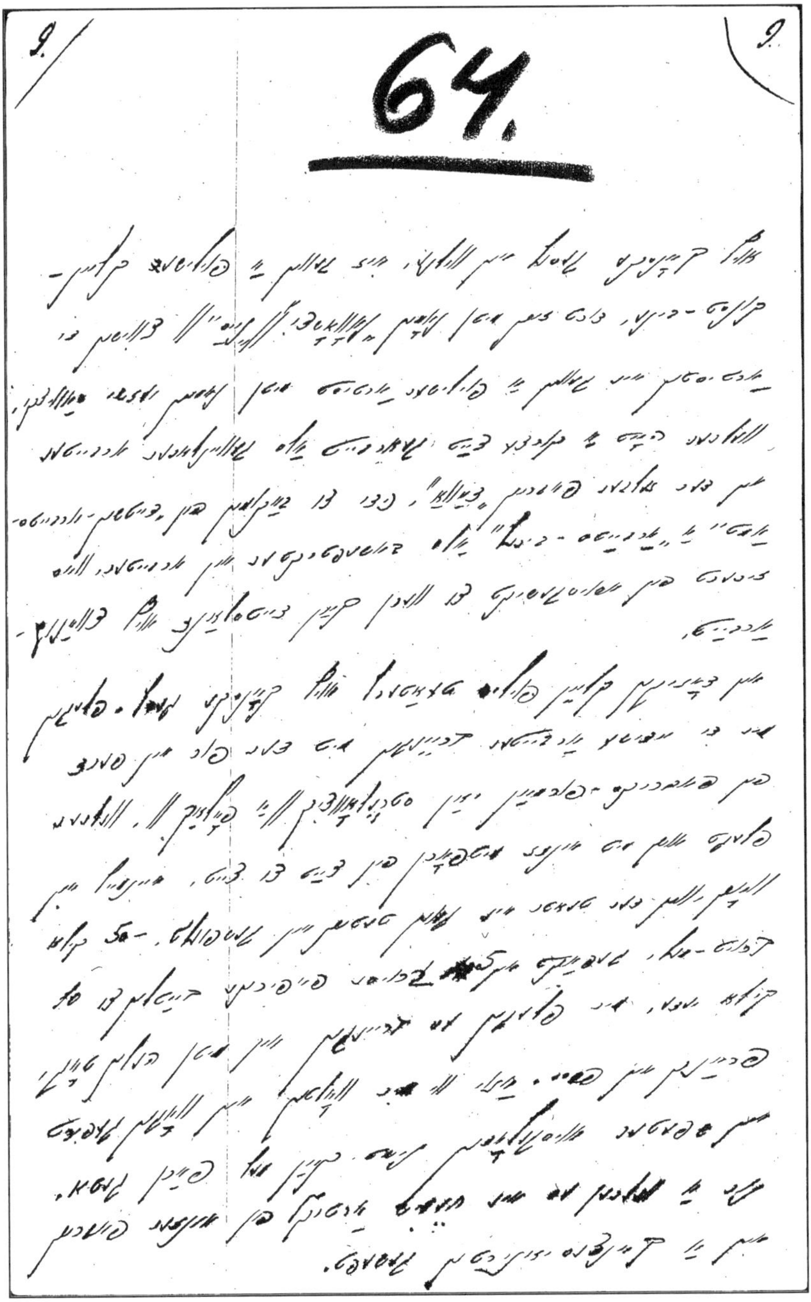
9.

64.

9.

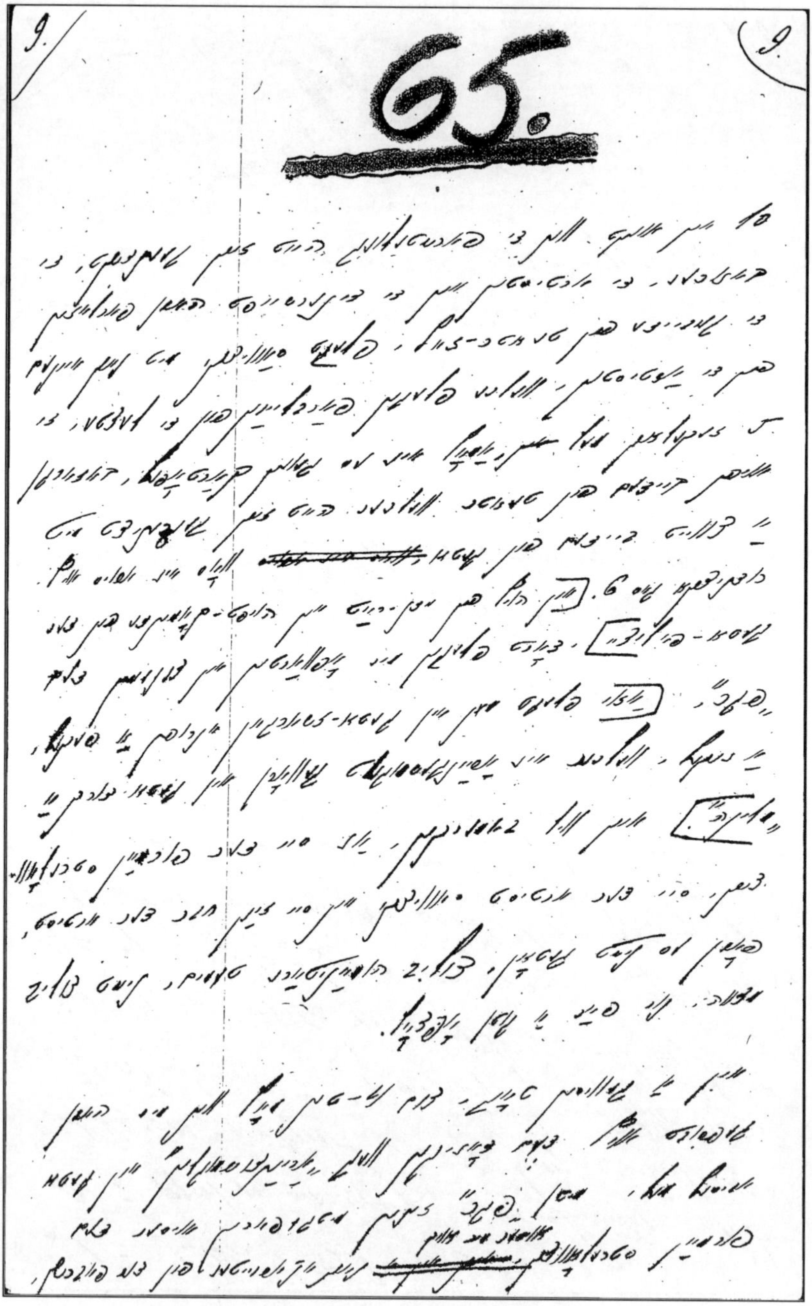

9. 9.

65.

[illegible]

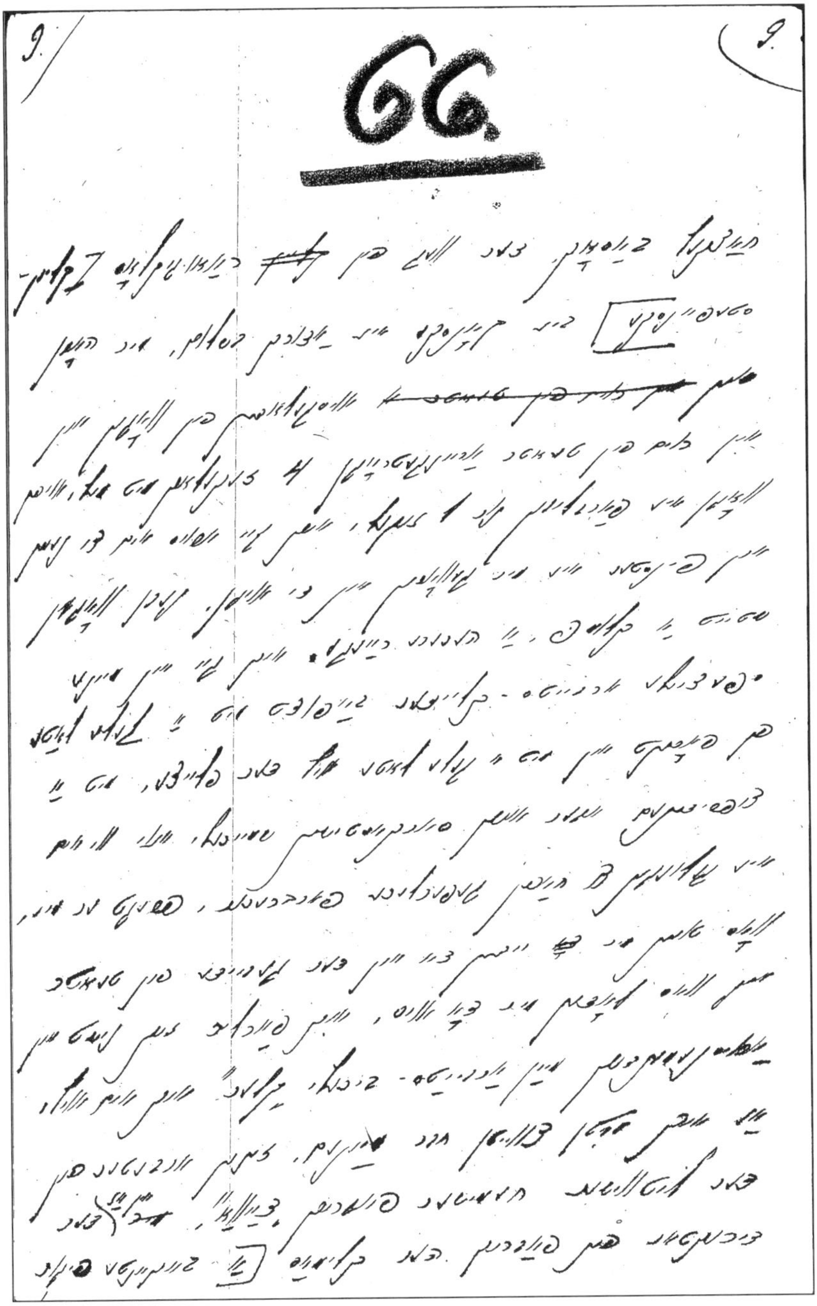

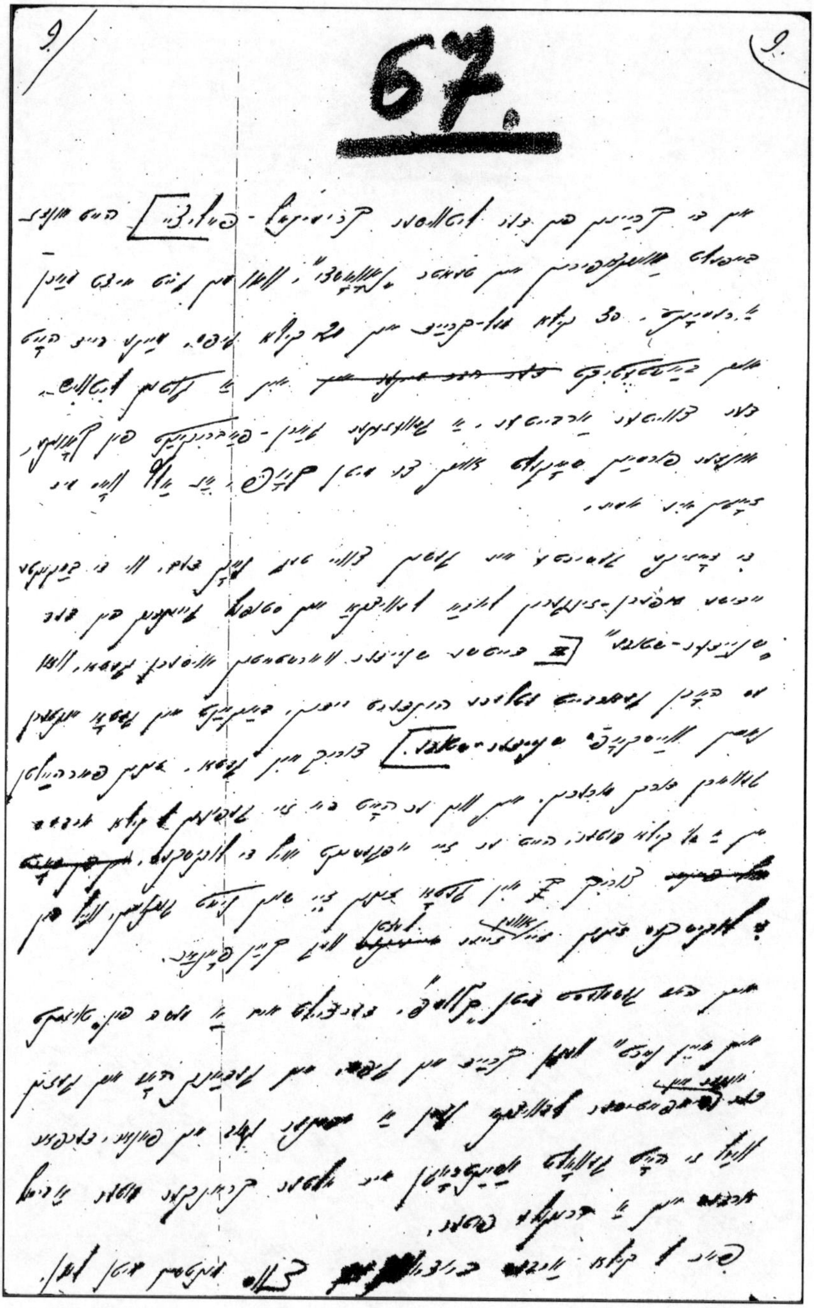
9/

67.

9.

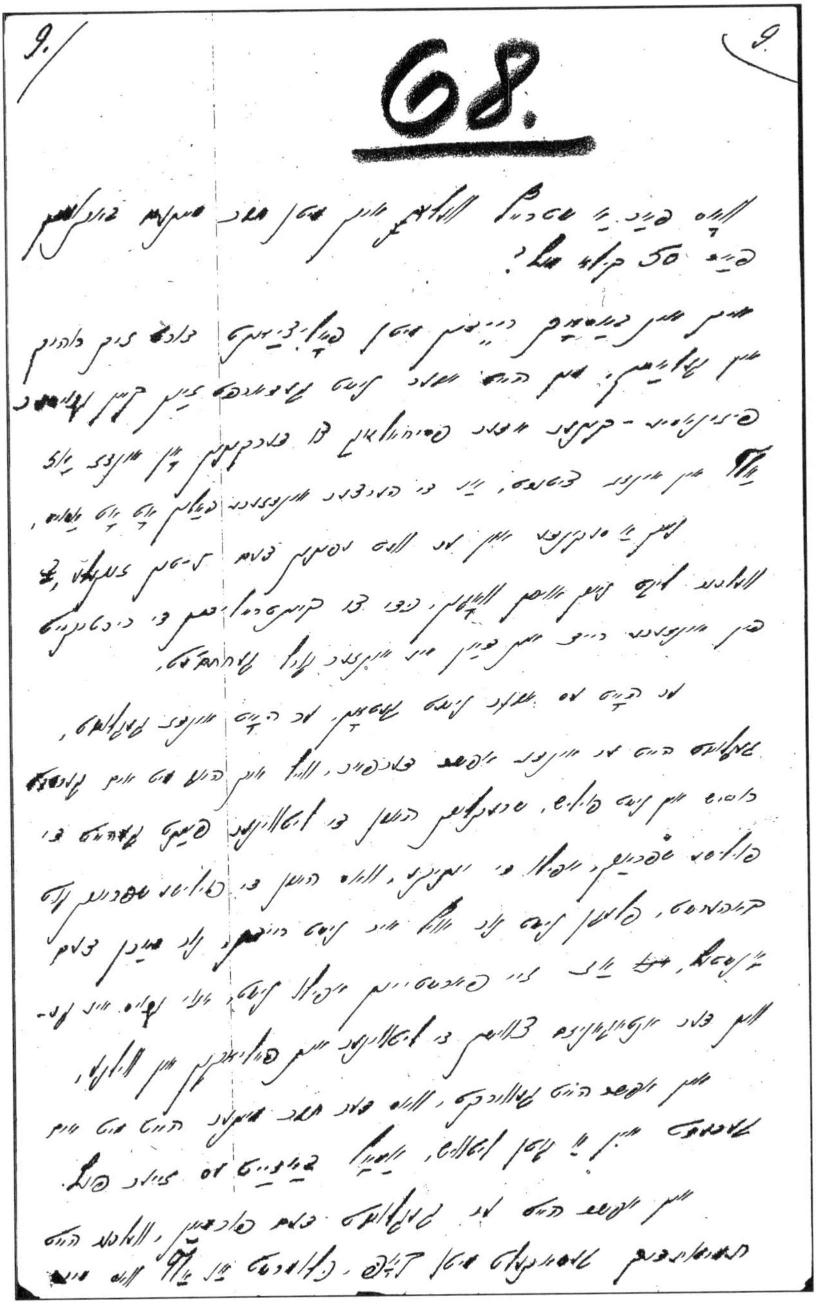

9. 9.

68.

[illegible]

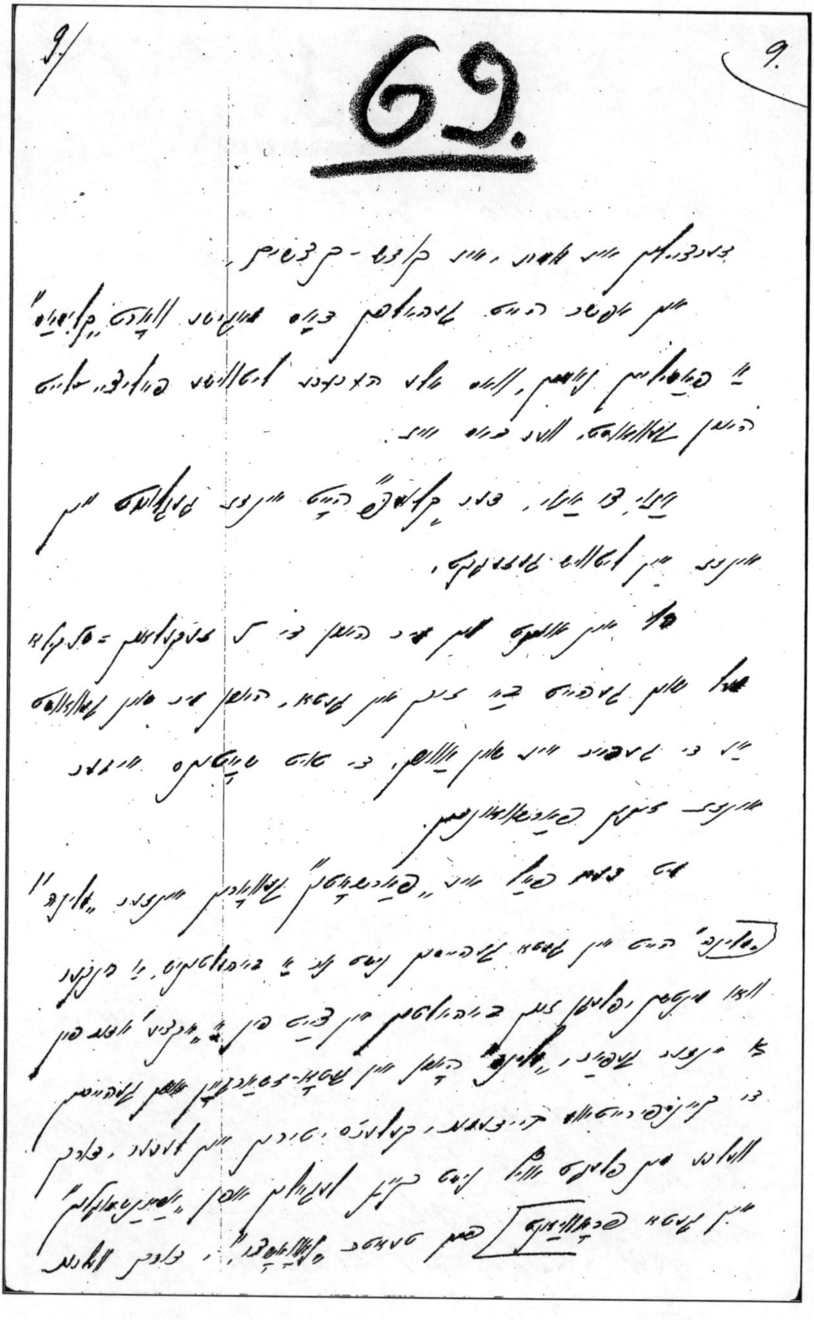
9/ 69. 9.

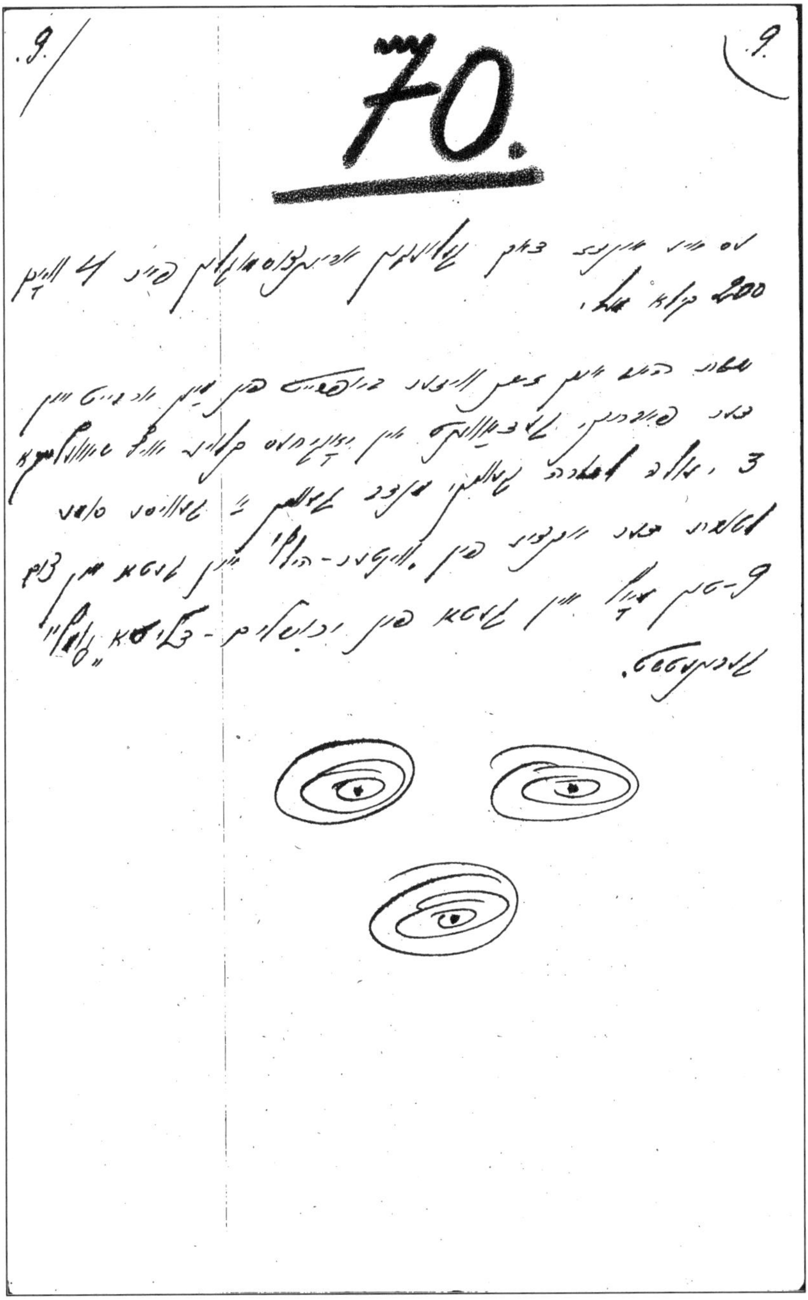

70.

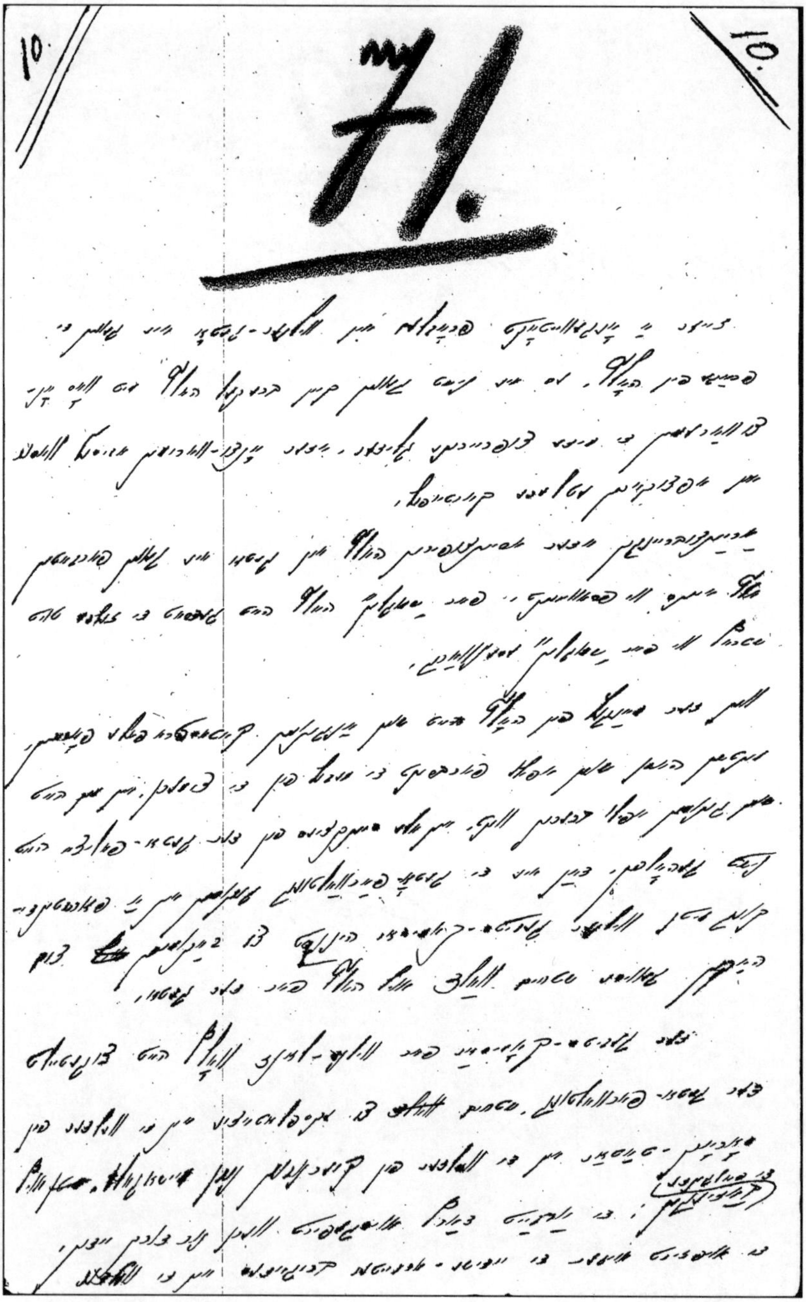

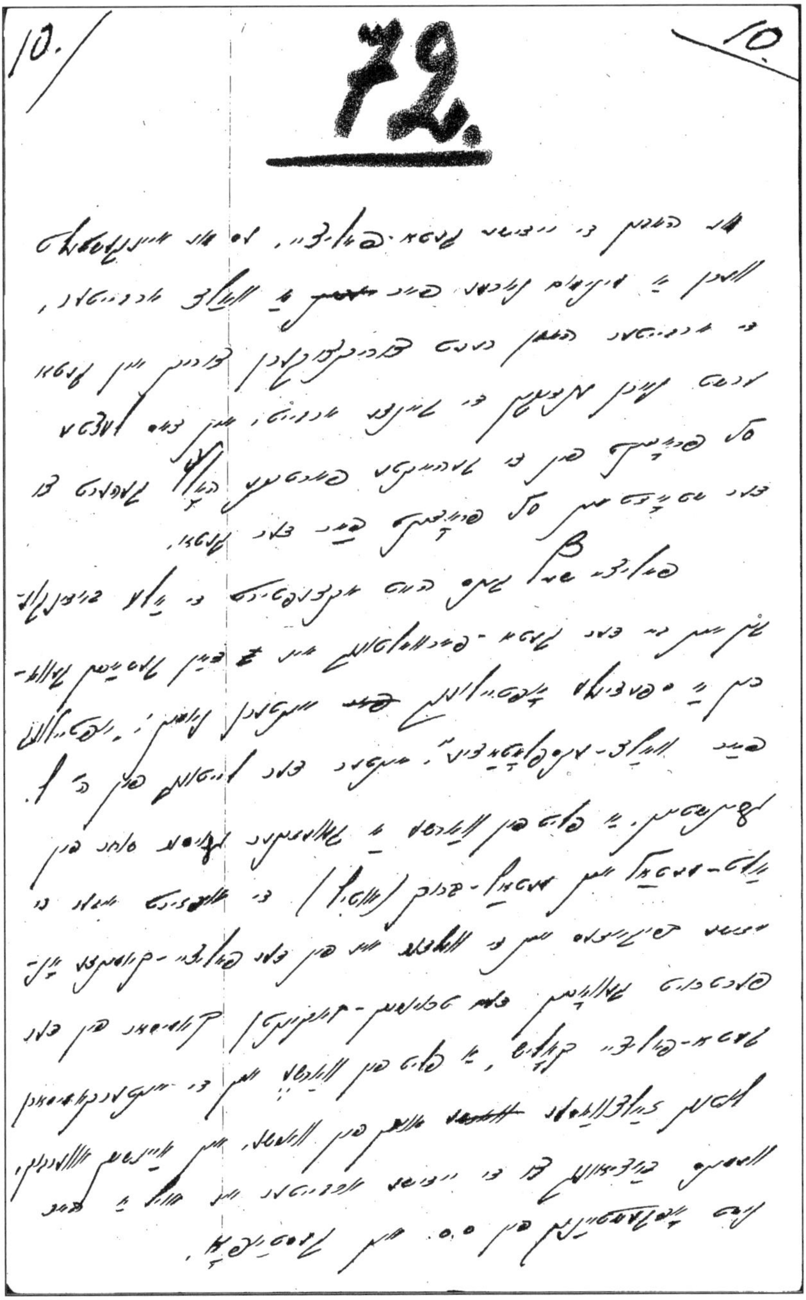

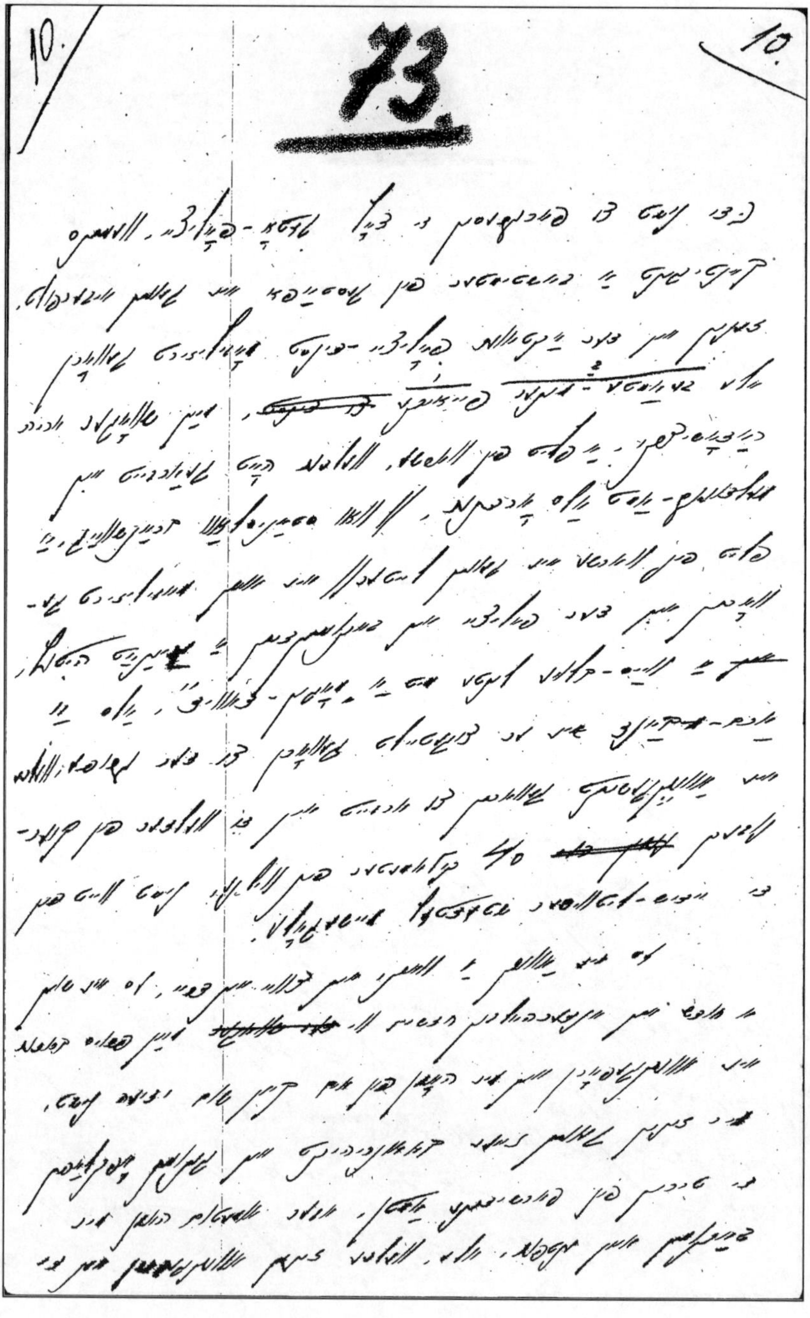
10.
73
10.

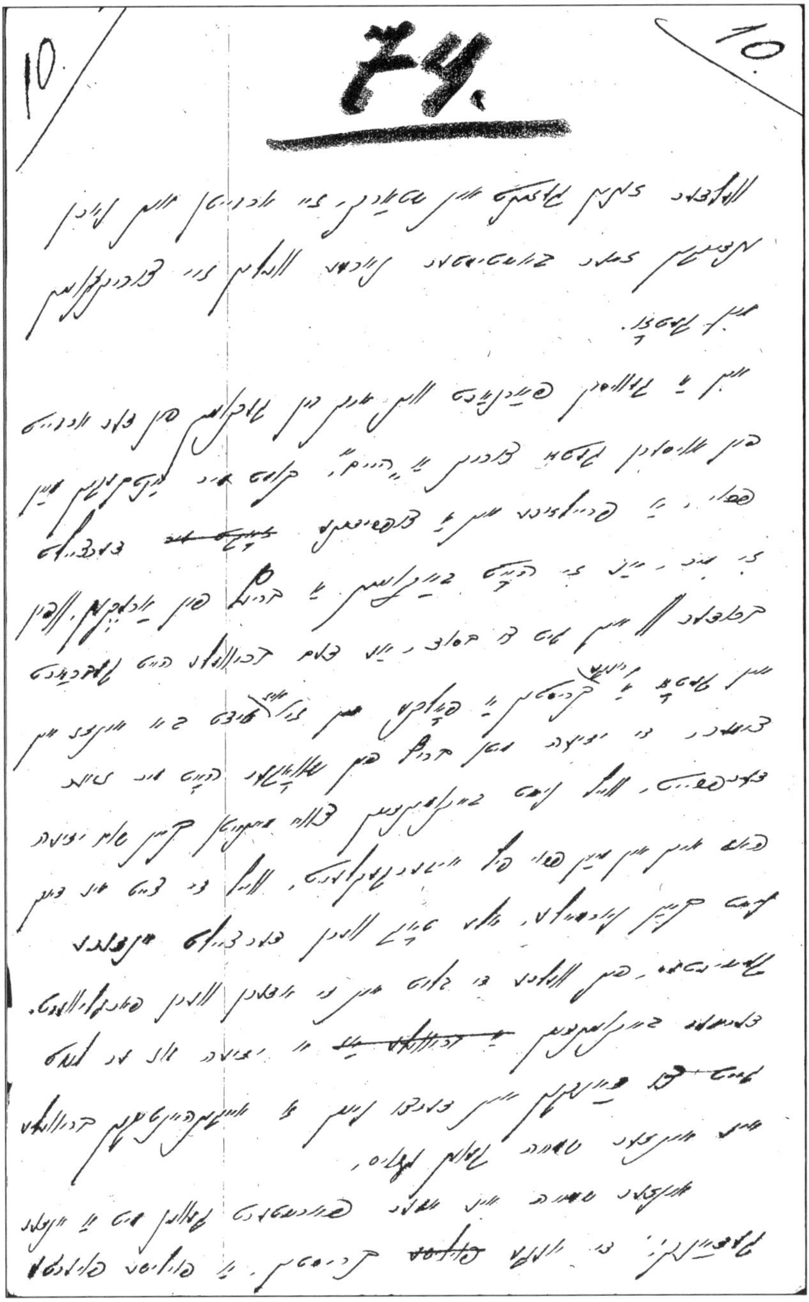
24.

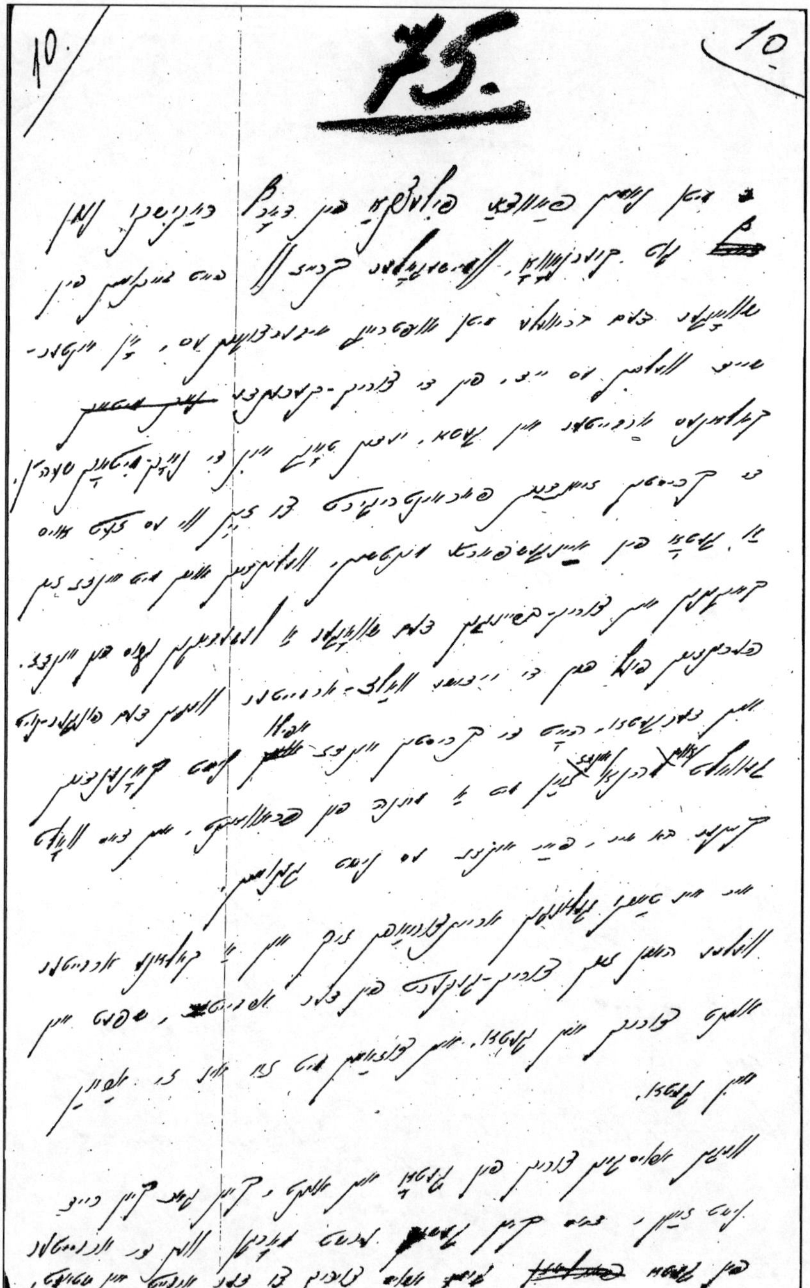
10.
75.
10

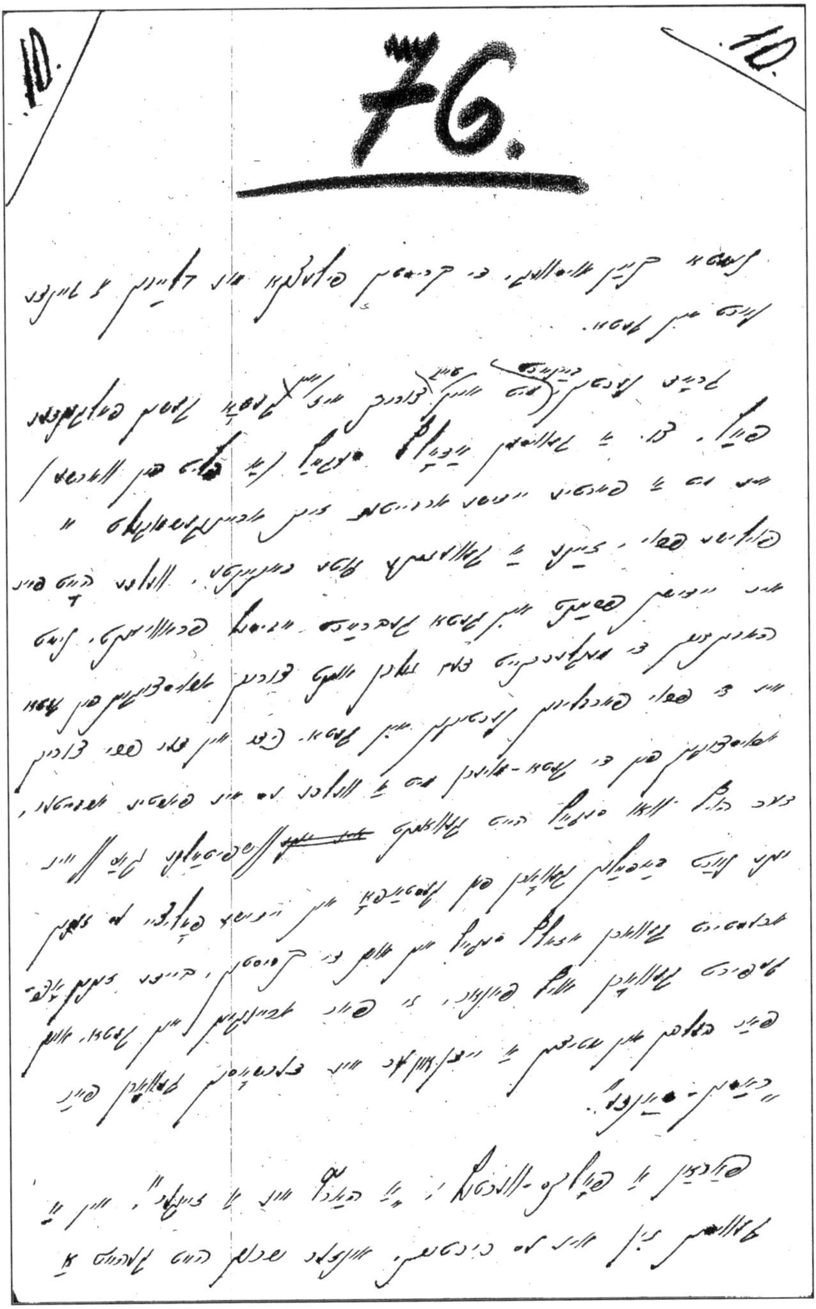

10.

76.

10.

[illegible]

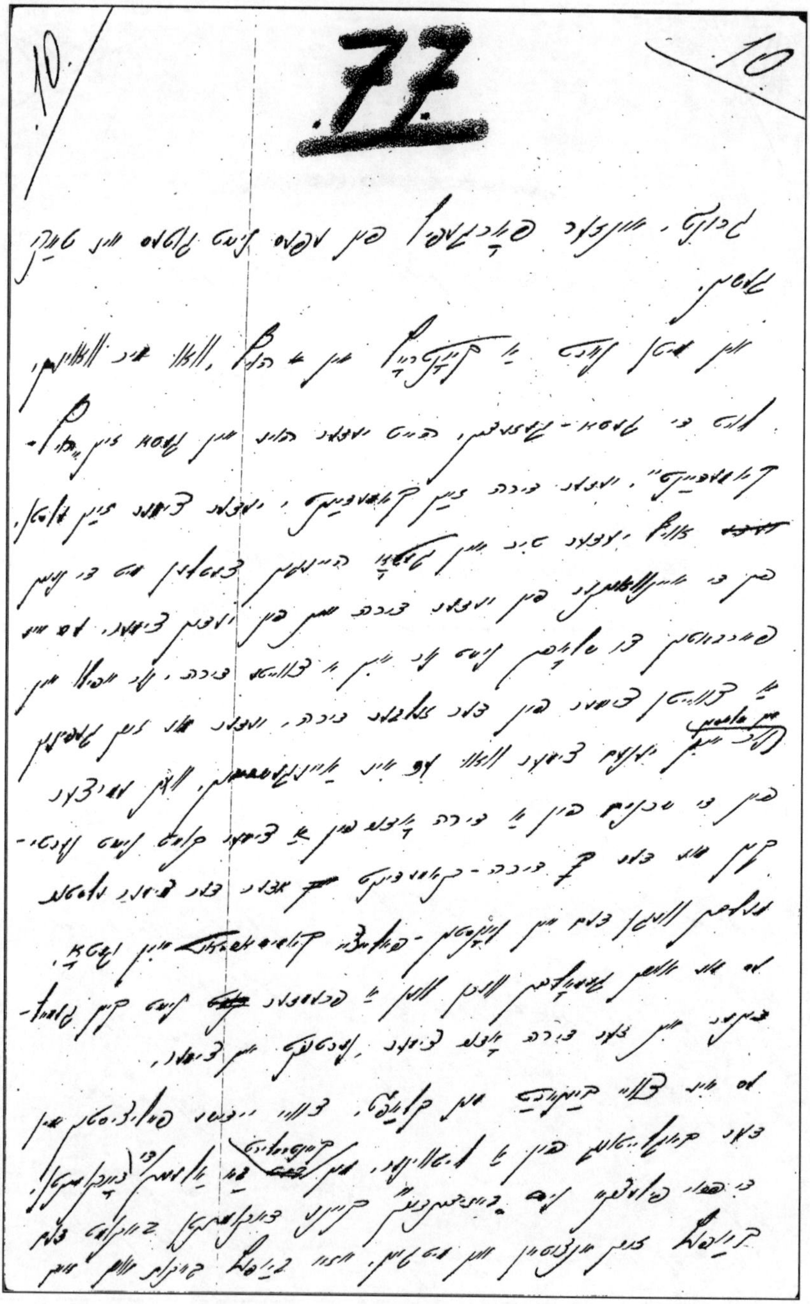

77

10.

10.

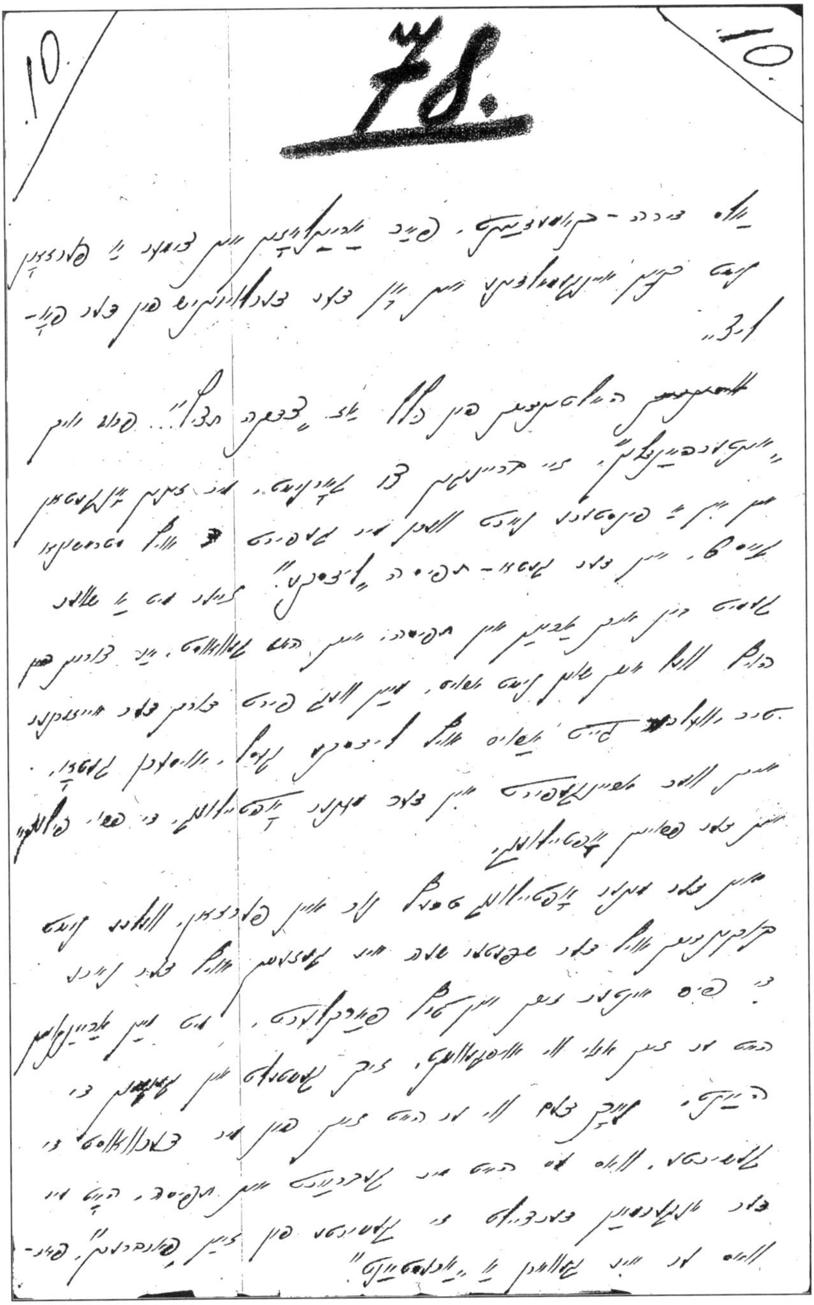
10.

78.

10.

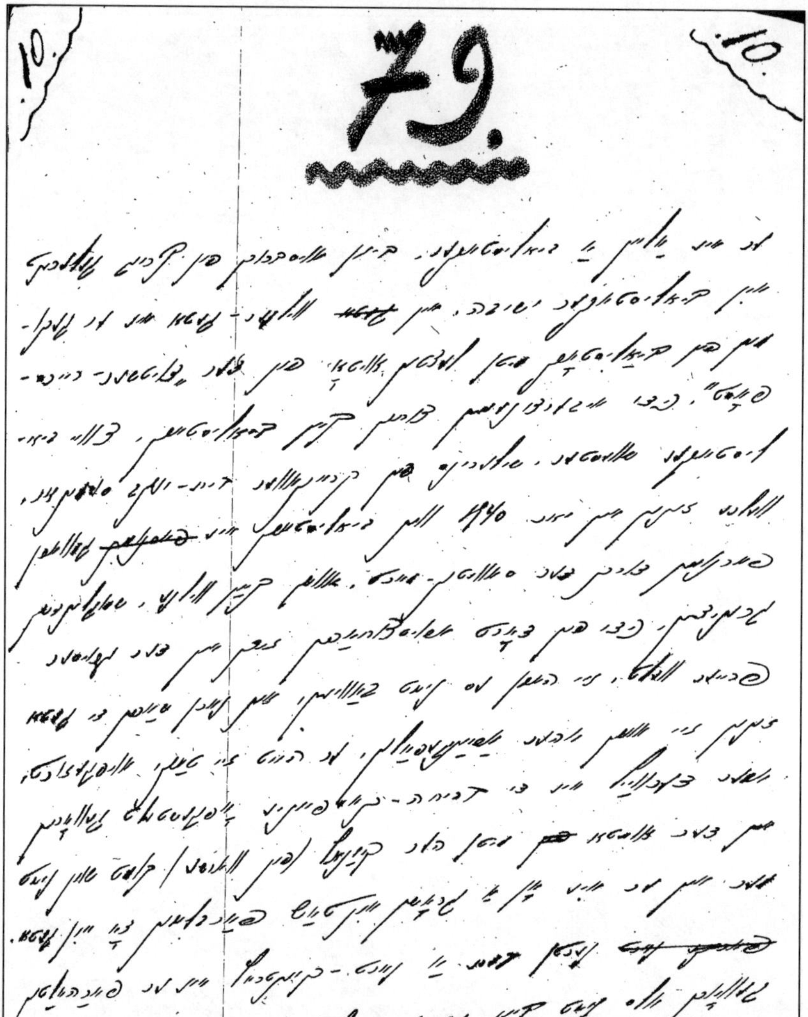

79.

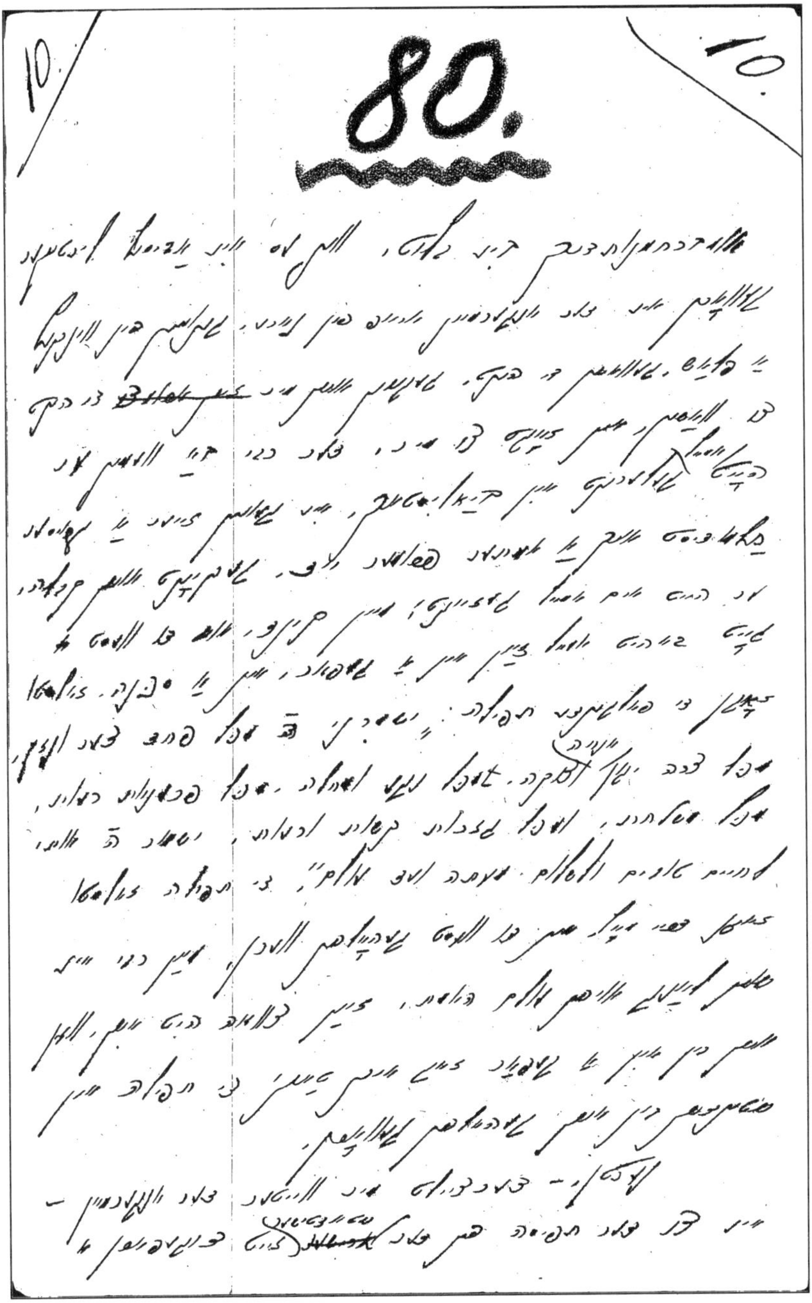
10.

80.

10.

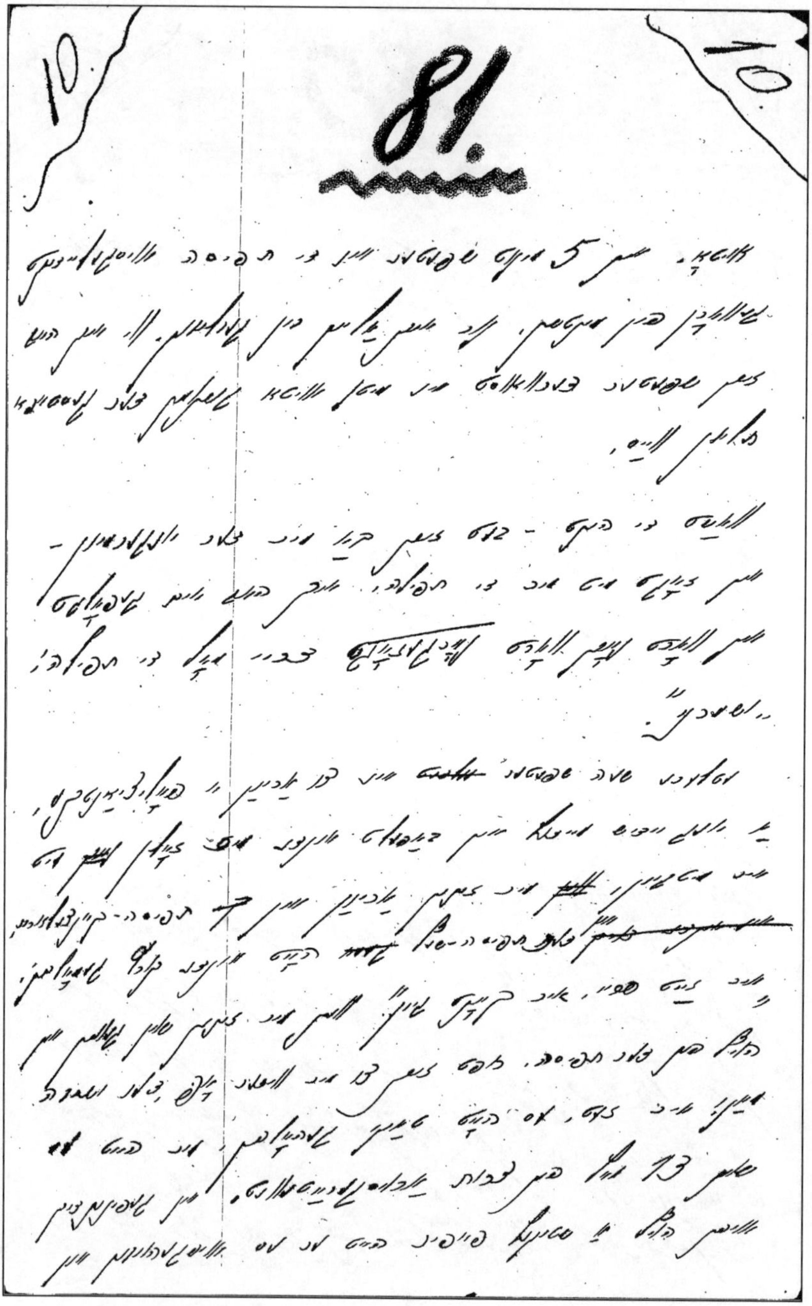
10.
81.
10.

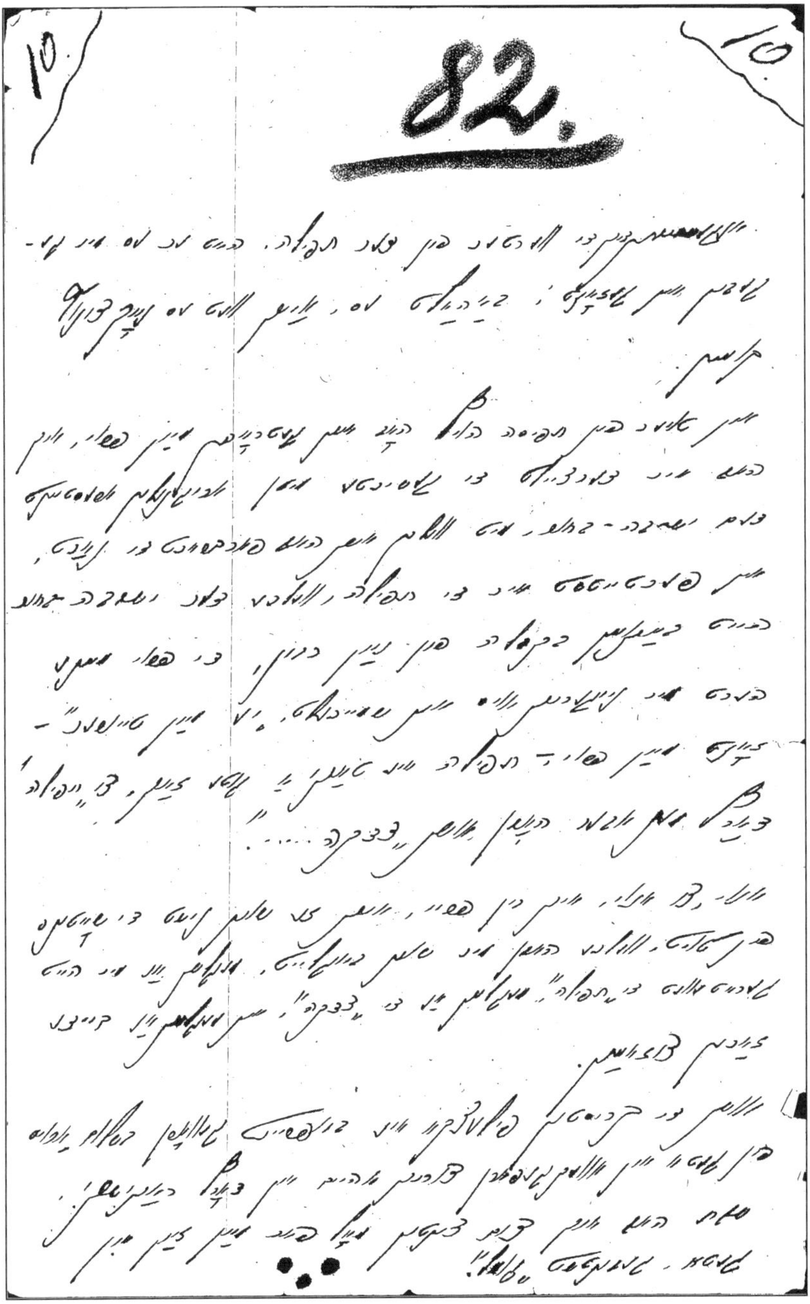

10.

82.

10.

[illegible]

[illegible]

[illegible]

[illegible]

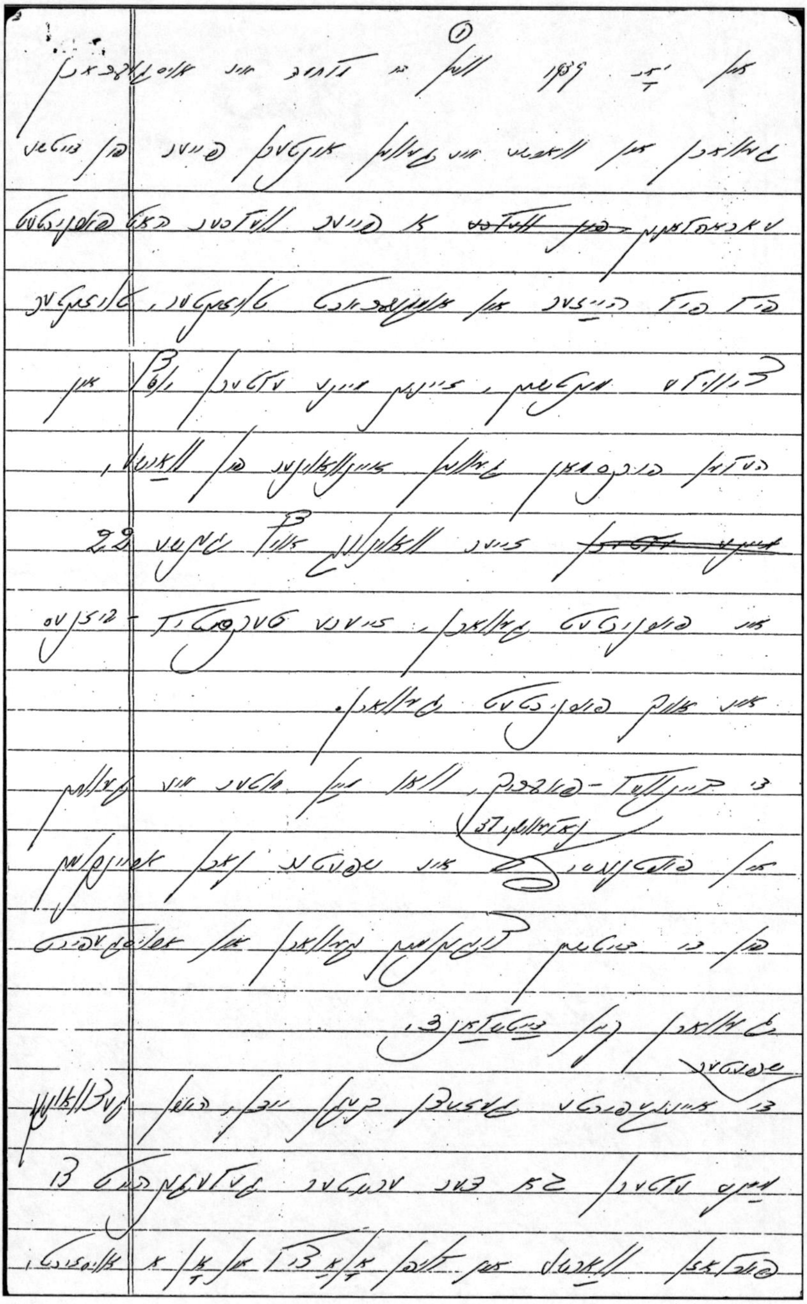

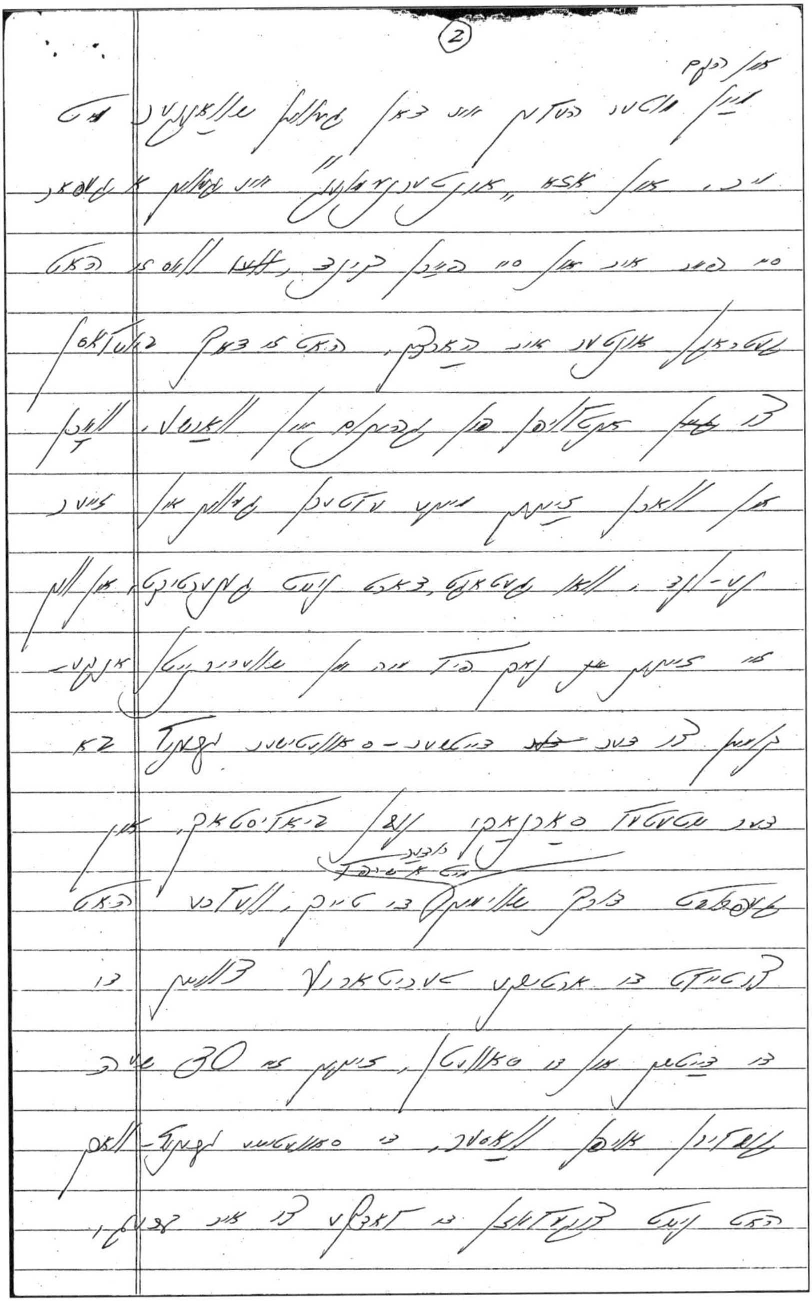
2

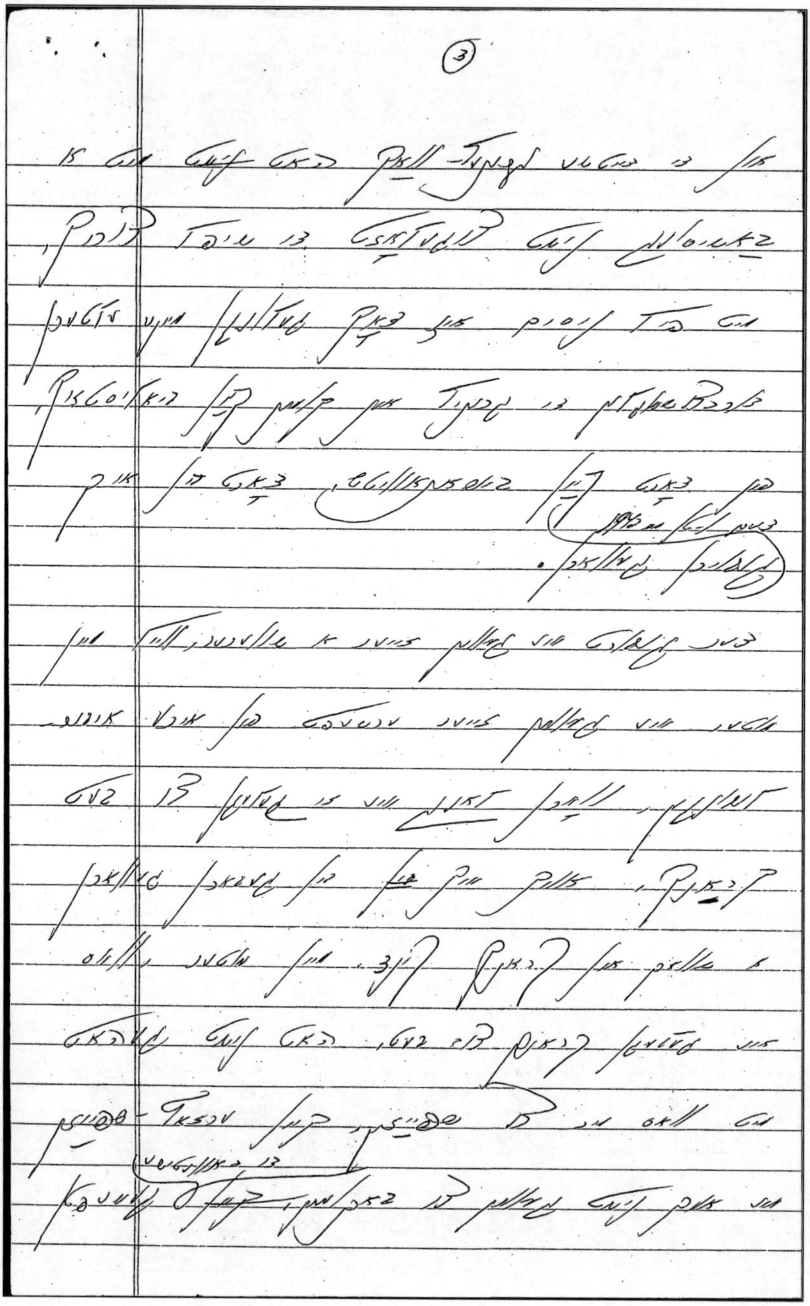

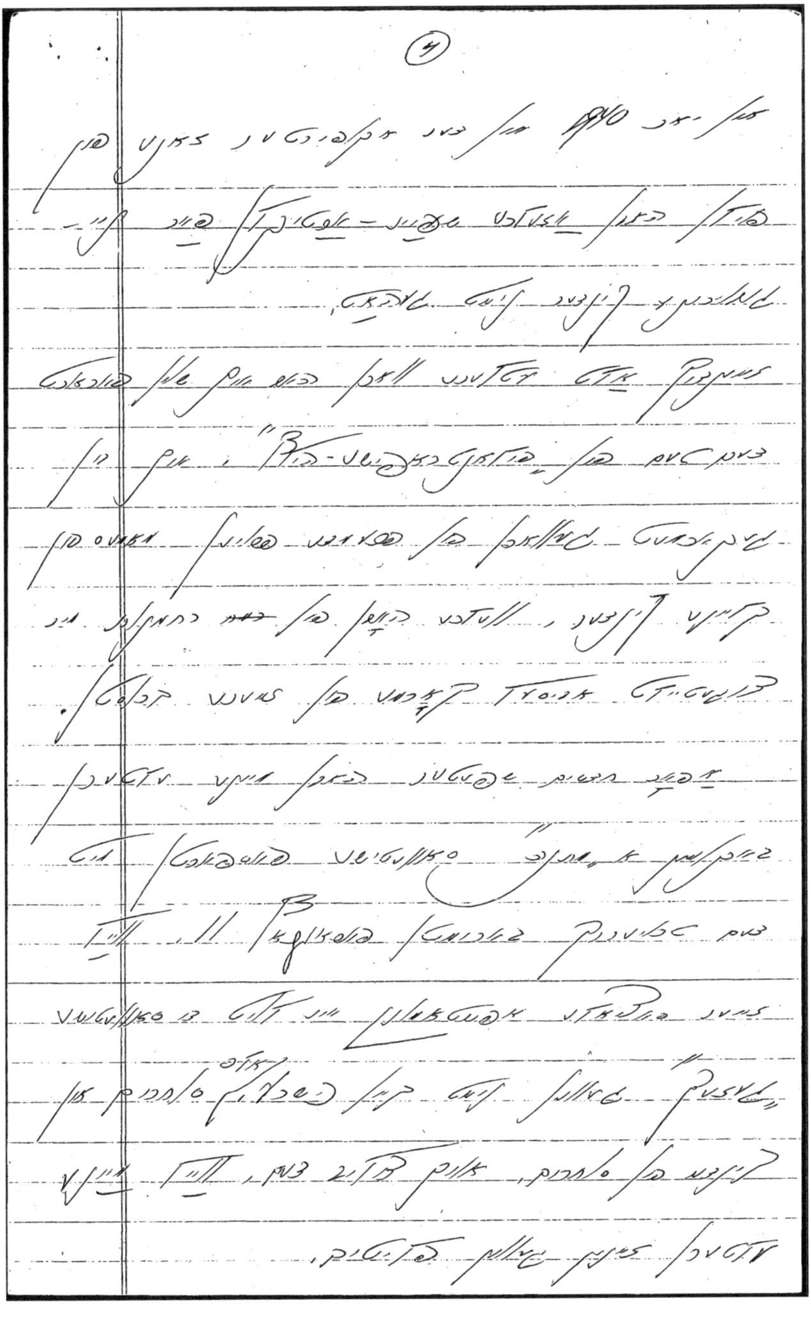

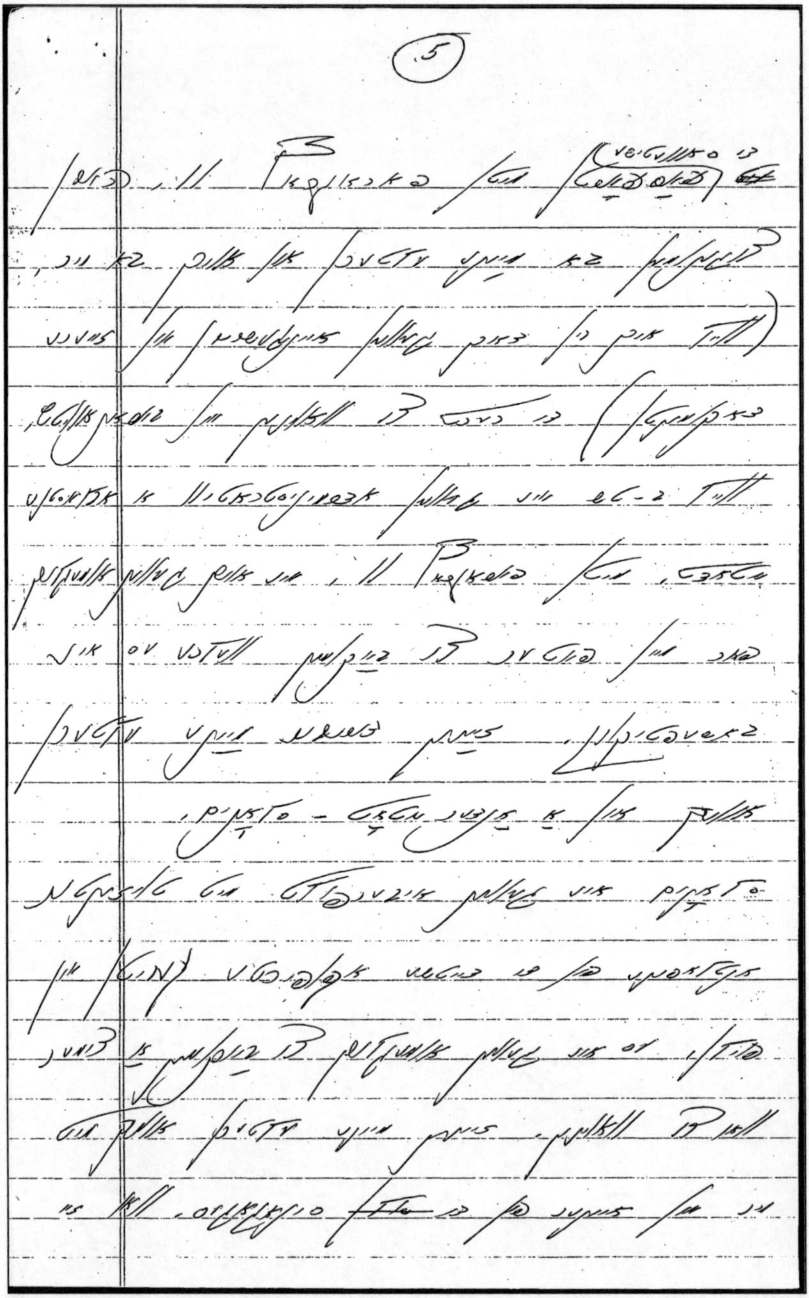

(6)

[illegible]

[illegible]

[illegible]

[illegible]

[illegible]

[illegible]

[illegible]

[illegible]

[illegible]

[illegible]

[illegible]

[illegible]

[illegible]

[illegible]

[illegible]

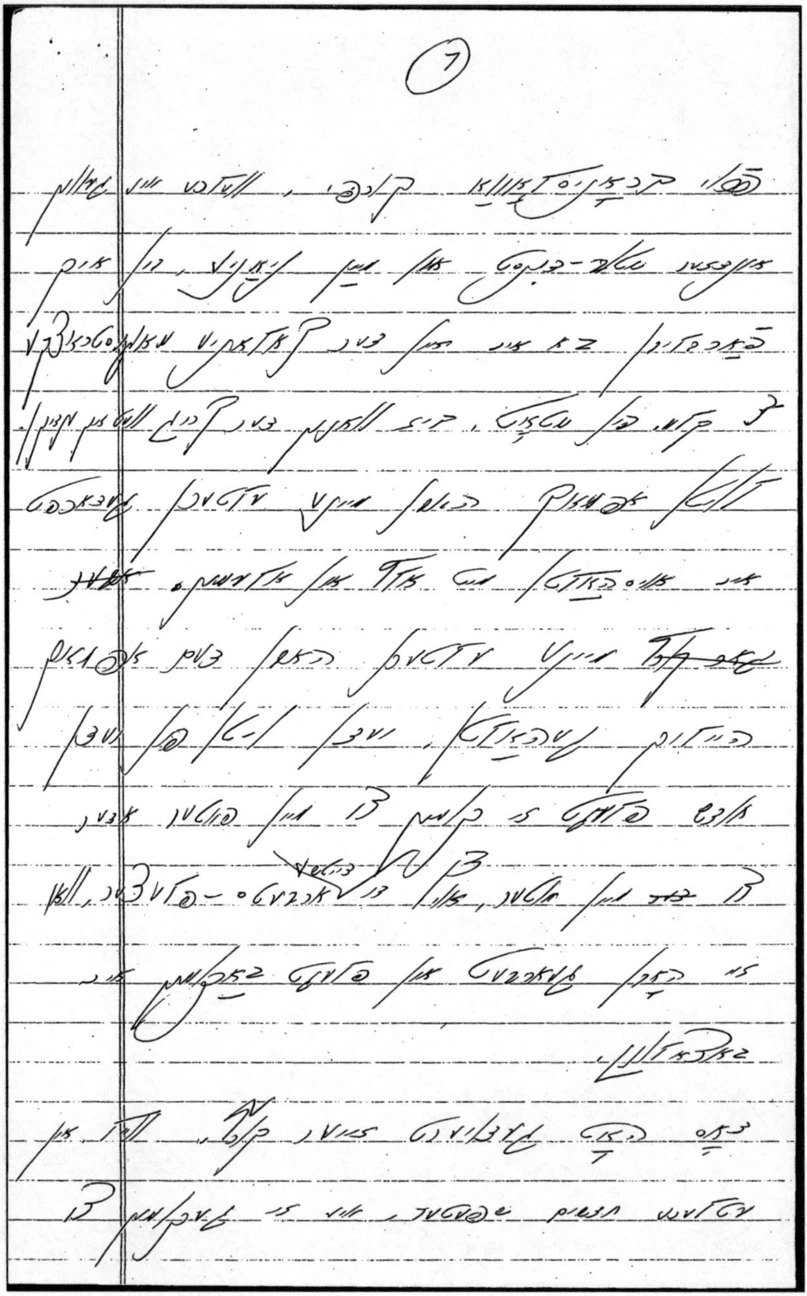

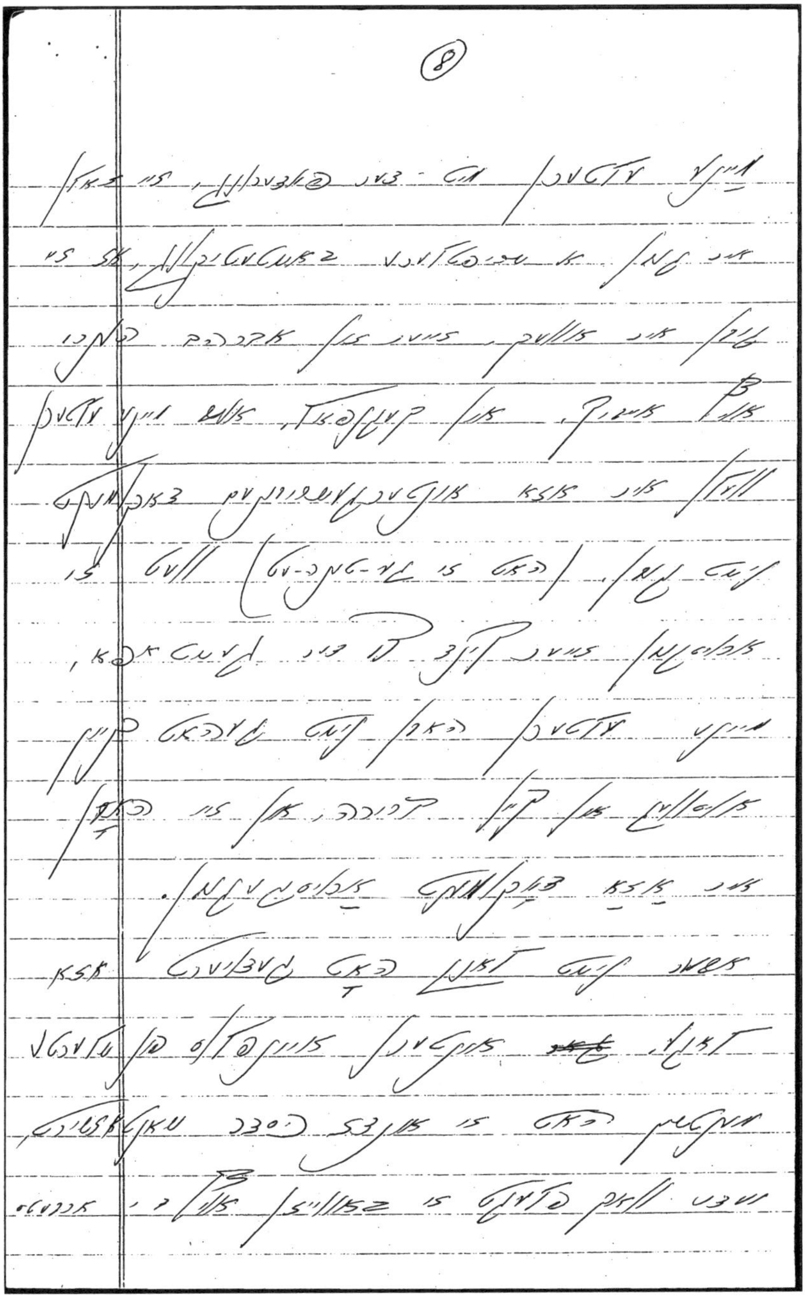

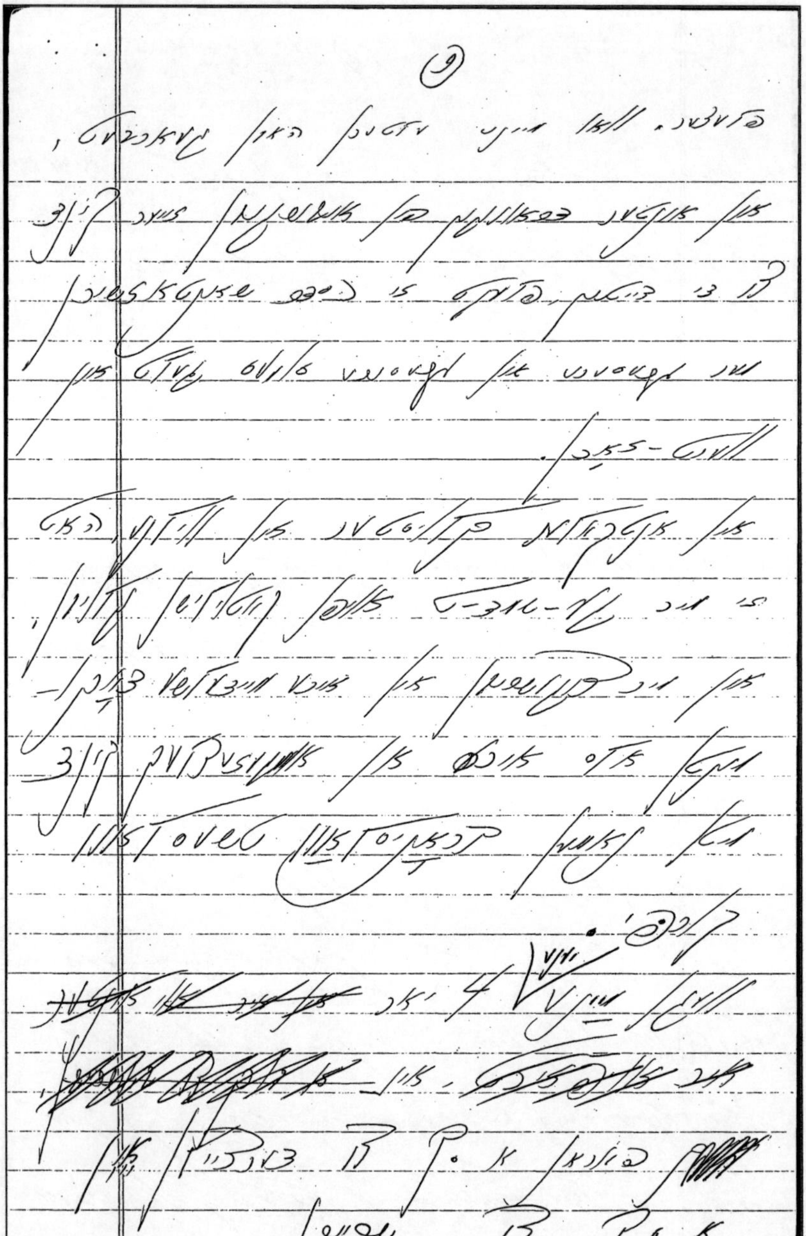

(9A)

און אפשר איז דאס גאר [illegible] צו
דערציילן. ווייל מענטשן, וועלכע האבן
געלעבט אין יענע יארן אין [illegible]
מענטשליכע [illegible] קענען דאס ניט
פארשטיין און ניט גלויבן.

און נאך פון 4 יאר [illegible]
[illegible] האט [illegible]
[illegible] [illegible] [illegible] און [illegible]
[illegible] און [illegible] [illegible] [illegible]
[illegible] [illegible] און [illegible] פון [illegible]
און א [illegible] [illegible]. פון [illegible]
און א [illegible], פון [illegible] [illegible] און
[illegible] [illegible].

[illegible] [illegible] [illegible] [illegible] [illegible]

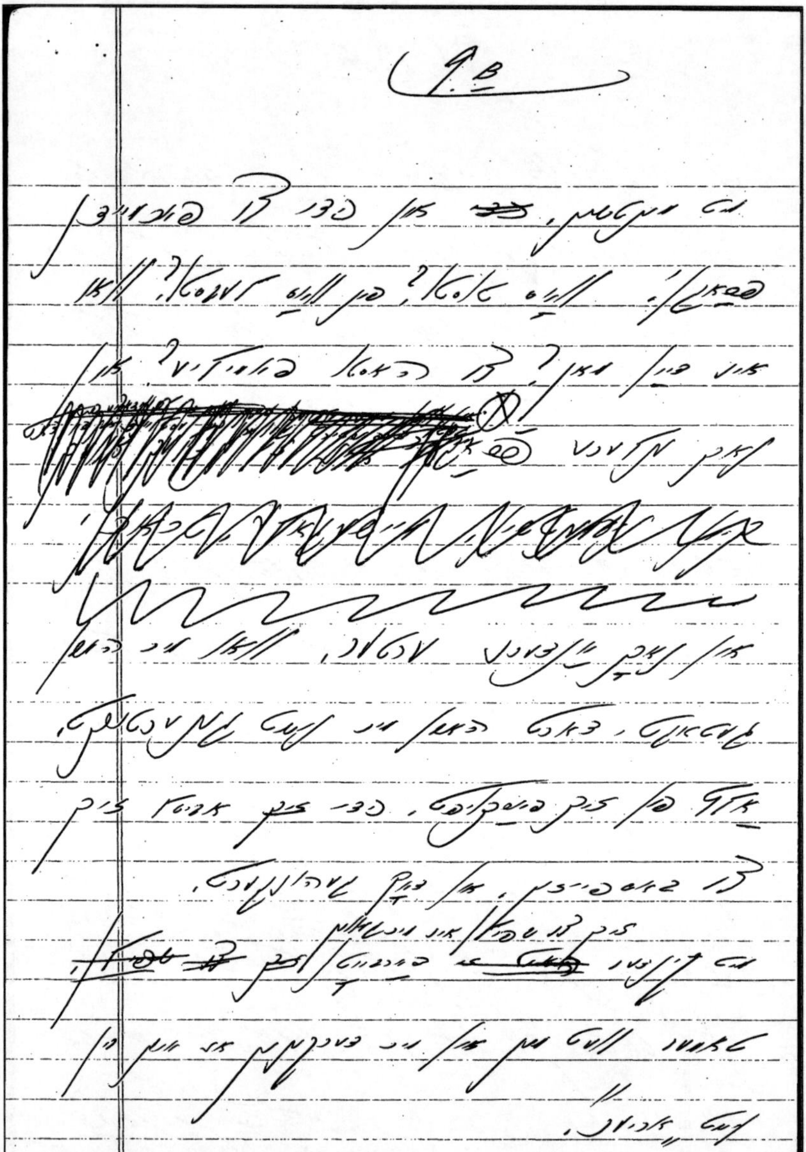

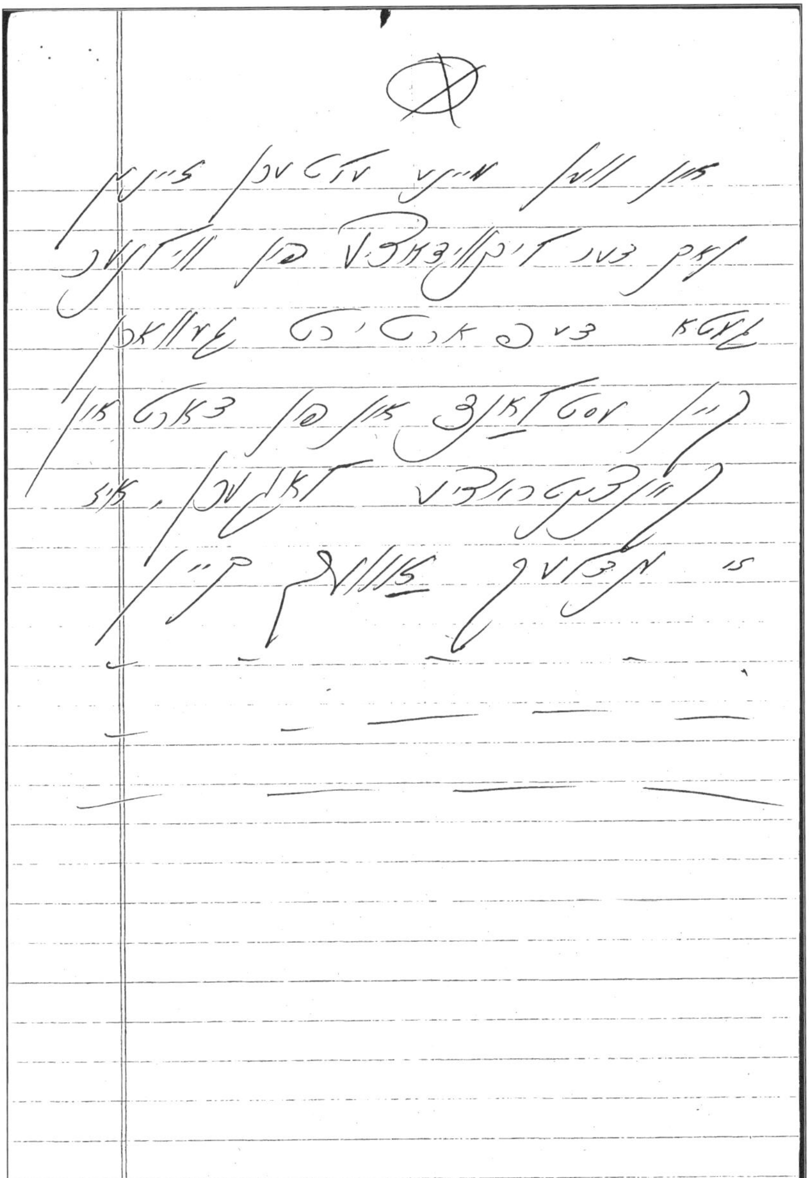

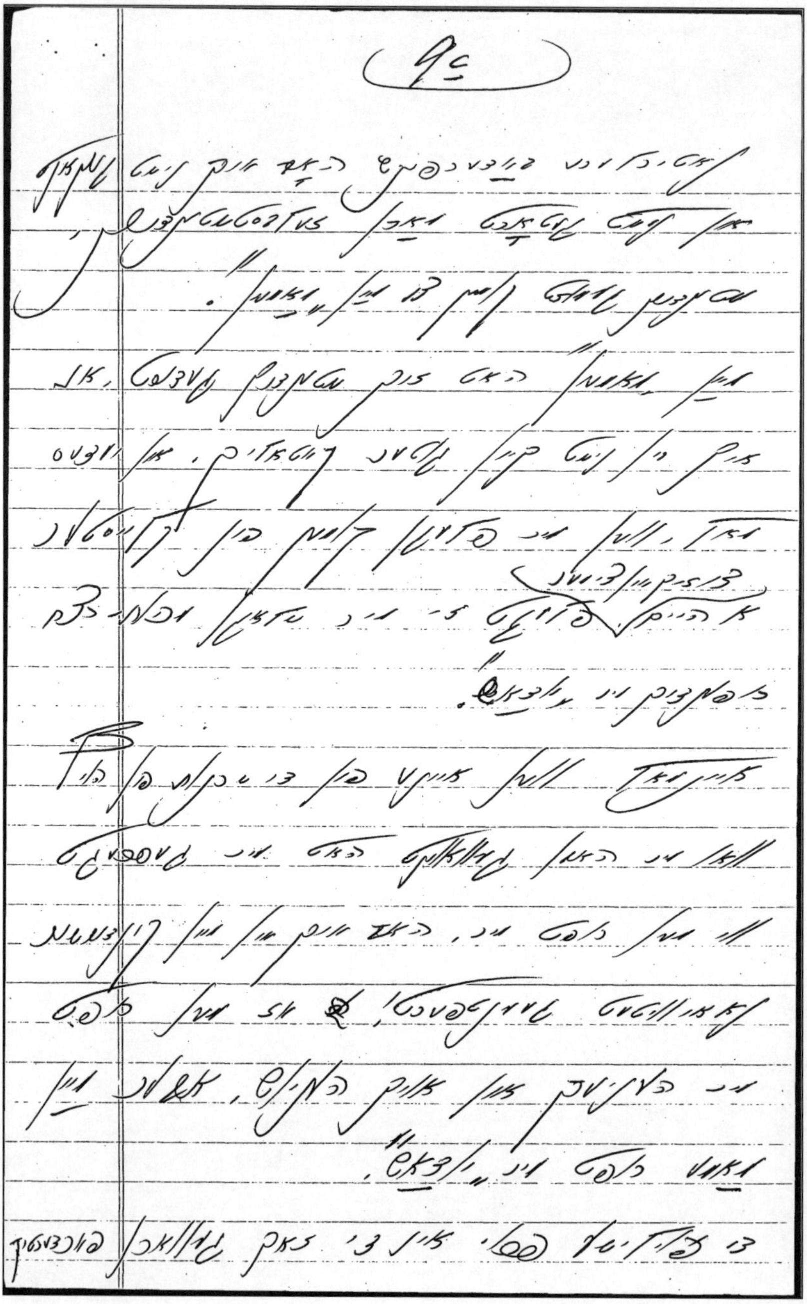

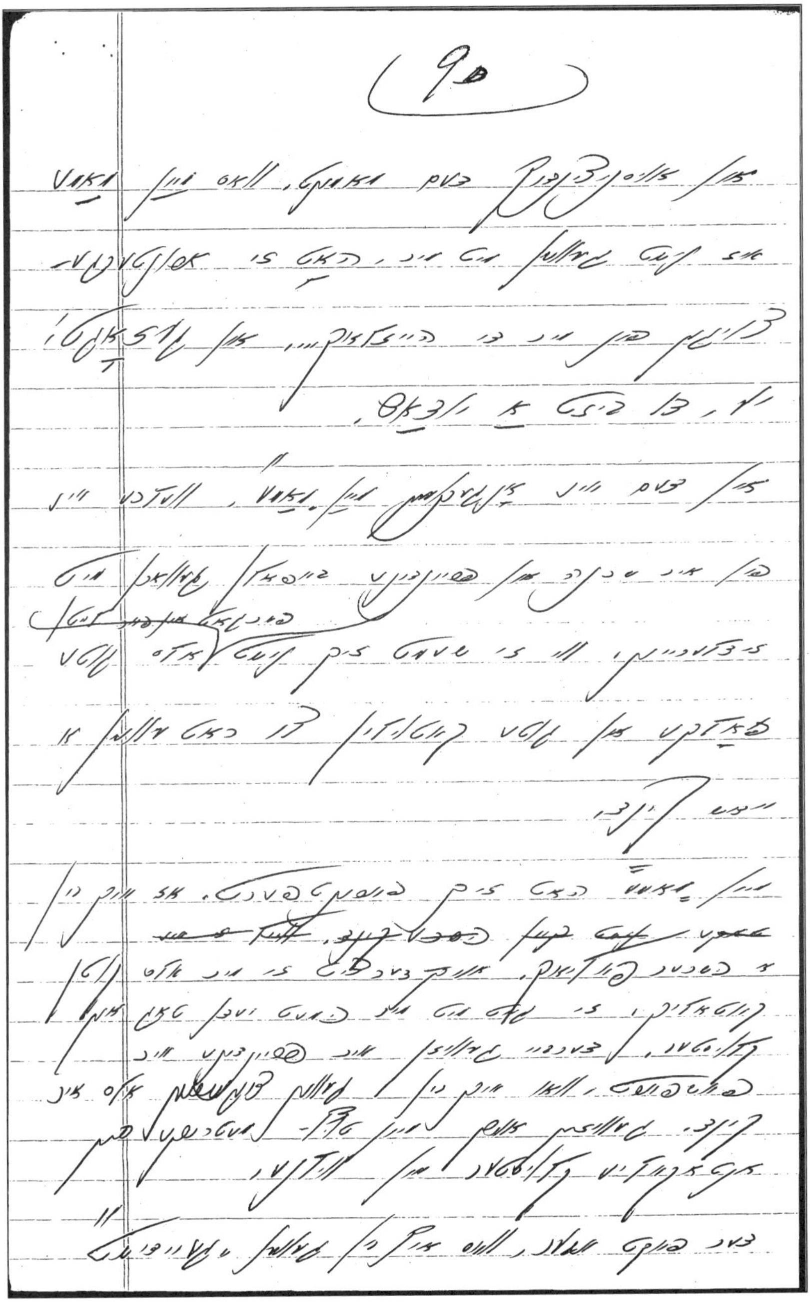

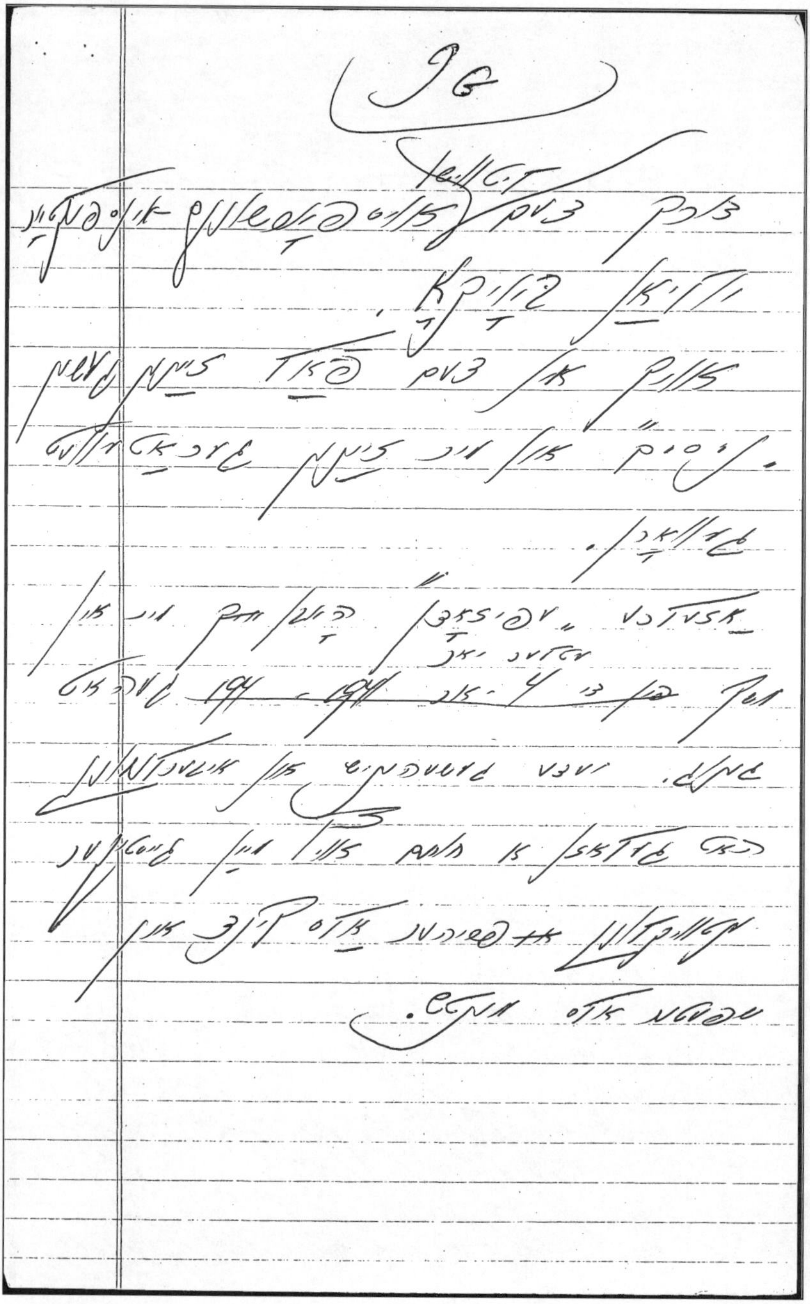

9E

אין פּלאַן דער היטלער פּאַרטיי געווען די אויסראָטונג,

וו די אַלטע, באַוואָרענע פֿון זייער מאַכט קאָרפּ,

קרייזע זיינען פֿאַרהאַלטן געוואָרן דורך

דער געסטאַפּאָ, דאָס לעבן פֿון אונדז ייִדן

איז געווען אין גרויס געפֿאַר, ווייַטער נאָך ווען

מען האָט אונדז געשלעפּט צו די פֿאַרהער,

זיינען מיר געווען זיכער, אַז מען נעמט אונדז

קיין פּאָנאַר, צו די י.פּ. אין ווילנע, וואו עס

זיינען אומגעבראַכט געוואָרן 100,000 אומשולדיקע

מענטשן, 90 פּראָצענט פֿון די ייִדן.

מיר זאָגן דער אינטעליגענץ און די אָנפֿירנדע

באַשטימונגען פֿון ווילנער געטאָ יודענראַט,

זיינען מיר אַרויסגעשמוגלט געוואָרן פֿון א

[illegible].

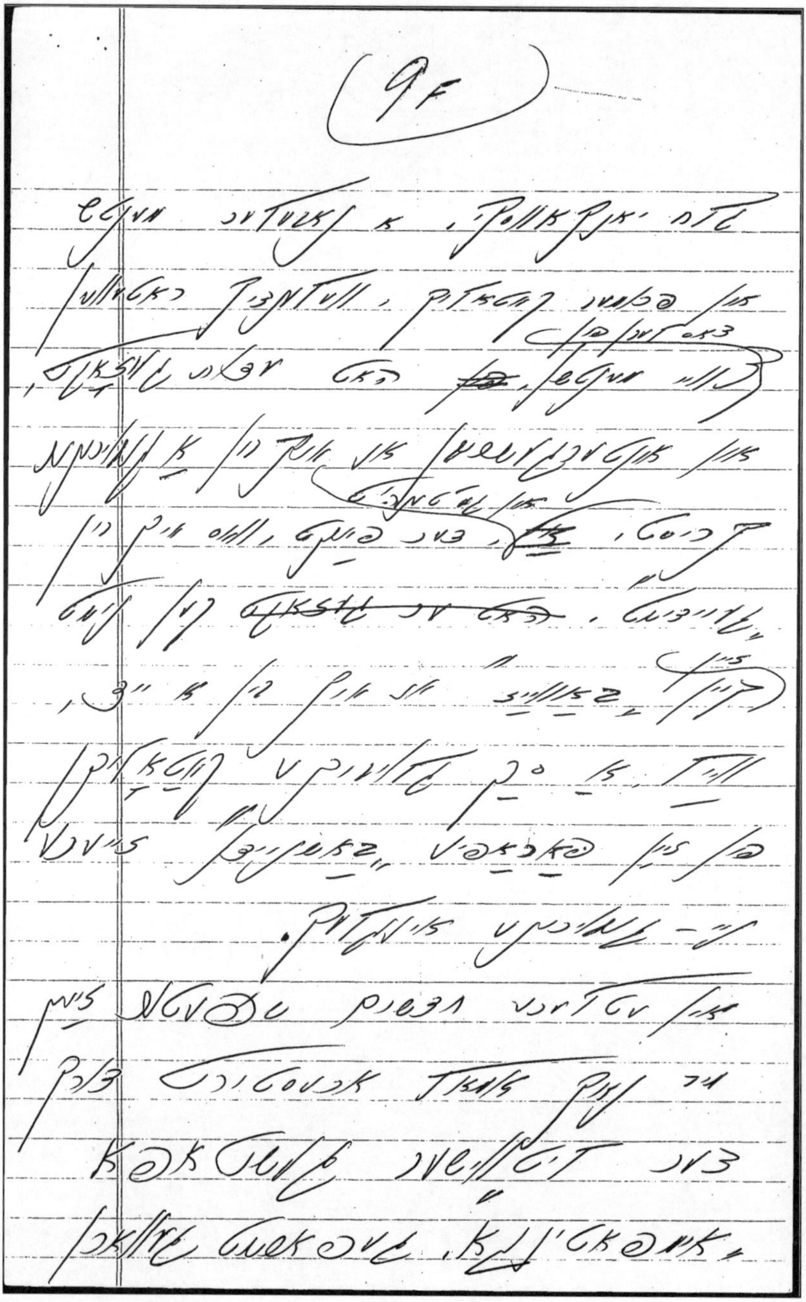

[illegible]

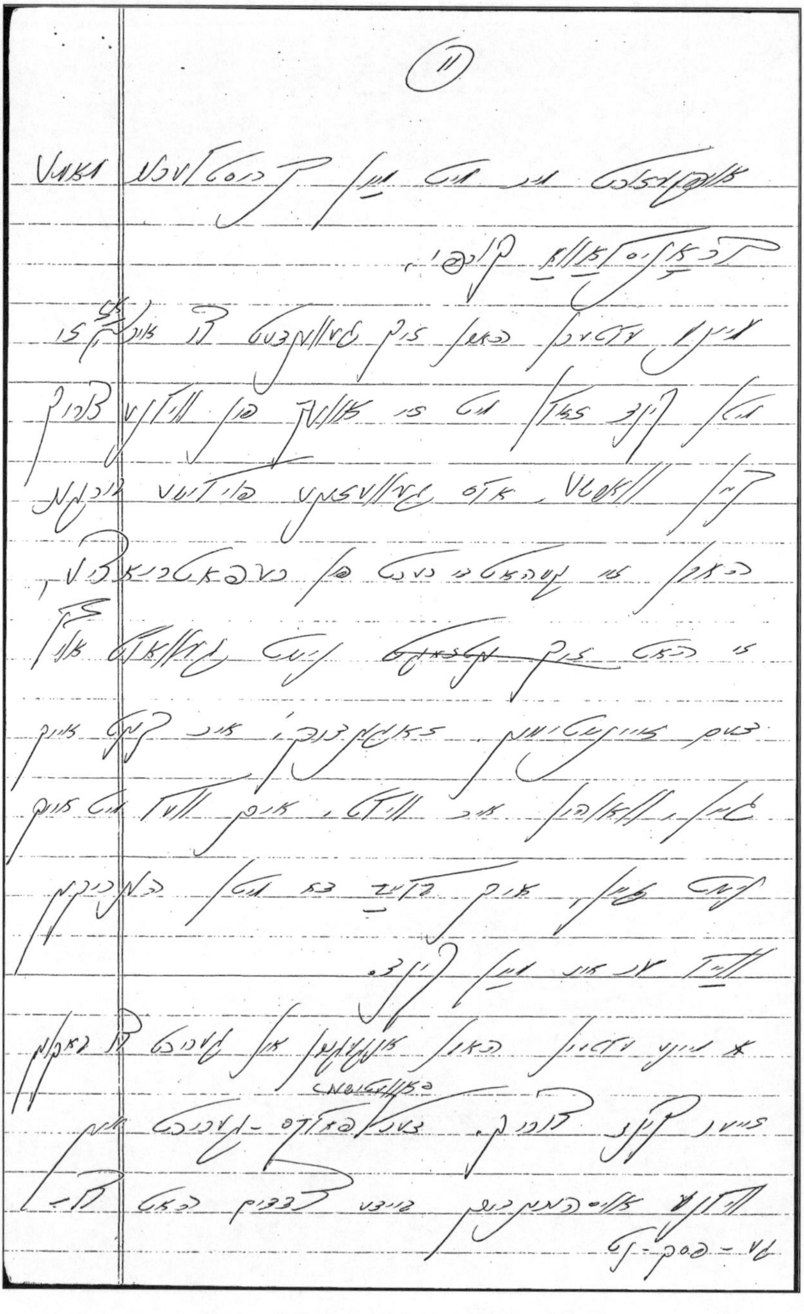

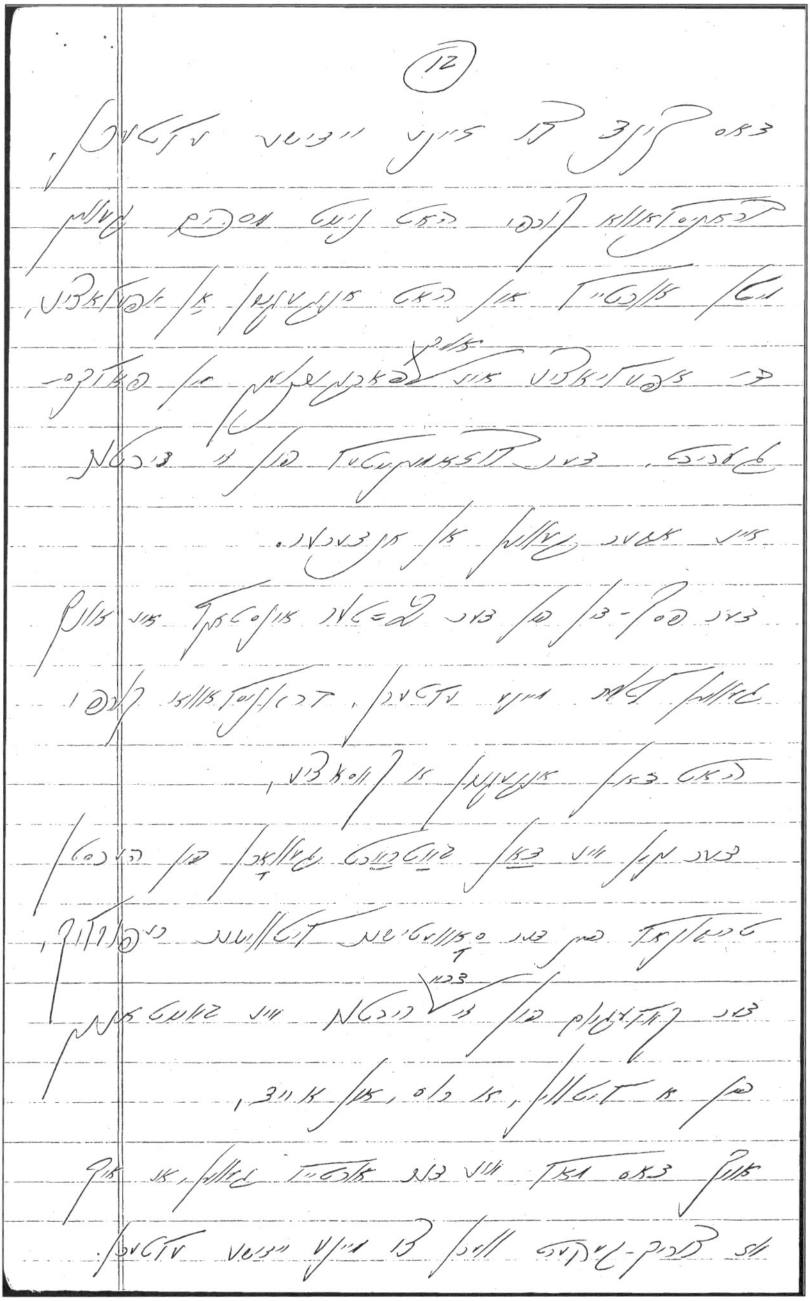

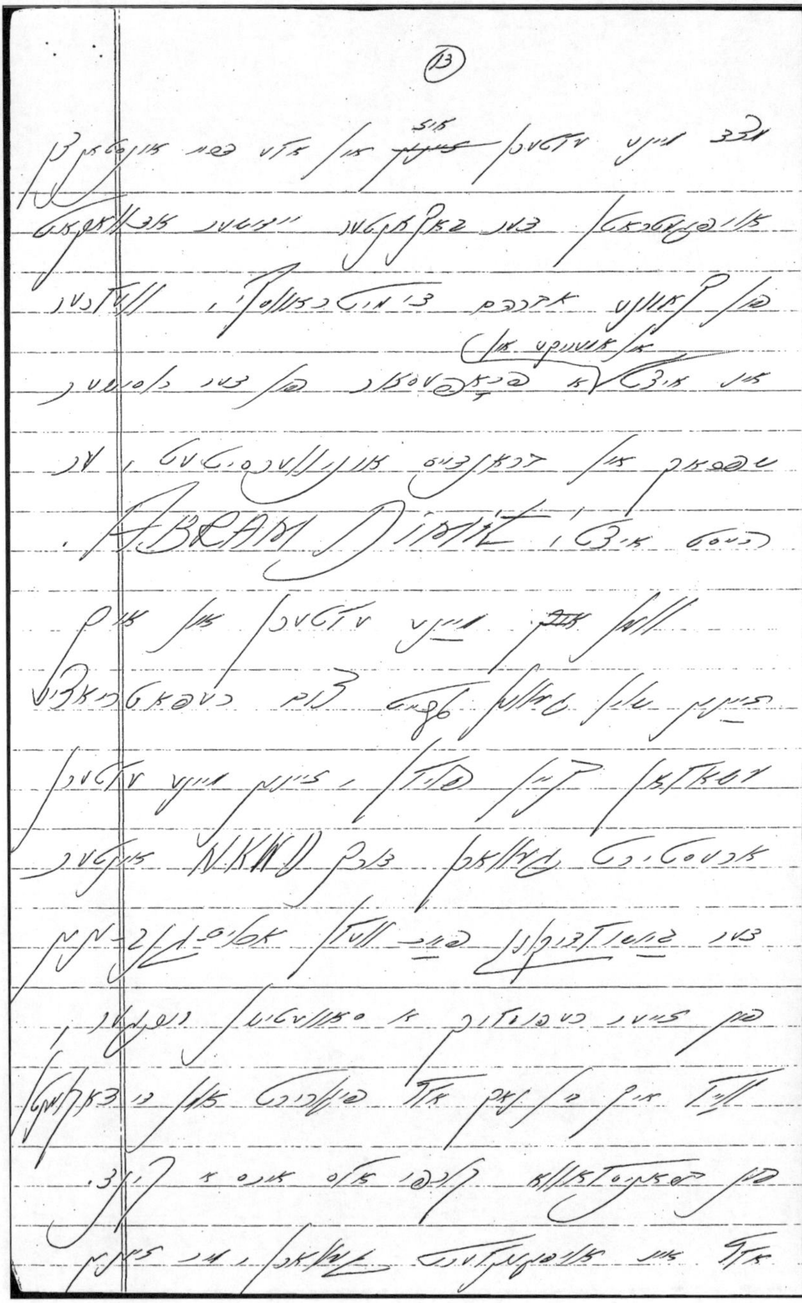
13

ABRAM DIMITZ

NKWD

(14)

אַוועק פֿון [illegible] (פֿורט), [illegible]

[illegible] און אַז די [illegible] שפּיטאָל [illegible]

פֿון [illegible] [illegible] און [illegible]

[illegible] [illegible], ~~[illegible]~~ פֿון [illegible]

[illegible] פֿון די אַנטיסעמיטישע פּאָליאַקן "A.K."

[illegible] [illegible], [illegible] און [illegible]

די [illegible] [illegible] [illegible] [illegible]

פֿון די [illegible], [illegible] [illegible] [illegible] [illegible]

[illegible],

אַ [illegible] שפּעטער [illegible] [illegible] [illegible]

[illegible] [illegible] [illegible] [illegible] [illegible],

פֿון [illegible] [illegible] [illegible], [illegible], [illegible],

[illegible], [illegible], [illegible], [illegible], [illegible]

[illegible] [illegible] [illegible] [illegible] [illegible]

[illegible] [illegible] [illegible] . . . . .

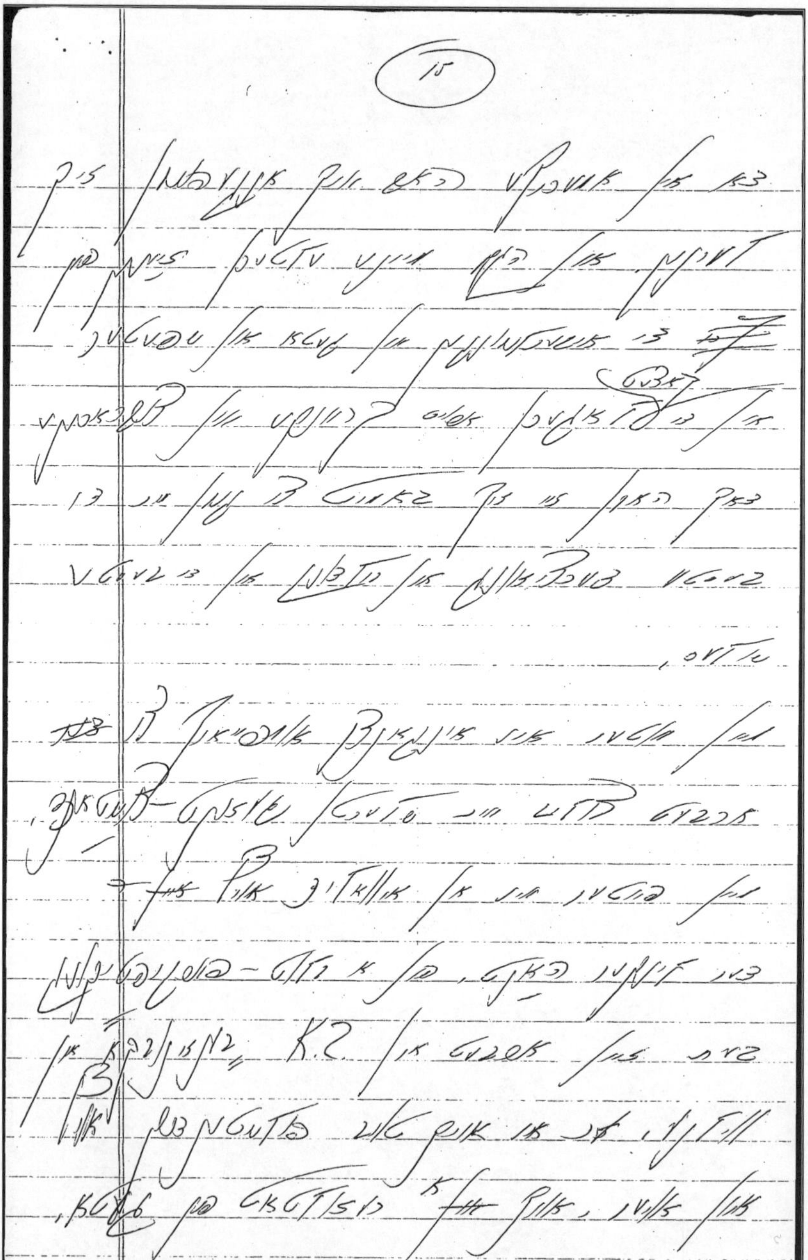

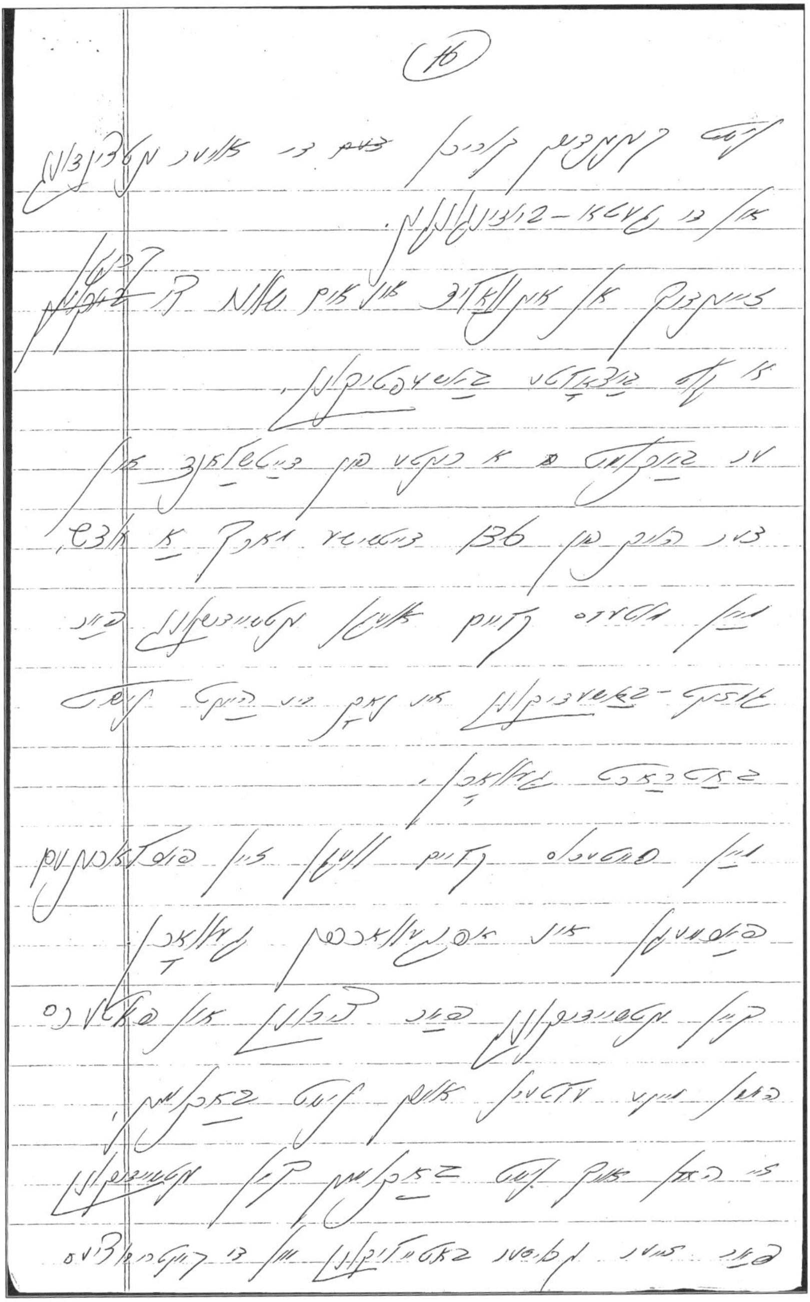
16

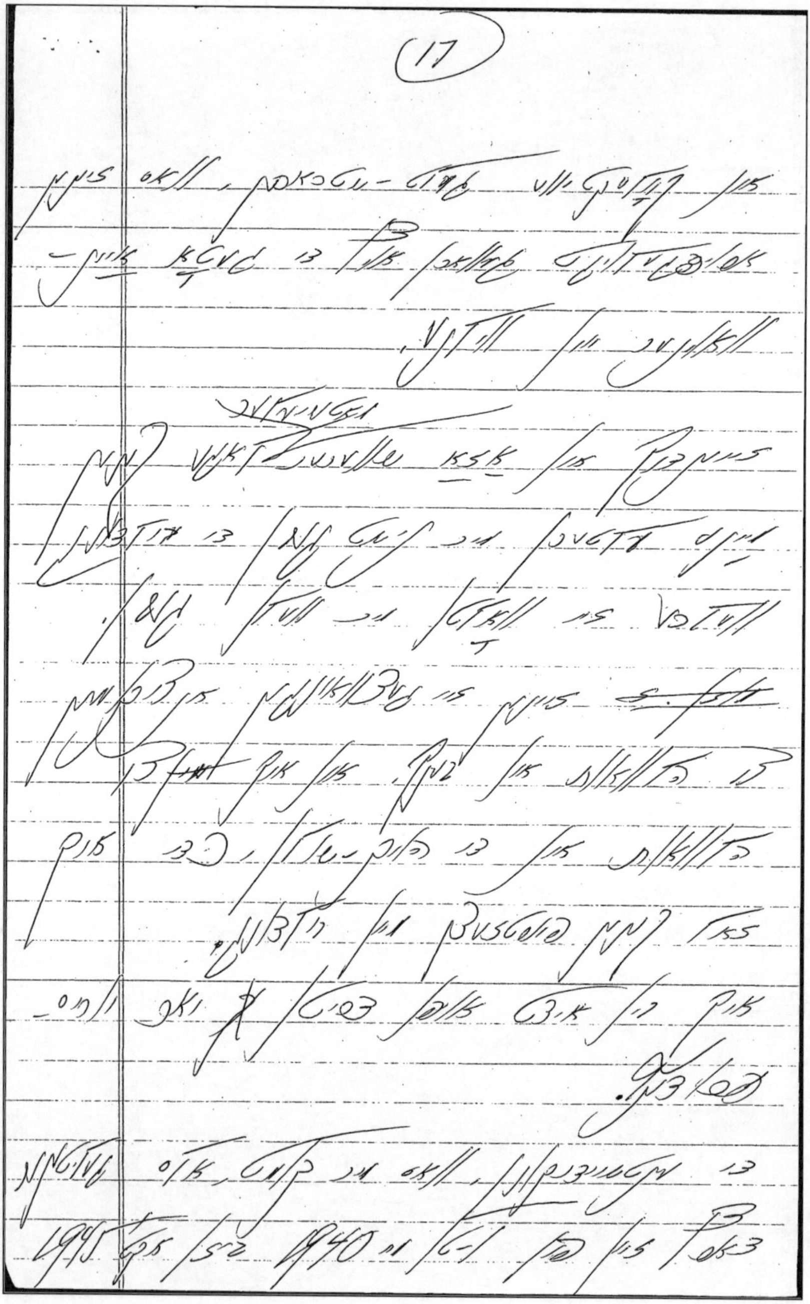

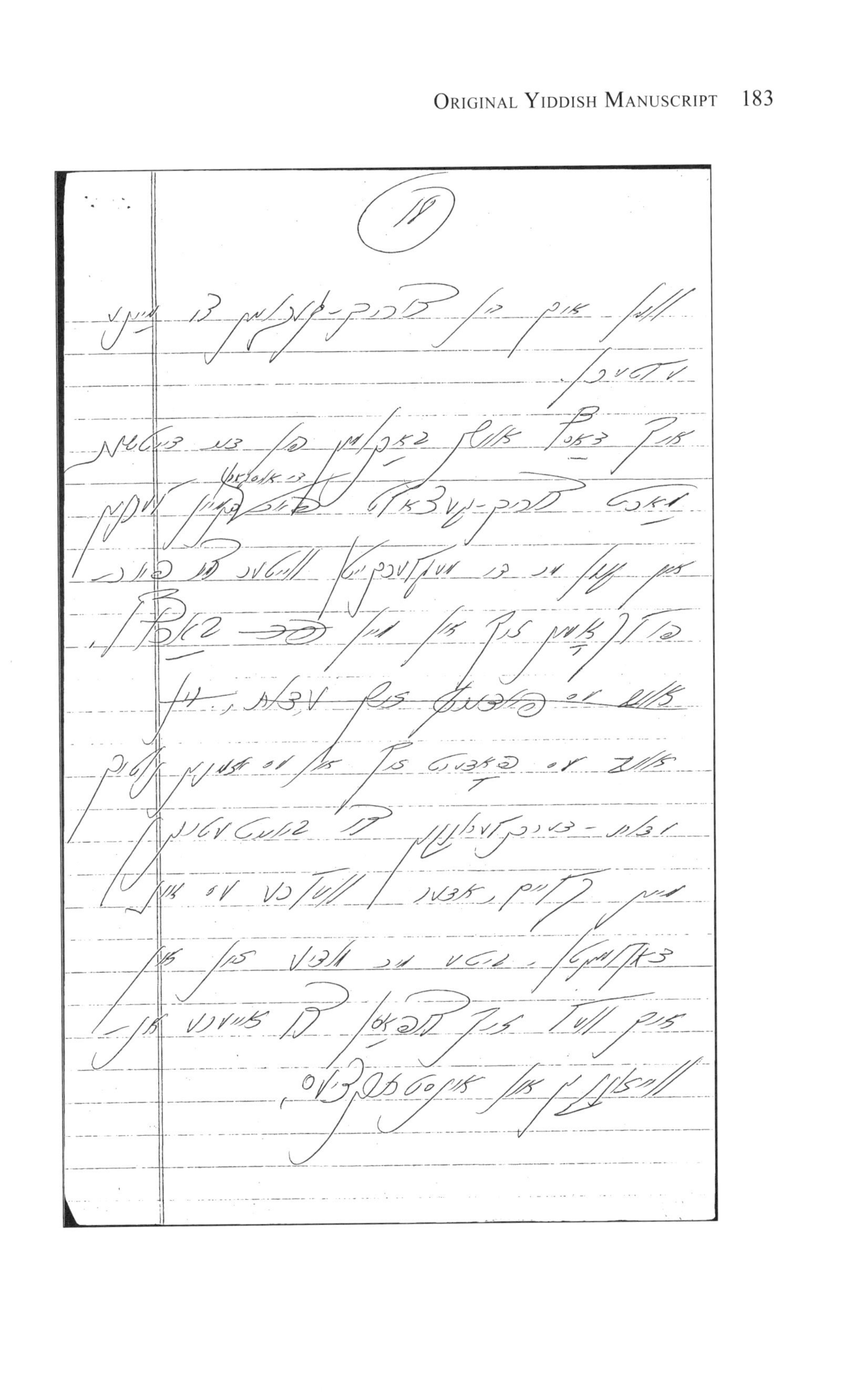

(יז)

ווען איך האָב [illegible] צו מײַנע
עלטערן.
[illegible]
[illegible]
[illegible]
[illegible]
[illegible]
[illegible]
[illegible]
[illegible]
[illegible]
[illegible]
[illegible]

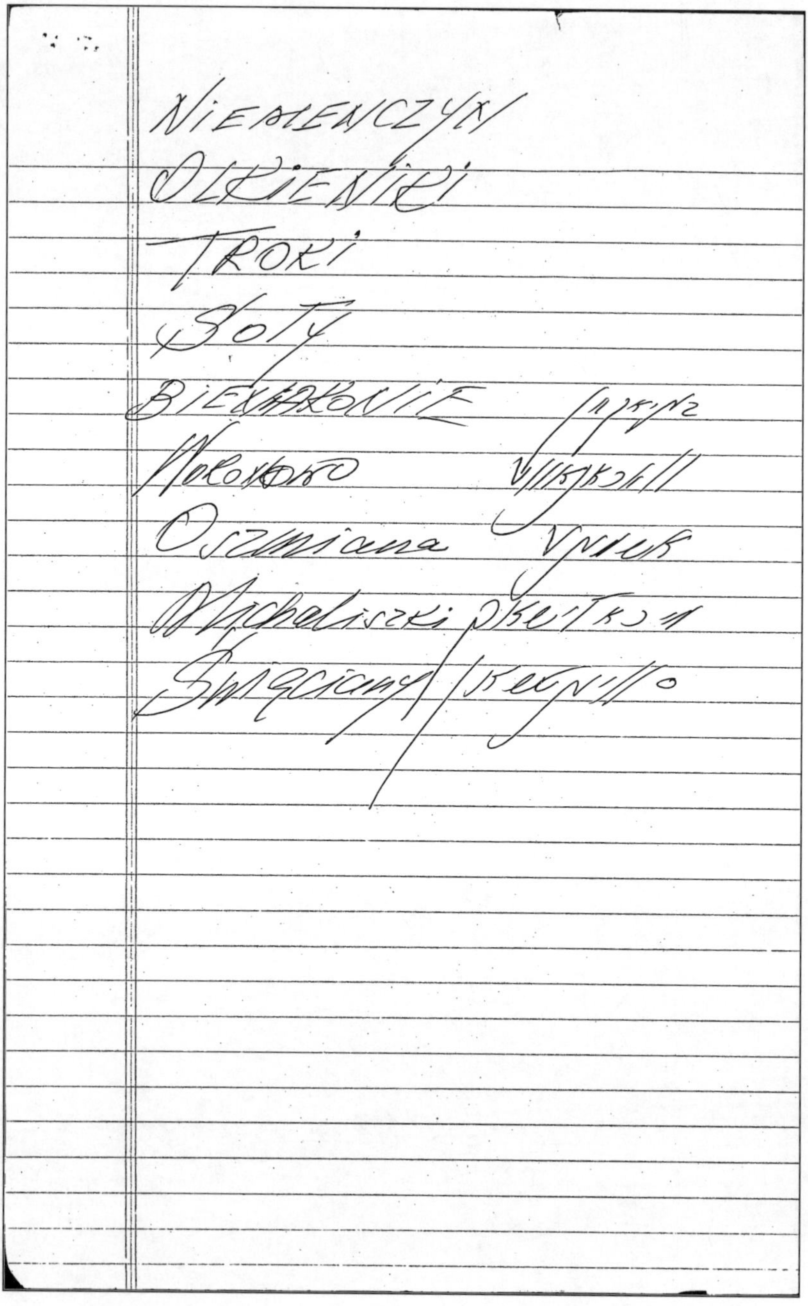
NIEMENCZYN
OLKIENIKI
TROKI
Soły
BIENIAKONIE
Oszmiana
Michaliszki
Święciany

C. Bylos Nr 2-370-45.
1945 m.

NUORAŠAS

Nutartis.

1945 metų gegužės mėn 10 dien.

L.T.S.R. Aukščiausiojo Teismo civilinių Bylų Teisminė Kolegija jo Pirmininkaujančio E. Mockio.
Narių J. Didžiulio ir J. Zimono.
Dalyvaujant Prokurorui. Advokatui E. Vidmantienei.
Viešame posėdyje Vilniuje išnagrinėjo civilinę bylą ieškovų Fuksmanų Elenos ir Juozapo su Atsakove Kupaite Brone dėl sūnaus grąžinimo.

Ieškovai padavė ieškinį pareiškime prašo Liaudies Teismą atiteisti iš atsakovės jų sūnų Abramą Fuksmaną, kurį jie 1941 metais, gelbėdami nuo vokiečių okupantų mirties, buvo palikę pas atsakovę Kupaitę Bronę. Dabar vokiečių okupantus išvarius ir ieškovams paliekus gyvims, atsakovė jų sūnaus Abramo grąžinti neatiduoda.

Vilniaus miesto 1 rajono Liaudies Teismas 1945 m. vasario mėn 26 d. sprendimu ieškovų ieškinį patenkino ir atiteisė jiems iš atsakovės grąžinti sūnų Abramą Fuksmaną.

Atsakovė padavė kasacinį skundą. prašo sprendimą panaikinti ir bylą grąžinti spręsti iš naujo, nes Liaudies Teismas neteisėtai atitiesė iš jos grąžinti vaiką ieškovams, kadangi jie jį buvo atidavę jai amžinai visados, ir ji esą vaiką augino ir išlaikė 3 metus savo lėšomis, todėl ji ir turinti teisę, kad vaikas būtų paliktas ir toliau jai auginti.

L.T.S.R. Aukščiausiojo Teismo Civilinių bylų Teisminė Kolegija, išnagrinėjusi bylą bei skundą ir išklausiusi advokato kuris prašė skundą atmesti, randa skundą atmestiną ir sprendimą tvirtintiną šiais sumetimais:

Iš bylos duomenų matyti, kad ieškovai gelbėdami savo sūnų nuo okupantų mirties, buvo priversti jį atiduoti atsakovei. Be to, ieškovai visą laiką vaiko išlaikymui atsakovei.

Sekretor

Kauen-Wilna Verlags u. ...-Ges. ... H. 1208-42

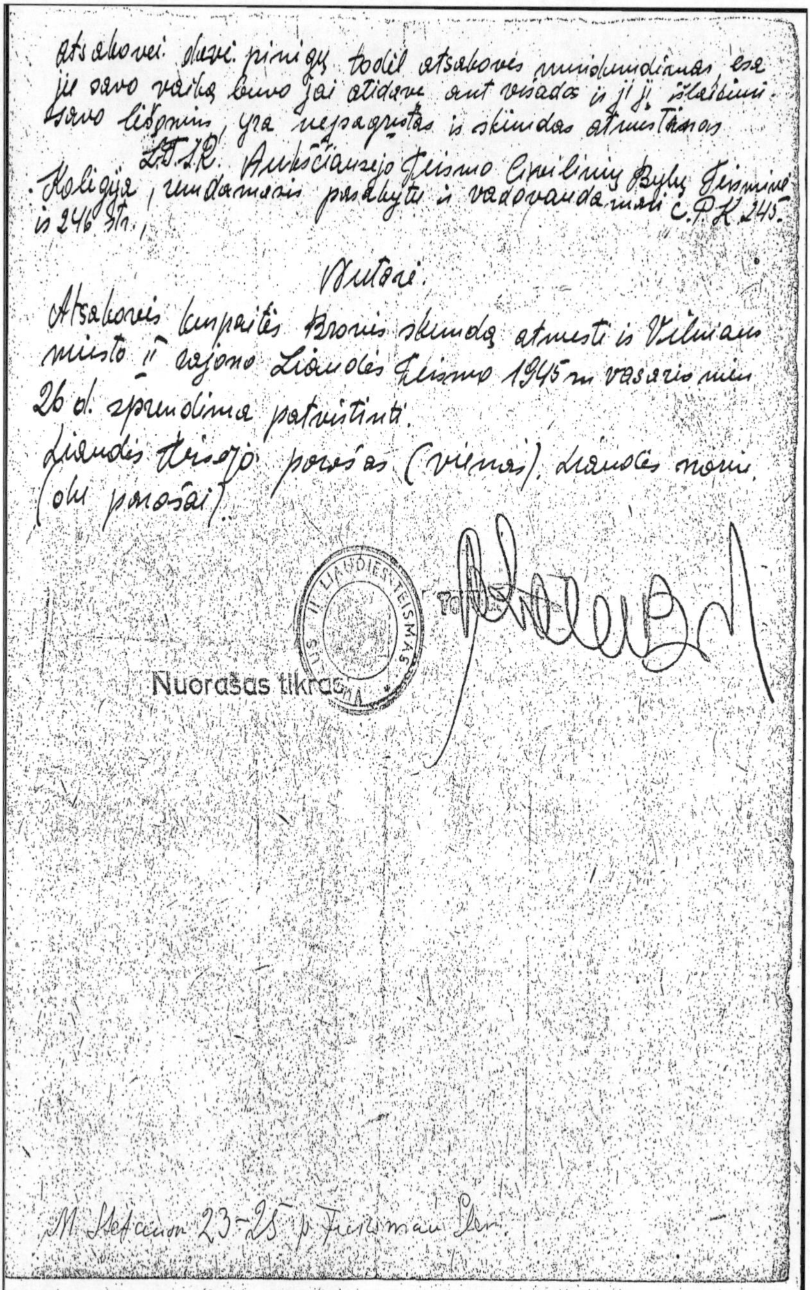

atsakovei davė pinigų, todėl atsakovės nusiskundimas, esą ji savo vaiką buvo jai atidavė ant visados ir jį jį išlaikiusi savo lėšomis, yra nepagrįstas ir skundas atmestinas.

L.T.S.R. Aukščiausiojo Teismo Civilinių Bylų Teisminė Kolegija, rasdama pasakyta ir vadovaudamasi C.P.K. 245 ir 246 str.,

Nutarė:

Atsakovės Kunpaitės Bronės skundą atmesti ir Vilniaus miesto II rajono Liaudies Teismo 1945 m vasario mėn 26 d. sprendimą patvirtinti.

Liaudies teisėjo parašas (vienas). Liaudies narių (du parašai).

LIAUDIES TEISMAS

Nuorašas tikras

M. Stefanon 23-25 p. Fischman Sar.

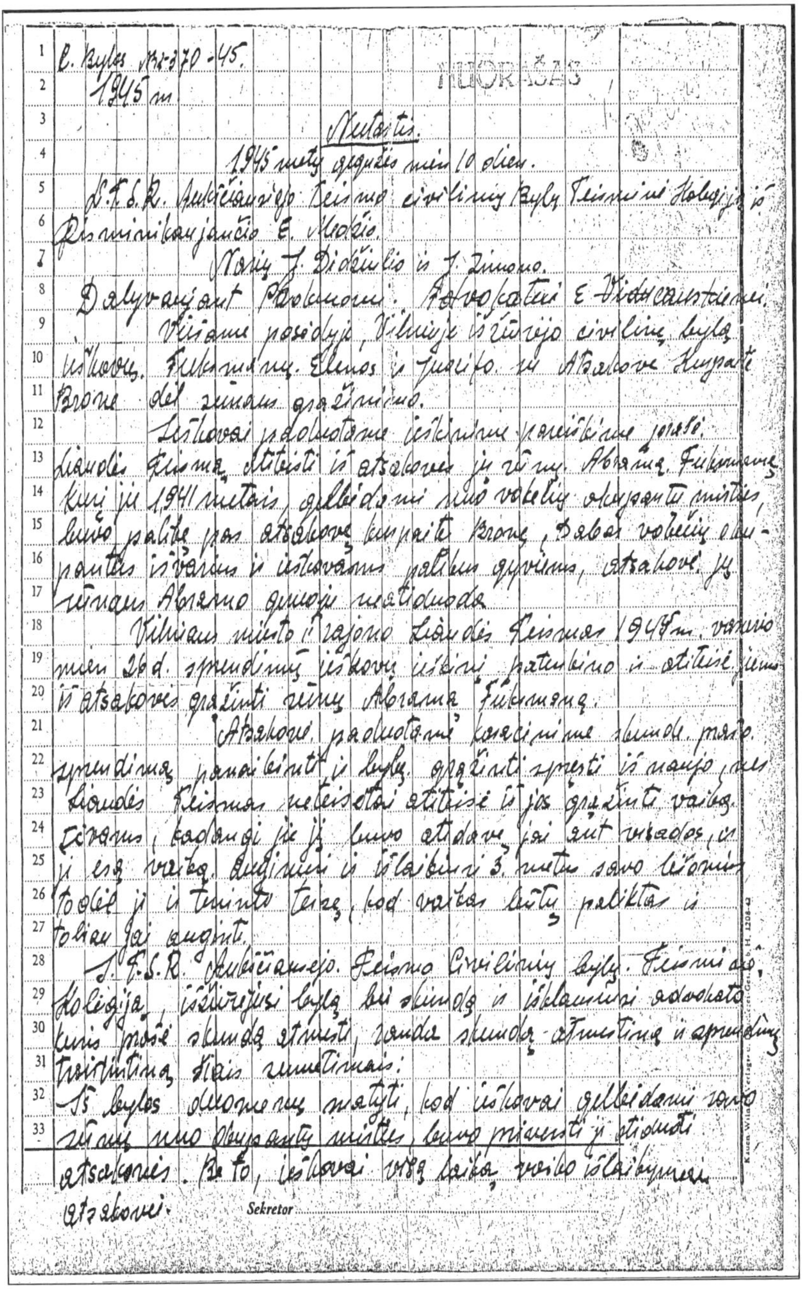

C. Bylos Nr. 3-370-45.
1945 m.

NUORAŠAS

Nutartis.

1945 metų gegužės mėn 10 dien.

L.T.S.R. Aukščiausiojo Teismo civilinių Bylų Teisminė Kolegija iš Pirmininkaujančio E. Meškio.

Narių J. Didžiulio ir J. Zimono.

Dalyvaujant Prokurorui. Advokatui E. Vidhcainstienei.

Viešame posėdyje, Vilniuje išnagrinėjo civilinę bylą ieškovų Fukmanų Elenos ir Juozifo su Atsakove Kupryte Brone dėl sūnaus grąžinimo.

Ieškovai paduotame ieškinime pareiškime prašė Liaudies Teismą atiteisti iš atsakovės jų sūnų Abramą Fukmaną, kurį jie 1941 metais gelbėdami nuo vokiečių okupantų mirties, buvo palikę pas atsakovę Kuprytę Bronę. Dabar vokiečių okupantus išvarius ir ieškovams palikus gyvims, atsakovė jų sūnaus Abramo grąžinti neatiduoda.

Vilniaus miesto ir rajono Liaudies Teismas 1945 m. vasario mėn 26 d. sprendimu ieškovų ieškinį patenkino ir atiteisė jiems iš atsakovės grąžinti sūnų Abramą Fukmaną.

Atsakovė paduotame kasaciniame skunde prašo sprendimą panaikinti ir bylą grąžinti spręsti iš naujo, nes Liaudies Teismas neteisėtai atiteisė iš jos grąžinti vaiką ieškovams, kadangi jie jį buvo atidavę jai amžinai visados, ir ji esą vaiką auginusi ir išlaikiusi 3 metus savo lėšomis, todėl ji ir turinti teisę, kad vaikas būtų paliktas ir toliau jai auginti.

L.T.S.R. Aukščiausiojo Teismo Civilinių bylų Teisminė Kolegija, išnagrinėjusi bylą bei skundą ir išklausiusi advokato kuris prašė skundą atmesti, randa skundą atmestina ir sprendimą tvirtintina šiais sumetimais:

Iš bylos duomenų matyti, kad ieškovai gelbėdami savo sūnų nuo okupantų mirties, buvo priversti jį atiduoti atsakovei. Be to, ieškovai visą laiką teikė išlaikymui atsakovei.

Sekretor

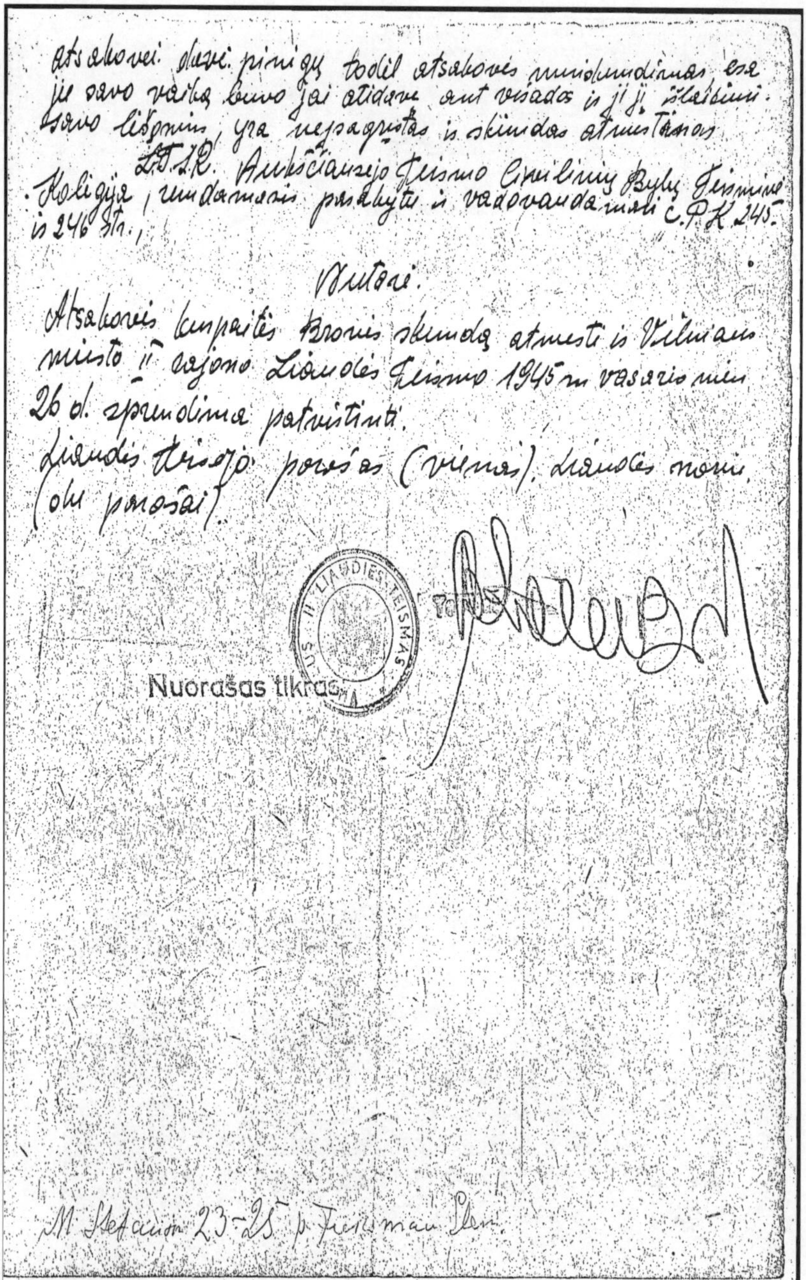

atsakovei davė pinigų todėl atsakovės nurodinėjimas esą
jie savo vaiką buvo jai atidavę ant visados ir jį išlaikiusi
savo lėšomis, yra nepagrįstas ir skundas atmestinas.
L.T.S.R. Aukščiausiojo Teismo Civilinių Bylų Teisminė
Kolegija, remdamasi pasakytu ir vadovaudamasi C.P.K. 245
ir 246 str.,

Nutarė:

Atsakovės Kupaitės Bronės skundą atmesti ir Vilniaus
miesto II rajono Liaudies Teismo 1945 m. vasario mėn.
26 d. sprendimą patvirtinti.
Liaudies teisėjo parašas (vienas). Liaudies narių
(du parašai).

M. Stefanion 23-25 p. Fiksman Elen.

PHOTOS

Bronislawa Kurpi and Abraham Foxman – Vilna,
Lithuania 1941 or 1942

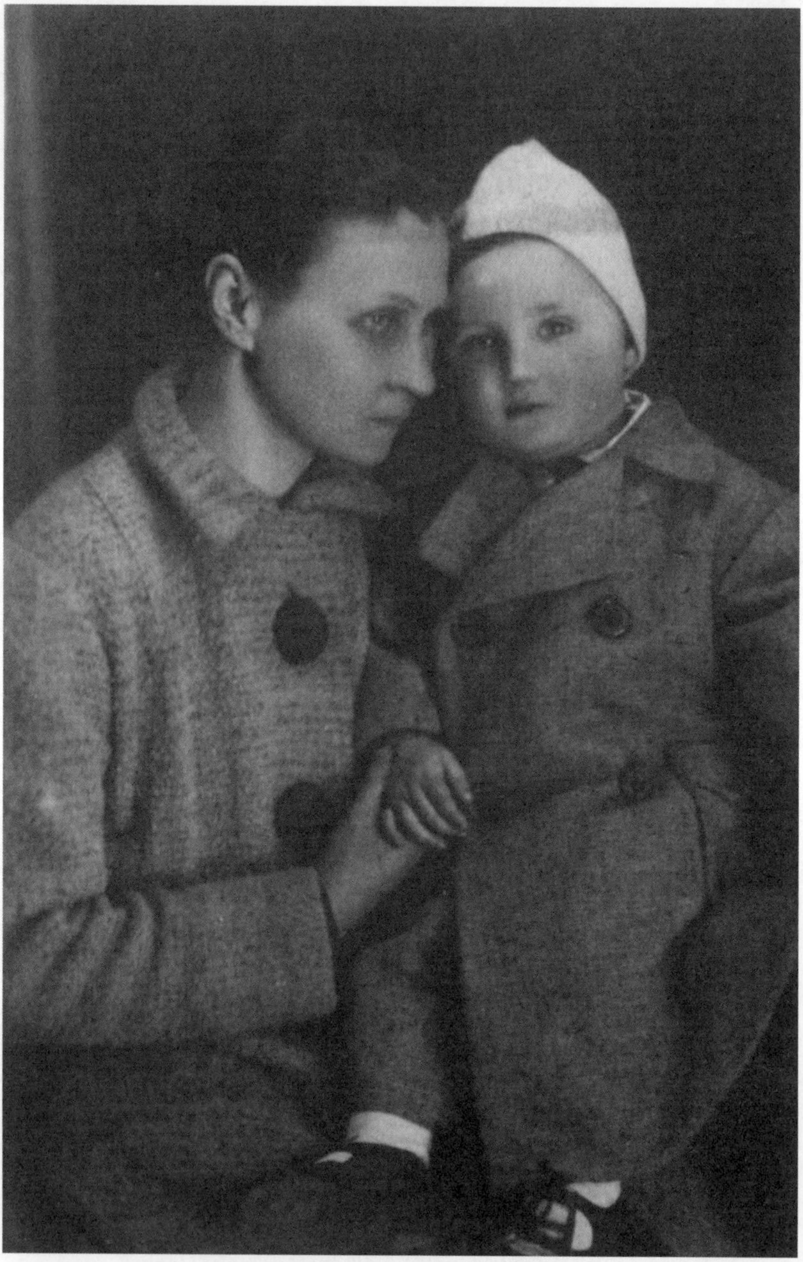

Bronia and Abraham, Vilna, Wartime

Bronia and Abraham, Vilna, Wartime

Bronia and Abraham, Vilna, Wartime

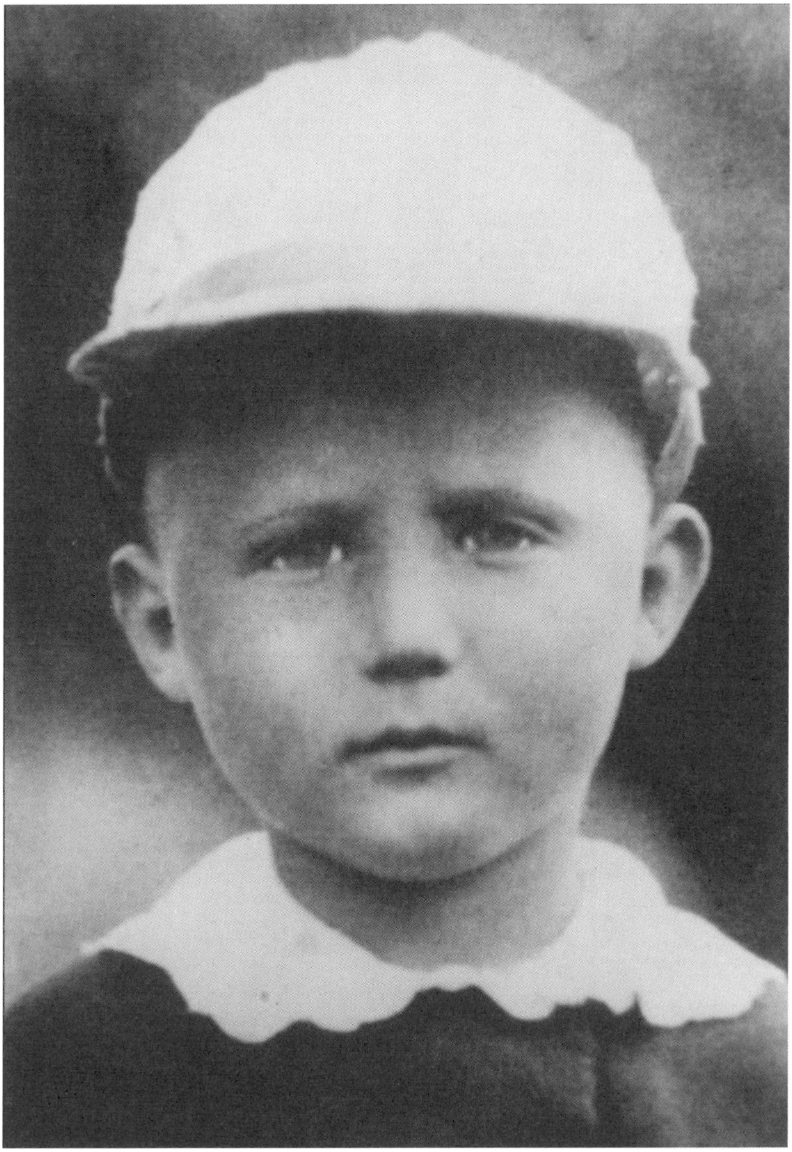

Henrik Stanislaw Kurpi — Aka: Abraham Foxman — Vilna, Lithuania 1944

Joseph and Abraham, Ebelsberg bei Linz DP camp

Joseph and Abraham, Ebelsberg bei Linz DP camp

Helen, Joseph and Abraham Foxman – DP Camp in Badgastein, Austria 1947

Helen, Joseph and Abraham Foxman — DP Camp in Badgastein, Austria 1947

Abraham Foxman's reunion with Rabbi Goldman, March 2010.
Photographed by David Brystowski.